Children as Consumers

The children's and teenagers' market has become increasingly significant as young people have become more affluent, and have an ever growing disposable income. *Children as Consumers* traces the stages of consumer development which children pass through and examines the key sources of influence upon young people's consumer socialisation.

Barrie Gunter and Adrian Furnham examine the kinds of things young people consume, how they use their money, how they respond to different types of advertising, and whether they need to be protected through special legislation and regulation. They also examine market research techniques which can work well with young people.

Children as Consumers will be useful to students of psychology, sociology, business and media studies, as well as professionals in advertising and marketing.

Barrie Gunter is Professor of Journalism Studies at the University of Sheffield. His previous publications include *Children and Television, 2nd edition* (with Jill McAleer) (1997).

Adrian Furnham is Professor of Psychology at University College London. His previous publications include *The Psychology of Money* (with Michael Argyle) (1998) and *The Psychology of Behaviour at Work* (1997).

INTERNATIONAL SERIES IN SOCIAL PSYCHOLOGY
Series Editor: Professor W. Peter Robinson, University of Bristol, UK

Adjustment of Adolescents: Cross-cultural Similarities and Differences (Scott and Scott)

Adolescence: From Crisis to Coping. A Thirteen Nation Study (Gibson-Cline)

Assertion and its Social Context (Wilson and Gallois)

Changing European Identities: Social Psychological Analyses of Social Change (Breakwell and Lyons)

Children as Consumers: A Psychological Analysis of the Young People's Market (Gunter and Furnham)

Children's Social Competence in Context: The Contributions of Family, School and Culture (Schneider)

Emotion and Social Judgements (Forgas)

Game Theory and its Applications in the Social and Biological Sciences (Colman)

Genius and Eminence, 2nd edition (Albert)

Making Sense of Television: The Psychology of Audience Interpretation (Livingstone)

The Psychology of Gambling (Walker)

Social Dilemmas: Theoretical Issues and Research Findings (Liebrand)

Social Groups and Identities: Developing the Legacy of Henri Tajfel (Robinson)

The Theory of Reasoned Action: Its Application to AIDS Preventative Behavior (Terry, Gallois and McCamish)

If you wish to contribute to the series please send a synopsis to Professor Peter Robinson, University of Bristol, Department of Psychology, 8 Woodlands Road, Bristol BS8 1TN.

Children as Consumers

A psychological analysis of the young people's market

Barrie Gunter and Adrian Furnham

1998 so good
Summary of
older research
but lacking
the post '98
research

Routledge
Taylor & Francis Group

LONDON AND NEW YORK

First published 1998 by Routledge
11 New Fetter Lane, London EC4P 4EE

Simultaneously published in the USA and Canada by Routledge
29 West 35th Street, New York, NY 10001

Reprinted 2004 and 2006 by Routledge
27 Church Road, Hove, East Sussex BN3 2FA
270 Madison Avenue, New York NY 10016

Routledge is an imprint of the Taylor & Francis Group, an informa business

© 1998 Barrie Gunter and Adrian Furnham

Typeset in Times by Avocet Typeset, Brill, Bucks
Printed and bound in Great Britain by TJI Digital, Padstow, Cornwall
This publication has been produced with paper manufactured to strict
environmental standards and with pulp derived from sustainable forests.

British Library Cataloguing in Publication Data
A catalogue record for this book is available from the British Library

Library of Congress Cataloging in Publication Data
A catalogue record for this book is available from the Library of Congress

ISBN 13: 978-0-415-18535-6 (pbk)
ISBN 10: 0-415-18535-1 (pbk)

Contents

Preface   vii

1 The Importance of the Children's Market   1

2 Socialization of Child Consumers   9

3 What Do Children Consume?   35

4 Children's Use and Understanding of Money   65

5 Advertising and Children: Attention, Awareness and Understanding   101

6 Advertising and Children: Influences and Effects   137

7 Reaching Child Consumers   155

8 Protecting Child Consumers   173

References   189

Author Index   211

Subject Index   214

Preface

Despite the importance of the children's and adolescent market to the educational, financial and retail sectors we know surprisingly little about where and how young people acquire their money. where and why they spend and save it, and their knowledge of the financial world and its opportunities. Before embarking on commercial or educational programmes, it is important to have an accurate picture of the beliefs and behaviours of young people and their parents, regarding money. In short. we need to know more about children as consumers.

Young people, or more specifically, children between 8 and 12 years and adolescents between 13 and 19 years are, because of their wealth, a very big market. It is difficult to estimate the market potential of young people. A recent American survey estimated that American children have around $9 billion from their families and directly influence $130 billion of parental purchases. At the beginning of the 1990s German 7–15-year-olds received 7.5 billion DM in pocket money and gifts, while the spending power of 12–21-year-olds amounted to 33 billion DM annually.

In Great Britain in 1990, it was estimated that 14–16-year-olds alone had nearly £10 per week in disposable cash. By 1996, the Walls survey showed even 5-year-olds had nearly £2.50 per week. The same survey showed that over a quarter save a considerable portion of their money in a variety of places. There is also concern, debate and speculation about how children and adolescents acquire and dispose of their money, as well as discussion about the hopes of their parents, but there are relatively few hard facts.

In this book, we have tried to bring together the very diverse literature and data on children as consumers spread over many different disciplines. Advertising and media specialists, sociologists and psychologists, political scientists and economists, all have a particular interest in how, why and where children develop into economically active members of our society. Policy makers too have taken an active interest in the way companies try to promote their products to children.

An overview of these discourses and an appreciation of the psychological factors involved in the role of children as consumers can help manufacturers, retailers, and those who advise them on their advertising and marketing strategies to design products and services which will appeal more effectively to their current tastes, and to plan promotional and marketing campaigns which will appeal to their core values and needs. Such information and understanding is equally important to those charged with regulating the marketing of products and services to this market segment. Regulations and public policy regarding advertising to young consumers should be informed by a proper understanding of the psychology of this age group, so that rules and regulations safeguard the public interest while placing no undue and unfair constraints on advertisers, and those whom they represent, to operate as openly as possible in a competitive marketplace.

A wealth of data has been collected from around the world by academic researchers who have approached their investigation of the young persons' market from a psychological perspective. This book represents an attempt to collate, review and critique this body of research. Having set the scene by examining the demographic and economic characteristics of the young consumers' market, the book then focuses on work conducted largely in the spheres of social and cognitive psychology, which has shed light on consumer socialization, particularly where learning about money is concerned, the psychological composition of young consumers as defined by their core values and needs, and their understanding of advertising. An important aspect of the interface between young consumers and the marketplace are the mass media. It is important, therefore, for marketers to have information about young consumers' media-related behaviours and preferences. There is an examination of how to conduct research on young consumers in order to obtain a better understanding of their consumer behaviour and the ways they think about consumerism. The book also takes a look at the issue of regulations and controls over marketing and advertising aimed at young consumers, which continues to be a major issue in the context of the rapid growth of mass media. While few people would argue against the protection of young consumers, there are different ways in which such protection could be implemented. In particular, we explore the tensions between the notion of tighter centralized regulation of consumer marketing and the idea of a more educated and consumer literate society for a deregulated consumer environment.

Barrie Gunter
Sheffield
Adrian Furnham
London

1

The Importance of the Children's Market

As the purchasing power of young people exhibits continued growth, marketers, manufacturers and advertisers have become increasingly interested in devising effective methods of reaching the young persons' market. Achieving this aim requires a full understanding of children as consumers: what they believe, what they want, and how they behave. The initial focus of this effort was upon teenagers who represent a substantial group of young people with considerable autonomy, distinctive tastes and perhaps more importantly money to spend. Lately, attention has also been directed at the *child market*, comprising young people up to the age of 12. This book will examine the nature of consumerism among young people up to their mid- to late teens. Young people, both children and adolescents, are richer and better informed than they have ever been. In some countries, particularly in the developing world, over half the population is under 21 years of age. With the globalization of mass media, the style of consumerism associated with modern industrialized societies of the western world has spread all around the planet. Young people can thus be recognized as a unique all-important market in their own right.

Interest in young consumers really began with the baby boom generation after the Second World War (McNeal, 1992). The idea of the 'teenager' as a distinct life cycle phase, for example, coupled with the emergence of a so-called 'youth market' did not really attract much specific marketing significance until the mid-1950s (Davis, 1990). The projection of youth or 'teenagers' as a distinct sub-culture, with its own consumer-related priorities was an outgrowth of the booming post-war economy in many industrialized societies. The United States probably led the way, but Europe soon followed. Full employment meant relatively high wages for the teenage worker, a situation which was in marked contrast to the depression years before the war. By the late 1950s in Britain, for example, average teenage earnings had increased by more than 50 per cent in real terms from pre-war levels (Davis, 1990). Earnings increased for everyone in work, in fact, meaning that family households in general were better off.

The booming economy spawned commercial interests across many sectors of society, creating faster-growing markets for an array of goods and services, from fashions and entertainment to food and drink. Many of these commodities were aimed specifically at satisfying the needs and aspirations of young con-

sumers (Stewart, 1992). Some markets, such as financial services, quickly realized that if customers could be captured early enough, they might remain loyal
consumers for life.

By the 1960s this generation was spending $2 billion a year in America alone.
By the end of the 1980s, this figure had risen to $6 billion among young
Americans. In addition to the amount they spend directly, it has been estimated
that children and teenagers exert a considerable indirect effect on consumer
activity, influencing annually some $132 billion worth of household purchases
in that country (McNeal, 1992). Later in this book we will examine both the
influence of parents on their children and the reverse influence of children upon
their parents' purchases in more detail. Further various changes that took place
in most developed countries in the 1980s contributed to the increased economic
power of children. These included fewer children per parent, the postponement
of having children, and dual-working families. Richer parents with fewer, but
better educated children, have created a more sophisticated young people's
market which comprises a body of individuals with money to spend and increasingly well-informed tastes and opinions in the sphere of consumerism.

The importance of the young people's market is underlined by the fact that
the older segment of it, namely the teenage market has become more affluent
while declining in number. In the United States, despite a 15.5 per cent drop in
the number of teenagers during the 1980s, their spending increased nearly 43
per cent, growing from $1422 to $2409 per capita (Tootelian and Gaedeke,
1992). Even considering the effects of inflation, this figure represents a real
growth in spending of nearly 25 per cent.

Whether this growth of the youth market will be sustained is another question.
The annual entry of people into the labour market has been declining throughout
the 1980s and 1990s (Ermisch, 1990). In the mid-1980s, 29 per cent of 16-year-
olds, 45 per cent of 17-year-olds, and 59 per cent of 18-year-olds in England and
Wales were in full-time employment. By 1993/4, these figures had dropped to
eight per cent, 15 per cent and 33 per cent respectively. Over the same period, the
number of teenagers remaining in full-time education increased dramatically.
Even those in full-time education, however, had sources of income, with around
one in five maintaining a part-time job (Department for Education and
Employment (DFEE), 1996). As a result of these demographic changes, one argument is that the commercial and cultural centre of gravity will shift up the age
spectrum to the middle-age group, or even to the late-middle-age/early old age
groups — the so-called 'grey market'—whose members are not only growing
rapidly, but whose discretionary spending power will become very significant.

Children and teenagers buy a wide range of products and services. Given the
size of the teenage market especially, in terms of spending power, considerable
attention has been directed towards understanding the types of products and services they purchase and the extent to which they influence family purchase decisions. Young people are major buyers of sweet things and play things. They
spend a lot on clothing, consumer electronics, entertainment and hobbies (Hall,

1987; Tootelian and Windeschausen, 1975). Figures for the United States have indicated that over 60 per cent of young people aged between 12 and 15 purchase groceries and make decisions, and over 50 per cent of all teenagers cook for their families at least once a week (Gonzales, 1988). They also make purchases from a wide range of retail outlets. The youth orientation has pervaded so many different product markets that it has spilled over into more mainstream culture, with images of youth in the mass media becoming dominant marketing icons (Stewart, 1992).

As we will see later, children's earliest experiences of consumer activity occur in the first few years of their lives. They have already begun to make independent purchases on a small scale and through local retail outlets by the age of four or five, and by the age of ten they have been found in the United States to make over 250 purchase visits a year to a variety of different kinds of stores (McNeal, 1992).

For McNeal (1992), children and teenagers are:

- a primary market in their own right;
- an influential market given their influence on parental household purchase;
- a market for the future of all nations;
- a particular demographic segment;
- a specific life-style segment according to the same criteria as their parents;
- a benefit segment such as educational benefits.

Modern marketing has, of course, clearly recognized for some time the important role children can play in influencing certain types of household purchases. Advertising for some fast-moving consumer goods, especially food-stuffs, attempts to embrace this role by portraying children prominently in commercial messages as models who encourage the purchase of certain commodities. Indeed an inspection of 'children's television' shows the number and range of products aimed specifically at younger people.

There is a distinction to be made, however, between children as mediators or triggers of household purchasing by parents, and children as consumers who purchase specific goods and services for personal use and satisfaction (see Chapter 3). Insofar as pre-teens have the desire and financial means to buy products for themselves they represent a potentially active consumer group in their own right.

A willingness to purchase is only part of the story. Children must have the financial ability to participate as consumers. This suggests that there must be a source of money and an understanding of money and of how to purchase. In this book we will examine how children develop as consumers. In doing so, we will discuss the major consumer socialization influences which work to shape children's consumerism. Research in the United States has noted that American children often make their first independent purchase by around the age of five (McNeal, 1965). Even earlier than this, parents can be seen training their children in various aspects of consumption. This preliminary training may involve allowing the infant to give money to a supermarket cashier or selecting items from supermarket shelves. Lessons may also be offered in testing for the quality of foods—the ripeness of fruits or freshness of bread. Furthermore, some schools offer courses in Consumerism (see Chapter 8). Banks, building societies and other financial institutions now provide educational packs and special accounts for children and teenagers across the age spectrum.

Size of the Child Market

There are two important questions to ask in establishing the size of the child market. First of all, how many children are there in a particular area, region or country? Second, how much money do they have to spend? The marketer and manufacturer need to know what proportion of this potential market will buy each product and how much they will buy.

A look at the population statistics reveals clearly that this represents a growing consumer group. This is true of many western industrialized countries. In the United States, for example, there were 36,732,000 children aged 5 to 13 years in 1967. By 1985 this group had grown to more than 40 million. According to McNeal (1992) American children's average annual income grew from $137 in 1984 to $229 in 1989 which represents over $8 billion. Their savings alone in 1989 were $2 billion. Table 1.1 below shows how children allocated this income to different items of expenditure. More than half their money was spent on snacks or sweets and toys or games. From 1984 to 1989, however, while overall expenditure increased by a significant margin, spending on video arcades and movies or sports dropped markedly. Although not shown in the table, McNeal also estimated a 50 per cent increase in the personal expenditure of American children had occurred during the six years up to 1984.

TABLE 1.1 *Products purchased by children with their own money, 1984 and 1989*

Product/service	Expenditure and share		Expenditure and share	
	1984	%	1989	%
Snacks/sweets	$1,440,600,000	(33.9)	$2,076,852,544	(34.6)
Toys/games/crafts	1,104,100,000	(26.0)	1,878,771,232	(31.3)
Clothes	NA		690,282,360	(11.5)
Movies/sports	771,200,000	(18.2)	606,248,864	(10.1)
Video arcades	765,900,000	(18.1)	486,199,584	(8.1)
Other	162,300,000	(3.8)	264,108,416	(4.4)
	$4,244,029,967	(100.0)	$6,002,464,504	(100.0)

Source: McNeal, 1992, p. 40

The children's market in the United Kingdom is also substantial. Marketing agency Mintel estimated in 1979 that there were around 10 million children aged 5 to 15 years, representing about 17 per cent of the population. This group was reckoned to have a total direct spending power of around £600 million. Population projections estimate that this age group will grow in number until early into the next century.

The new teen explosion has already begun in the United States where advertisers and marketing corporations have woken up to the demographic wave that will form the most important American spending group in the next century. The ageing Baby Boomers, whose aspirations have dominated popular culture for the past 25 years, are in for a shock, as are today's so-called Generation X of disaffected teenagers bemoaning how life is passing them by.

In America the number of teenagers has started to grow at such a rate that by 2010 there will be more than ever before, peaking at 30.8 million, 900,000 more than the Boomer height of 1976, according to the latest census projections. In Britain, the teen wave will be less of a 'surfer's dream'. Projections suggest there will be 5.6 million teenagers in 2010, 800,000 (16%) more than 1992 but 300,000 fewer than the British Boomer year of 1976. All these youngsters have cash to burn; last year America's 28 million teenagers were estimated to have spent $57 billion of their own money and influenced much more of their parents' expenditure. They are used to deciding what stereo is best, what car is 'cool', what vacation to go on.

Many organizations are desperate to discover how to tap this market and have been disconcerted by the emergence of 'slackers', today's sub-culture of teenagers who appear to have rejected conventional working lives. They are supposed to be the heirs of Generation X, the bunch of angry, disengaged youths immortalized in Douglas Coupland's eponymous novel published in the early 1990s. Neither idle nor stupid, they are sceptical, well educated, computer-literate and take a perverse enjoyment in television trash-culture. In addition they are characterized by a potentially considerable purchasing power.

In general, although population growth has slowed down in most developed industrialized countries in Europe and America it is growing substantially in the rapidly developing countries of the Pacific Rim. Nevertheless, even in those countries where populations in general are stabilizing, the affluence of young people continues to grow. Tootelian and Gaedeke (1992), examining American data, found that despite a 15 per cent decline in the number of teenagers in the 1990s, their spending power increased by 43 per cent, which (taking inflation into consideration) is a real growth of nearly 25 per cent. They also noted that an astounding 20 per cent of American teenagers had access to credit cards. This growth is now occurring across Europe, especially in the wealthier nations such as Germany.

Establishing how much money youngsters have to spend is not easy. Children have a number of sources of purchasing power. These include gifts of money from parents or relatives, earned income from odd-jobs, and allowances or pocket money which may also be partially earned. Although the amount of disposable cash that children have varies considerably over time there is a clear pattern of growth especially in early adolescence. Income data for this group, however, is not always available and often only rough estimates exist. How children use their money is examined in more detail in Chapter 3.

Children represent a current market; a potential future market but also an influential market (McNeal, 1987). That is, children have substantial influence on the purchases of their parents. The increase in the pocket money of British children is considerable (see Table 1.2). This means that a 12-year-old may have well over £200 per annum to spend.

TABLE 1.2 *Average weekly total income 1990/91 by age and sex*

Year	All children	Boys	Girls	5–7	8–10	11–13	14–16
1987	220p	219p	220p	84p	121p	228p	458p
1988	208p	213p	201p	100p	154p	236p	351p
1989	271p	273p	269p	124p	161p	280p	605p
1990	354p	323p	385p	129p	190p	353p	916p
1991	396p	411p	381p	148p	235p	401p	920p
% change							
1990/91	+12%	+27%	-1%	+15%	+24%	+14%	+0.5%

Source: Walls Pocket Money Monitor by Gallup

A large scale survey of children's 'pocket money' conducted on behalf of Walls Ice Cream (Birds Eye Walls, 1990) provides some useful data on the average spending of 14- to 16-year-olds. By 1990 the average weekly total income for this age group was £9.16p, representing a 51 per cent increase on 1989. Of this, earnings accounted for about 40 per cent, parental contribution for a further third, the balance being accounted for by 'hand-outs' from family friends and relatives. This gave 14- to 16-year-olds an average annual per capita income of £476.32p. Multiplied by the number of 14-16s in the population at the time, this age band had a total annual spending of around £1 billion (Stewart, 1992).

Thus, children have considerable spending power in their own right. A subsequent analysis reported that pocket money for British children rises from 58p average per week at age 5 to £3.85p at 14, but that this forms less than half the total income. This money is enhanced by earnings from part-time jobs, errands and gifts, which boost the total to £1.72p on average for five-year-olds, £3.80p for 10-year-olds and £9.57p for 14-year-olds. Extrapolated to the total population for a year this represents some £1.5 billion (James, 1994). Indirect spending by children adds hugely to these figures. Gift purchases, entertainment and purchase of food, drink and in-house products reflect the persuasive powers of children and their involvement in family discussions about what to do and what to buy.

In 1991 the Halifax Building Society conducted a major survey of British youngsters. They found that eight out of ten British children regularly got pocket money, which averaged £1.40 a week. Of these, 51 per cent earned part of the money in return for doing household chores such as washing the dishes, keeping their bedrooms tidy and making their own beds. In all, 23 per cent claimed to save all the money they received, while 9 per cent said they spent all their money. For teenagers (12–16s), average earnings reached £4.20 a week. One in three teenagers, however, had a part-time job which brought in an average of £12.70 per week. Finally, girls tended to earn more than boys. These findings underline the spending potential associated with the young people's market.

Demands of the Child Market

In many respects, the child consumer resembles all other consumers. Children want to purchase things to satisfy various needs. Satisfaction may be gained directly from the items purchased. This may be particularly true of foods and toys, and also of clothes, books, magazines and personal entertainment items as they grow older. Satisfaction may also be obtained from the act of purchase itself rather than solely from what is purchased.

It has been observed, however, that the inherent value of the consumption act declines with age, while satisfactions obtained through owning certain possessions and using particular products become increasingly important (McNeal, 1969). As the child's needs change, so too do the nature and pattern of consumption. What children buy and consume at different stages is discussed more fully in Chapter 3.

Surveys of young people have revealed them to be sophisticated consumers with a high level of interest in shopping, able to distinguish between what they like and dislike, and quite capable of rejecting hype. In the United States, for example, a 1993 Yankelovich Partners Youth Monitor survey among 6- to 17-year-olds found children and adolescents to be enthusiastic and discerning shoppers. Young people expressed a firm interest in advertising, which they claimed to use for information to guide their buying decisions. Young consumers are not brand loyal, however, and tend to make many different brand choices in response to rapidly changing fads and fashions. In this sense they are probably less consistent, but paradoxically easier to predict than their parents because of their sensitivity to fashion trends.

The Yankelovich Monitor yielded a profile of young people as knowledgeable consumers who often held pragmatic attitudes about the future. Even pre-teenage children, for instance, indicated saving for the future. They were often self-reliant, with 36 per cent claiming to prepare meals for themselves in 1993, compared with 13 per cent in 1987. Sixty-two per cent said they had visited a supermarket in the previous week.

Young people can be active and discerning consumers. Their consumer behaviour, however, develops gradually and progressively throughout childhood, and it yields and is susceptible to many social influences. Consumer socialization is characterized by a number of key influential agents, including parents, peers and various mass media, as well as direct experience. This book will examine the character of children as consumers, indicate how young consumers develop consumer awareness, and consider what freedoms they should be allowed and what controls should be implemented to protect the child consumer.

Overall the results suggest, as McNeal puts it:

> before there is a geographic culture there is a children's culture; that children are very much alike around the industrialized world. The result is that they very much want the same things that they generally translate their needs into similar wants that tend to transcend culture. Therefore, it appears that fairly standardized multinational marketing strategies to children around the globe are viable.
>
> (1992, p. 250)

If McNeal is right, findings on children as consumers will translate well across countries and across time. But parental habits and beliefs as well as the influence of the media are not likely to yield universal findings. Young people may not be the same everywhere, but the growth of the world economy and the increase in wealth particularly of the Pacific Rim countries means that young people as consumers worldwide are likely to share more common interests and tastes than did their parents' generation.

Given the nature of an increasingly consumer-oriented society, the commercial influences on young people's lives have grown to a point where they can have a profound impact on them (Gardner and Sheppard, 1989). Consumption fulfils symbolic needs as well as bodily ones. The influences of consumption-related messages in the news media and points of purchase may reach into young people's beliefs and value systems, cultivating social and moral norms with far-reaching implications for society. This situation creates an obvious need to understand as much as we can about children and consumerism.

2

Socialization of Child Consumers

As children grow up, they increasingly become involved in decisions related to the purchase of products or services. They may observe, request and select goods with permission while accompanying their parents shopping as well as make independent forays to shops themselves (McNeal, 1992). Effective decision making requires having in place the necessary skills to make judgments about different aspects of consumerism. These skills are acquired through a process of consumer socialization. This can be defined as the process by which children acquire the skills, knowledge and attitudes necessary to function fully as consumers. A variety of studies have focused on how and when children develop consumption skills involved in earning and understanding money, attending to advertisements, making consumer choices and purchasing goods. This process is shaped by a number of sociocultural forces including parents, peers, school, shopping experiences and the mass media (Carlson and Grossbart, 1988; Peracchio, 1992). Inevitably the process is also influenced by the prevailing state of the local, national and global economy.

Children's consumer socialization begins at a very early age. Long before children are able to purchase products they are already expressing their preferences to parents (Reynolds and Wells, 1977). Involvement with the consumption process has been observed to occur as early as age five (McNeal, 1969). Research has indicated that mothers may instruct their children about brand preferences, frequently by having potential young consumers observe their own brand choices (Bahn, 1987). Mothers take their children shopping from two to three years of age onwards and often explain to them what they are doing, thus providing a powerful role model. By the time children have reached nine years most have acquired fairly sophisticated consumption orientations though this may differ by gender and class. Consumer attitudes and values are likely to undergo change during childhood, in line with cognitive development theory which postulates successive stages in the development of cognitive ability with age.

Co-shopping experiences (i.e. when mother and child shop together) have been found to give children an opportunity to acquire in-store shopping skills. Possibly because of their more harried life styles, working mothers are more likely to undertake co-shopping with their children than are non-working mothers (Grossbart et al., 1988). This style of shopping enables mothers to get certain domestic chores done, while spending important time with their children from which the latter can benefit as young consumers.

The consumer knowledge structure of children becomes more sophisticated and global as they grow older. Thus, young children (4–6 years) describe grocery shopping with their mothers in highly specific (i.e. episodic) terms. Older children (7–10 years), on the other hand, tend to give very general (i.e. categorical) descriptions (John, 1984). In fact McNeal (1992) found 4- to 12-year-old children amazingly brand conscious as Table 2.1 illustrates.

Young children have been found to display consumer-related skills beyond what would be expected given their theoretical stage of cognitive development (Ward et al., 1977). With appropriate tuition, pre-school children can acquire a degree of consumer literacy which would not develop naturally before the age of eight (Moschis et al., 1980).

The early school years also find the child changing in the way he or she interacts with agents of socialization. Television viewing increases throughout childhood years and so does its use as a source of consumer information (Adler et al., 1980). Similarly, the use of newspapers, magazines and books appears to increase between the ages of 5 and 11 (Wartella et al., 1979). Peer influence, on the other hand, seems to begin at about mid-childhood (McNeal, 1969). Parents also seem to treat their children differently according to the child's age. Overt parent-child interaction about consumerism is likely to be of importance during early childhood; it may be supplemented or followed by observation of parental behaviours in later childhood (Ward et al., 1977).

Adolescence, the period covering ages 12 to 18, is an important area for illustrating the socialization perspective in relation to consumerism. Adolescence is a period of rapid change in consumer behaviour. In the short space of half a dozen years, the relatively dependent child is transformed into the relatively autonomous young consumer.

Several patterns of consumer behaviour appear to undergo formation and change during the adolescent years. The adolescent's discretionary income as well as expenditures constantly rise with age during this period (e.g. Moore and Moschis, 1978, 1979) (see Chapter 4). In addition, preferences for products and brands are likely to be formed and changed (Moschis and Moore, 1981d; Reynolds and Wells, 1977). During adolescence, the young person generally acquires several consumption-related skills and is transformed into a fairly sophisticated consumer (e.g. Moschis, 1978, 1981; Moschis and Moore, 1979a). Furthermore, several of the consumer-related orientations adolescents acquire are likely to persist well into adulthood. For example, a study of brand loyalty prepared for Yankelovich, Skelly and White for *Seventeen* magazine found that a significant percentage of adult women were using the same brands they first chose as teenagers (Madison Avenue, 1980).

TABLE 2.1 *Extent of brand consciousness among children*

Product	Brand indicated	Frequency
Foods		
Cereal	Yes	5
Candy	Yes	4
Cookies	Yes	4
Soft drinks	Yes	4
Chips	Yes	3
Ice cream	Yes	3
Fruit juice	Yes	2
Peanut butter	Yes	2
Bakery foods	No	–
Bottled water	No	–
Butter	No	–
Canned vegetables	No	–
Coffee	No	–
Detergent	No	–
Eggs	No	–
Fish	No	–
Fruits	No	–
Meat	No	–
Milk	No	–
Popcorn	No	–
Vegetables	No	–
Nonfoods		
Toys	Yes	16
Clothing	Yes	8
Records/cassettes	Yes	7
Video games	Yes	7
Sporting goods	Yes	6
Cosmetics/toiletries	Yes	5
Shoes	Yes	4
Stereos/jam boxes	Yes	3
Bicycles	Yes	2
Computer/software	Yes	2
Skate Boards/skates	Yes	2
Television sets	Yes	1
Books	No	–
Jewellery	No	–
Stickers	No	–
Telephones	No	–

Source: McNeal,1992, p. 561

With increasing age adolescents are likely to develop more egalitarian sex roles regarding decision making (e.g. Moschis and Moore, 1979a). They also exert greater influence on adult and family purchases. Adolescence is a period of rapid change in interaction patterns with socialization agents. With respect to the adolescent's interaction with the mass media, research shows that television viewing and use of books declines, whereas radio listening, record playing and newspaper reading all increase (e.g. Avery, 1979; Lyle and Hoffman, 1971; Moschis and Moore, 1981a; Moschis and Churchill, 1978).

During this period, the adolescent's need for independence from his or her parents leads to greater dependency on peers (Coleman, 1961). In consequence, adolescents spend more time away from their family and home. This seems to affect adolescents' frequency of interaction with parents and peers. Thus, it is not surprising that age has been found to be associated negatively with frequency of communication about consumption with parents and positively with peers (Moschis and Churchill, 1978). While the frequency of communication with peers and parents seems to change, it is not quite clear whether the actual influence of these agents undergoes corresponding changes with age. Some studies have shown that parents are still the main influence affecting buying decisions (e.g. Moschis and Moore, 1979a), although their significance may be declining (Gilkison, 1973). Other evidence also suggests that such influence may be situation specific (e.g. Moschis and Moore, 1979a). Much may also depend on differences between the social background and status of the child's parents and his or her friends. Parents have a tendency to worry about their children mixing with the 'wrong crowd' who may exert more influence over their children's attitudes and behaviour than they do.

Consumer socialization can serve as a tool by which parents influence other aspects of the socialization process. For instance, parents frequently use the promise or reward of material goods as a device to modify or control a child's behaviour. A mother may reward her child with a gift if the child does something to please her, or may withhold or remove it if the child disobeys.

Research has supported this behaviour controlling function (Kourilsky and Murray, 1981). Specifically, adolescents reported that their parents frequently used the promise of chocolate as a means of controlling their behaviour (e.g. to complete homework or clean their rooms). Others have found that parents can teach children to apply economic reasoning. Children who were taught that they cannot have everything and must choose between realistic alternatives were found to be more satisfied with their choices (Kourilsky and Murray, 1981).

Consumer socialization has two distinct components: direct socialization related to consumption, such as the acquisition of skills, knowledge and attitudes concerned with budgeting, pricing and brand attitudes; and indirect socialization related to consumption, such as the underlying motivations that spur a male adolescent to purchase his first razor or a young girl to want her first bra. While both are significant, the indirect component of consumer socialization is of most interest to marketers, who want to understand why people buy their products.

Consumer Socialization

The term 'socialization' refers to the process by which young people acquire various patterns of beliefs and behaviours (e.g. Goslin, 1969), while 'consumer socialization' refers specifically to the process of learning consumer-related skills, knowledge and attitudes (Ward, 1974). Socialization explanations of human behaviour make the following key assumption: 'To understand human behaviour we must specify its social origins and the process by which it is learned and maintained.' (Mcleod and O'Keefe, 1972, pp 127–128.)

The adaptation of the socialization approach to consumer research was only proposed as a vehicle for the study of consumer behaviour in the mid-1970s (Ward, 1974). The area commonly known as consumer socialization has received considerable interest and attention mainly as a result of various contemporary issues related to public and corporate policy formulation. *Public policy makers* have developed an interest in the area because of various issues surrounding the effects of marketing activities (advertising in particular) on young people and their families. *Marketers* are primarily interested in understanding how young people develop consumer-related thoughts and behaviours, as a means of improving their communication campaigns directed at this rather lucrative segment of the market. *Consumer educators* need to understand consumer socialization in order to design appropriate consumer education materials and prepare young people for efficient and effective interaction with the marketplace. Finally, the area has become of interest to students of socialization and consumer behaviour because it seems to present new directions and opportunities for studying and understanding consumer behaviour.

Consumer socialization research is typically based on two models of human learning: the *social learning model* and the *cognitive development model*. Studies using the social learning approach attempt to explain socialization as a function of environmental influences applied to the person. Learning is assumed to take place during the individual's interaction with socialization agents in various social (structural) settings. The cognitive development model, on the other hand, seeks explanations for the formation of cognitions and behaviour on the basis of qualitative changes (stages) in the cognitive organization occurring between infancy and adulthood. These stages are defined in terms of cognitive structures that a child can use in perceiving and dealing with the environment at different ages (Kohlberg, 1969). There is considerable criticism of stage-wise theories, however (Furnham and Stacey, 1991). Learning is viewed as a cognitive-psychological process of adjustment to one's environment.

A model of consumer development has been produced by Moschis and his colleagues (Moschis and Churchill, 1978; Moschis and Moore, 1978, 1979a). This conceptual model consists of five types of variables derived from general socialization theories: socialization agents, learning processes, social structural variables, age or life cycle, and content of learning. It represents a clear way of thinking about how the process works (see Figure 2.1).

Antecedents	Socialization Processes	Outcomes
Social structural variables		
	Agent-learner relationships	
		Learning properties
	– Modelling	
	– Reinforcement	
	– Social interaction	
Age or life cycle position		

FIGURE 2.1 A conceptual model of consumer socialization. Moschis and Churchill, 1978

Socialization agents may refer to a person or organization. In the life of every person there are a number of people and institutions (e.g. family members, school, clubs, neighbours) directly involved in socialization that have great influence because of their frequency of contact, primacy, and control over rewards and punishments given to the individual.

Learning processes refer to the mechanisms through which the agent influences the learner. They can be classified into three categories: modelling, reinforcement, and social interaction. Modelling, which is also known as observational learning, involves imitation of the agent's behaviour (i.e. doing what parents do). Reinforcement involves either reward or punishment. Social interaction is less specific and it may involve a combination of modelling and reinforcement (i.e. conforming to peer group norms of purchasing and consumption).

Social structural variables are factors, such as socioeconomic status, sex, and birth order, that help locate the learner within his or her social environment, where learning takes place. These demographic variables are powerful partly because they relate so closely to disposable cash available.

Age or life cycle position refers to a person's lifetime span during which learning occurs; it is used to index a person's cognitive development or life cycle stage(s).

Learning properties refer to a variety of consumer-related cognitions and behaviours that comprise the concept of consumer behaviour, such as attitudes toward saving and spending and brand preferences. This is frequently a mixture of abilities and attitudes developed often at an early age.

The Role of Parents

Families are an important influence in consumer socialization of children. For many years, sociologists speculated that young people learn basic 'rational' aspects of consumption from their parents (Parsons *et al.*, 1953; Reisman and Roseborough, 1955). Later research on consumer socialization also supported this view. Ward and Wackman (1972) showed that parents' 'general consumer goals' included teaching their children about price–quality relationships. Similarly, Moore and Stephens (1975) showed that overall parent–adolescent communication about consumption predicts fairly well a child's knowledge of prices of selected products. These findings suggest that parents may encourage their youngsters to use price as a criterion in evaluating products. The adolescent's frequency of communication with his or her parents about consumption is expected to be related positively to the strength of the individual's economic motivations for consumption.

Parents can and do play a major role in relation to the child's consumer-related attitudes and values. This influence may be felt throughout the child's daily living experience. Parents may, for example, play a key role in the formation of the child's knowledge about nutritional values by commenting on the nutritional quality of various food products (Schneider, 1987). The foods usually purchased or the comments made by parents about food products when actually shopping with their child in grocery stores and supermarkets may have a powerful influence on the child's knowledge about nutritional values and attitudes towards various types of foods.

Not all parents adopt the same patterns of consumer socialization with their offspring. Family influence on consumer socialization of young people is often related to demographic characteristics such as the socioeconomic status of the household and the gender and age of the child. Independence in consumer decision making, for example, becomes greater as the child gets older (Moschis and Moore, 1979b), although the degree of independence varies with the type of product under consideration.

Social class is an important factor in relation to consumer socialization. Middle-class adolescents appear to attain less independence in purchasing as they grow older than do adolescent consumers in lower and upper social classes. This finding has been attributed to the normative standards of their class, and the greater desire of middle-class parents to supervise their children's activities generally in an effort to socialize them into the class norms (Moschis *et al.*, 1977; Psathas, 1957).

Parental influence on the development of the consumer behaviour of their offspring is also affected by the gender of the child. Among adolescent girls, for example, parental influences may often be far weaker than they are among adolescent boys because of the powerful effects of the need to conform to peer group norms among girls, especially when purchasing items related to physical appearance, such as clothing and health care products (Moschis *et al.*, 1977).

[handwritten marginalia: Research 'till 1998 about Parent/family role in cons. socialisation.]

Family influences on adolescent consumer behaviour vary by type of product. There is evidence that parental influence is less likely to be present during the purchase of such items as records or tapes, sporting equipment and movie tickets. The opposite is likely to be true when the young person is shopping for clothes (although adolescent girls often present an exception to this rule) (Mehotra and Torges, 1976; Moschis et al., 1977; Saunders et al., 1973). The extent to which adolescents take parental suggestions into account in choosing among brands is associated with the perceived risk or long-term consequences connected with the specific decision. Parental influence tends to be greater with high risk purchases (Moschis and Moore, 1979a). Considerable influence of parents has also been observed in respect of less risky areas such as bank patronage (Fry et al., 1973). There is reasonably good supportive evidence that the family is instrumental in teaching young people basic rational aspects of consumption. It influences behaviours related to saving and spending, expenditure allocation and product decisions.

Parental influence is not invariably purposive and instructional, however, tending rather to be incidental in nature. Parent–child discussions about consumption are most actively initiated as a result of the child's request for a product that he or she sees advertised. Reinforcement mechanisms (e.g. giving the child an allowance) are likely to be frequent during early childhood (Ward et al., 1977). With increasing age children often find other sources of income, thus reducing their economic dependence on their parents. This, in turn, may diminish the importance of parental control over the child's consumerism. In fact the study by Ward and his associates suggests the ways children learn consumer skills from their parents through observation. The child's acquisition of economic independence from his or her parents is often combined with parental permissiveness. McNeal (1969) found that with increasing age there is not only an increasing desire among children to assume independent purchasing activities, but also an increasing parental permissiveness in children's independent consumer behaviour.

The family appears to remain a significant source of consumer information throughout adolescence. In one study of adolescent decision-making patterns, Moschis and Moore (1979a) found the family to be the most important source of information regarding consumer decisions. The fact that the adolescent's frequency of interaction with his or her family regarding consumption matters declines with age (e.g. Moschis and Churchill, 1978) does not necessarily imply that the family's influence over the youth's consumer behaviour declines. Moschis and Moore (1980b) examined the effects of various socialization practices among families, including overt communication, observation of parents' consumer behaviours and reinforcement mechanisms (positive and negative) used by parents. Although overt communication about consumption appeared to decline with age, the adolescent's tendency to observe parental behaviours was not affected by age. This observational measure was a strong predictor of some aspects of adolescents' consumer behaviours, especially consumer role perceptions.

Overt communication with parents was found to be a relatively weak predictor of consumer behaviour. The frequency of talk within the family about consumption was positively associated with the adolescent's tendency to use advertising and price reduction ('sales') as criteria for choosing among brands; it was negatively related to the adolescent's tendency to use brand name as a criterion and did not affect their level of brand preferences (Moschis and Moore, 1980a). Instead, brand preferences were found to be associated with the adolescent's frequency of viewing television, reading newspapers and interacting with peers about consumption matters (Moschis and Moore, 1981b).

Effective consumer learning has also been found to be related to the patterns of *quality* (rather than the quantity) of communication that takes place within the home (Moore and Moschis, 1978; Moschis and Moore, 1979b, 1980a). This is in line with family communications patterns research in political socialization, where patterns were found to have a more significant influence than frequency or amount of parent–child interaction (McLeod and Chaffee, 1972). These findings suggest that not only may the relative importance of consumer socialization agents vary during adolescence, but also the impact of the various learning processes.

Furthermore, it is not quite clear from the available research findings how various socialization processes interact to affect consumer learning. For example, while much research has treated family influences as a mediating variable of media effects, especially television (Robertson, 1979), there is some evidence to suggest that the mass media may also mediate the effects of parents on consumer behaviour (e.g. Churchill and Moschis, 1979). In fact, as Moschis and Moore (1981b) found, different patterns of communication occur in households exhibiting different newspaper readership and television-viewing patterns, and which in turn lead to the development of various consumer orientations among adolescents.

Moschis and Churchill (1978) found that the family seems to be important in teaching adolescents 'rational' aspects of consumerism. They also found a strong positive relationship between family communication about consumption and the adolescent's propensity to perform sensible consumer acts such as spending within their means. At odds with some earlier research findings that parents taught their children very little about consumer skills (e.g. Ward and Wackman, 1973), Moschis and Churchill found that parents did try to teach consumer skills to their teenagers, though this is probably class related and differs from country to country. Thus, different consumer skills, such as judging good value for money, spending to a budget, and comparing prices before buying something, seem to be learned at different ages from parents and through different learning processes. Social class differences may explain equivocal findings: middle-class parents are more likely overall than are working-class parents to attempt to teach their children to become consumer literate.

Churchill and Moschis (1979) reported that family communication was related to adolescent consumer socialization. Interactions with parents apparently contributed to the child's learning of the 'goal-oriented' or rational elements of consumption. Their findings indicated a significant link between the amount of family communication about consumption and the extent to which adolescents held economic motivations for consumption. This finding appeared to be consistent with speculations of early sociologists with respect to the kinds of consumer behaviour young people learn from their parents, as well as with respect to the role television plays in this process (Parsons *et al.*, 1953; Riesman and Roseborough, 1955). This complex and highly political issue will be discussed further in Chapters 6 and 8.

Many studies have looked at the influence of parents (particularly mothers) on children's and adolescents' consumer decisions (Bocker, 1986; Rust, 1993; Saunders *et al.*, 1973). Research in this area dates back nearly 30 years and most researchers have attempted to identify key characteristics or variables. Thus, Ward and Wackman (1972) examined three variables thought to effect children's purchases: the demographic characteristics of the mother, the usual parent–child interaction style and the mothers' mass communication behaviour. The latter proved by far the most influential. The more television the mother watched the more her child attempted to influence consumer decisions and the more likely it was that the mother yielded to influence. However, as Caron and Ward (1975) have shown, social class is a determinant of television watching which also relates to consumer behaviour.

In an observational study of parent–child interaction in a supermarket, Atkin (1978) found for each decision either the child initiates a request or demand (and the parent agrees, denies or suggests another choice) or the parent initiates by inviting or directing the child's selection (which the child can agree or disagree with). The most common pattern for young children is the parent yielding to children's demands, followed by children selecting after the parental invitation to choose.

Belch, Belch and Ceresino (1985) looked at the influence of fathers, mothers and teenage children. They found parental influence strong but sex-linked; hence fathers were influential on automobiles and television sets and mothers on household appliances and food. Teenage children's influence seems greatest at the initiation phase. Further, the teenagers' influence was strongest for aesthetic qualities like style, colour and model, and weakest as regards when and where to purchase and how much to spend. Interestingly, children believed that they themselves had greater influence over decision making than was attributed to them by their parents. However, as various authors note, parents may underplay the actual influence of the children in the decision-making process. Thus, the influence of parents and teenage children on family consumer decisions is a function of product class, decision stage and sub-decision area. Swinyard and Sim (1987) found that for child-centred (toys, clothing, food) and child-used products or services (holidays, restaurant choices, outside-the-home entertainment) children are perceived as most influential. They also provide a very useful summary table of findings from the 1970s (see Table 2.2).

TABLE 2.2 *Studies examining child interaction with family purchase decisions*

Study	Key Findings
Hempel, 1974	Children are more likely to participate in the need identification stage than in later stages.
Ward and Wackman, 1973	In mother-child interactions, children most often request food, toys, and clothing. As children's age increases, their requests decrease and parental yielding increases.
Szybillo and Sosanie, 1977	Children and parents interact to a high degree in all stages of the decision-making process.
Filiatrault and Ritchie, 1980	The relative influence of husband and wife are about the same in families with and without children, and children's influence is greatest in need identification stage, less in later stages.
Jenkins, 1979	Children were found to have minimal influence in the choice of household durables (furniture, major appliances, automobiles, life savings, selection of a family doctor), but were more influential on the choice of family 'activities'.
Nelson, 1979	In decisions for a pizza restaurant, children over 5 are as involved as their parents in all decision areas except final decision and amount spent.
Mehotra and Torges, 1977	In a study designed to isolate factors that affected mothers' yielding to children's purchase requests, no factors were identified.
Deering and Jacoby, 1971	In a mother-and-child decision simulation, children contributed almost half of the joint total.

Source: Swinyard and Sim, 1987

The details of their own study are however important (see Table 2.3). Note that the respondents in the study ranged from 3 to 30 with over 50 per cent between 12 and 19 years.

Some products, of course, cause more parental concern and hence conflict than others (Grossbart and Crosby, 1984). Some researchers through observation, interview and diary methods have tried to model the process. Isler, Popper and Ward (1987) provide a useful model of the process which describes how the decisions are made (see Figure 2.2).

From their study Isler *et al.* (1987) concluded:

Older children do not have to ask for particular products, because their mothers already know their desires and frequently buy accordingly. Our data also indicated that older children ask less frequently—perhaps because they have fewer opportunities since they may accompany their parents on shopping trips less frequently. Requests for cereals and snack foods remain relatively constant for all three age groups studied, while request frequency for other products varies with age. Most requests occur at home, although a large percentage of requests made by younger children are made while shopping with the mother.

TABLE 2.3 *Summary of results by product*

	Product	Category %
Children's products		62.92*
Child(ren)'s toys	72.78#	
Child(ren)'s clothing	69.48	
Food and nonalcoholic beverages	46.50	
Activities		50.04
Outside entertainment	62.45	
Conventional restaurants	43.40	
Family vacation	44.28	
Children's Education		43.33
Courses for child(ren)	56.55	
Child(ren)'s school	34.00	
Private tutors for children	39.45	
Durables		17.46
Television	32.40	
Refrigerator	14.00	
Household appliances	10.60	
House/apartment	27.50	
Living room furniture	21.18	
Furniture for kitchen	11.90	
Other furnishings	15.50	
Automobile	19.60	
Life insurance for husband	4.50	
Nondurables		10.97
Household cleaning products	15.60	
Kitchenware	9.75	
Drugs and first-aid items	23.35	
Wife's clothing	7.30	
Husband's clothing	5.70	
Cosmetics	11.80	
Alcoholic beverages	3.30	

* Indicates that 62.92 per cent of parents reported that their children were influential in decisions for 'child(ren)'s products'.
# Indicates that 72.78 per cent of parents reported that their children were influential in decisions for 'child(ren)'s toys'.
Source: Swinyard and Sim, 1987

The most frequently used request strategy is 'just asking'. The most common response by mothers is to accede to their children's requests. This response may be due to several factors: mothers may wish to please their children, to reward them, or simply to buy products which they feel are reasonable for their children. The extent of yielding is dependent upon the type of product requested and is higher for less expensive products and services. The most common agree-to-buy response is 'didn't mind buying, said yes right away', while refuse-to-buy responses are more likely to be characterized by discussion or stalling.

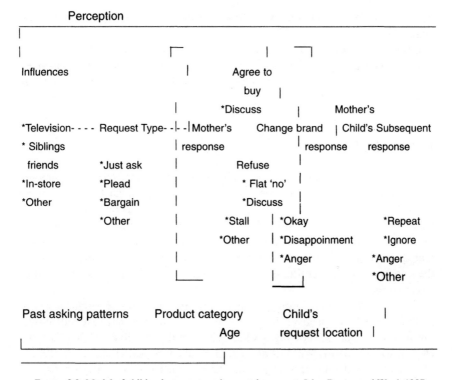

FIGURE 2.2 Model of children's requests and parental response. Isler, Popper and Ward, 1987

Reports of mothers' refusals leading to conflict are rare. In the few instances where children argued or got angry, the mother's most common response was to repeat what she had said.

Mothers feel that most requests stem from the child's seeing the item in the store or from 'other' reasons. The incidence of citing television advertising as the main influence decreases with the child's age.

Requests by children, then, do not seem to take the form of a constant barrage of demands directed toward parents, nor is television advertising perceived as the major influence in stimulating product requests. We should note, however, that it is not possible to examine secondary influences (i.e. did the child ask for the item in store because the child had previously seen an ad for the item on television?) from the data reported. Mothers generally accede to children's requests, and the amount of conflict caused by requests appears to be quite low.

(pp. 38–39)

A problem with much of these data, however, resides in the fact that there is disagreement between mothers, fathers and children about how much influence they actually do have on the decision-making process. Foxman *et al.* (1989) found considerable differences between the three, and it remains difficult to ascertain who was correct. They also note the family 'communication environment' (conforming versus non-conforming) and the child's personal resources (such as income and school grades) as well as perceived product knowledge are important in determining the extent to which adolescents influence family purchase decisions.

Childers and Rao (1992), however, demonstrated that an adolescent's peer reference group may be extremely important in determining his or her consumer decisions. They believed that peers have a particularly strong influence when it comes to luxury goods that are publicly displayed.

Parental Styles

Parents have been found to vary in their styles of consumer socialization with their children. These can give rise to different attitudes towards consumerism and different consumer practices on the part of young people. Carlson and Grossbart (1988) found that mothers with alternative parental styles differed in communicating with children about consumption, in the way they managed their children's consumer-related behaviour, in the manner in which they controlled their children's media usage and in their attitudes towards advertising.

Various studies had previously revealed differing attitudes of parents towards children and television advertising. Parents tend to be either negatively disposed towards television advertising (Atkin, 1978; Burr and Burr, 1976; Clancy-Hepburn et al., 1974; Ward et al., 1977) or unconcerned (Enis et al., 1980). More will be said about this subject in a later chapter which focuses on the role of television in shaping children's consumer attitudes and behaviour. It is appropriate at this point, however, to examine more closely the issue of parental styles in connection with consumer socialization practices.

The socialization of children by their parents is aimed at instilling in children the predominant habits and values of the culture in which they live (Baumrind, 1980). As such, it reflects varying cultural values and norms and is therefore unlikely itself to take on a single form. Some scholars have observed that parents can be classified according to the way they handle their children's misbehaviour, to show warmth towards their children, or anxiety about them, or in the way they protect them (or in some case overprotect them) (Gardner, 1982). These different styles of parental socialization have been given various labels such as: restrictiveness versus permissiveness (Armentrout and Burger, 1972; Baumrind, 1968, 1971; Bronson, 1972; Gardner, 1982; Kagan et al., 1962), warmth versus hostility (Armentrout and Burger, 1972; Becker, 1964; Hower and Edwards, 1978; Roe and Siegelman, 1963), and calm detachment versus anxious emotional involvement (Armentrout and Burger, 1972; Becker, 1964; Hower and Edwards, 1978; Roe and Siegelman, 1963).

Becker (1964) offered a three-dimensional model which includes eight ideal parental types that reflect combinations of structural components of socialization. In his model, *warmth* denotes accepting, child centredness, use of explanation and reasoning, praise in discipline, and low reliance on physical punishment; *restrictiveness* signifies enforcement of demands regarding manners, neatness, care of family items, obedience, and so forth; and *anxious emotional involvement* indicates high emotionality in babying, protectiveness, and solicitousness for the child's welfare. Such a typology has been investigated in relation to consumer socialization.

Authoritarian parents seek high levels of control over children because they view children as dominated by egotistical and impulsive forces (Gardner, 1982). These parents judge children's conduct by religious or other standards endorsed by authority figures (Baumrind, 1968), expect unquestioned obedience, strictly enforce rules, and discourage and punish wilful behaviour. Authoritarians believe in parental omnipotence, keeping children in subordinate roles, restricting expression of autonomy, and not encouraging verbal exchanges between parents and children (Baumrind, 1978; Crosby and Grossbart, 1984). Authoritarians believe children have few rights, but have adult responsibilities (Baumrind, 1980). *Rigid controlling* parents are similar to authoritarians, except that calm detachment limits their emotional involvement in children's socialization.

Like authoritarian and rigid controlling parents, *neglecting* parents also maintain distant relations with children. However, they neither seek nor exercise much control over children, perhaps because they are self-involved and deny or wish to avoid obligations to provide guidance. Their limited restrictiveness is coupled with a relative lack of warmth or anxious concern about the child's development. They see children as having few rights or responsibilities that require parental attention, as being capable of meeting many of their own needs, and requiring little communication reinforcement. Hence, neglecting parents do little to monitor or directly encourage their children's capabilities to function autonomously.

Authoritatives are inclined to view rights and responsibilities of adults and children as complementary. They foster a balance between parents' and children's rights that changes as the child develops. They encourage self-expression and value self-will and autonomy, but also expect disciplined conformity (Baumrind, 1968, 1978). Authoritatives do not impose any restrictions merely to exercise power, but they use firm control and confront disobedience when they think overt intervention is needed. They are warm, conscientious and supportive, but expect from children the maximum in mature behaviour (Gardner, 1982). Authoritatives explain rules, offer alternatives to blind obedience, and solicit the child's opinion. They attempt to enrich the child's environment with cultural and educational activities (Gardner *et al.*, 1978).

Ward *et al.* (1977) identified five methods mothers use to teach children consumer skills:

(1) prohibiting certain acts;
(2) giving lectures on consumer activities;
(3) holding discussions with the child about consumer decisions;

(4) acting as an example;
(5) allowing the child to learn from his or her own experiences.

Their research showed that most mothers used relatively few teaching methods and that there was considerable variation between them in how they taught their children consumer skills.

Carlson and Grossbart (1988) developed and tested a variety of hypotheses about parental styles of child consumer socialization and control (see Table 2.4). What is significant about this work is its demonstration of how important parenting is on various aspects of children's consumption behaviour. That is, parenting styles are extremely powerful forces in shaping a child's perception, understanding and experience of the economic world. Predictably, parental values, lifestyles and socialization patterns have considerable effects on their children's purchasing behaviour. Thus, authoritarian parents might in fact restrict the economic and consumer knowledge of their children while permissive parents encourage early consumerism believing informed choice comes from experience. But what right have parents favouring one style to impose their views, values and preferences on another? If they are in large part responsible for their children's beliefs and habits it is to them that education (rather than regulation) ought to be applied (see Table 2.4).

Social Class

Socioeconomic background may affect decision-making patterns as well as the development of such patterns. From a learning theory point of view, it has been argued that because adolescents from low-income homes have less experience with money, and may be less aware of the range of consumer goods, their learning of some aspects of consumption may be less adequate than that of adolescents from upper-income homes who have more opportunities for consumption (Ward, 1974).

While working-class parents may have lower incomes than middle-class parents they may nevertheless often give their children greater exposure to the economic world and consumer experiences than middle-class parents do. Thus, working-class children receive more pocket money/allowances and undertake more purchasing trips on their own (frequently at their parents' bequest). Because they are exposed to the market-place earlier and more extensively than middle-class children, frequently working-class children are better informed about and experienced at commercial consumption.

Earlier, Riesman, Glazer and Denney (1953) also speculated that in the more affluent families, children acquire some understanding of the purchasing processes at a relatively early age. Other research findings appear to support this line of reasoning, showing that young people from upper socio-economic backgrounds have greater awareness of, and preference for, commercial stimuli in their consumer environment (Moschis and Churchill, 1978; Moore and Moschis, 1978; Ward, 1974). Specifically, some research suggests that young people from upper social classes may have stronger brand preferences (Guest, 1964) and are more likely to seek information prior to decision-making (Moore and Moschis, 1978) than their lower-class counterparts.

TABLE 2.4 *Hypotheses about parental styles of child consumer socialization*

Children's Consumption Autonomy
- Authoritarians grant less consumption autonomy to their children than *rigid controlling, authoritative, permissive* or *neglecting* parents.
- *Rigid controlling* parents grant less consumption autonomy to their children than *authoritative, permissive* or *neglecting* parents.
- *Authoritatives* grant less consumption autonomy to their children than *permissive* or *neglecting* parents.

Parent–Child Communication about Consumption
- *Authoritatives* communicate more with their children about consumption than *permissive, authoritarian, rigid controlling* or *neglecting* parents.
- *Permissives* communicate more with their children about consumption than *authoritarian, rigid controlling* or *neglecting* parents.
- *Authoritatives* have more consumer socialization goals for their children than *permissive, authoritarian, rigid controlling* or *neglecting* parents.
- *Permissives* have more consumer socialization goals for their children than *authoritarian, rigid controlling* or *neglecting* parents.

Restriction and monitoring of consumption and media exposure
- *Authoritatives* restrict and monitor children's consumption and media exposure more than *authoritarian, rigid controlling, neglecting* or *permissive* parents.
- *Authoritarians* restrict and monitor children's consumption and media exposure more than *rigid controlling, neglecting* or *permissive* parents.
- *Rigid controlling* parents restrict and monitor children's consumption and media exposure more than *neglecting* or *permissive* parents.
- *Authoritatives* have a less positive attitude about advertising than *authoritarian, rigid controlling, neglecting* or *permissive* parents.
- *Authoritarians* have a less positive attitude about advertising than *rigid controlling, neglecting* or *permissive* parents.
- *Rigid controlling* parents have a less positive attitude about advertising than *neglecting* or *permissive* parents.

Source: Carlson and Grossbart, 1978

Theory and research indicate that upper-class and middle-class families, as opposed to lower-class families, are more conscious of the normative standards of their class and are more likely to supervise closely their children's consumption activities in an effort to socialize them into the class norms (Moschis *et al.*, 1977; Psathas, 1957; Robertson and Rossiter, 1975). This parental involvement in adolescent consumer behaviour may result in more frequent discussion of consumption with the child (see Ward *et al.*, 1977).

Churchill and Moschis (1978) found that socioeconomic status was not related to family communication about consumption. Moschis and Churchill (1979) reported that socioeconomic background was related to brand prefer- ence, suggesting that children from higher socioeconomic backgrounds have more opportunities for consumption and are more aware of their consumer envi- ronment, including the availability of products in the marketplace, than children of lower socioeconomic backgrounds. The questions in understanding this socialization process relate to *what*, *when* and *why* parents communicate to their children about the commercial world.

Another study of adolescents examined relationships between measures of adolescent–parent interactions and several dependent variables among lower-, middle-, and upper-class adolescents (Moschis and Moore, 1979c). Findings showed that parent–child communication about consumption was associated with the youth's consumer role perceptions only among children from upper social classes, suggesting that purposive consumer training may occur only in the upper social strata. In lower social classes, family communication appears to focus upon product brand names. Discussions about consumer matters with parents among middle-class adolescents tended to focus upon product attributes (e.g. prices).

Indirect influences

In addition to the direct effects that family communications appear to have on consumer learning, such processes may affect consumer behaviour indirectly. Indirect influence can take place when family communication processes influ- ence the offspring's interaction with other sources of consumer information which, in turn, directly (or indirectly) affect the development of consumer behaviour. The findings of several studies have established the presence of rela- tionships between family communication processes—including family commu- nication patterns—and the individual's interaction with other socialization agents (e.g. Lull, 1980; McLeod *et al.*, 1982) that subsequently affect behaviour. This indirect pattern of family influence has also been found in studies of con- sumer socialization. There are indications, for instance, that different styles of family communication within the home may lead to differential exposure to and use of the mass media (newspapers and television) which, in turn, could lead to the development of various consumer orientations (Moore and Moschis, 1981). Thus, family communication may indirectly influence the child's interaction with other socialization agents, which may then influence consumer learning.

With respect to the influence of specific parent–child communication processes on mass media use, one study examined whether motivations for tele- vision viewing could be the result of family communication structure at home

(Moore and Moschis, 1981). It was speculated that a socio-oriented communication structure may implicitly encourage the child to pay attention to the mass media as a means of learning how to behave in various social settings. The results were in line with this expectation, suggesting that families may be encouraging their children to turn to the media to learn social orientations or consumption behaviours appropriate to certain roles. This may then lead to the learning of materialistic orientations, since people are believed to learn the 'expressive' aspects of consumption from mass media (e.g. Moschis and Moore, 1982; Riesman and Roseborough, 1955).

Additional support for these speculations comes from previous research (Ward and Wackman, 1972) which also found materialistic attitudes to be related to social motivations for watching television commercials and programmes (e.g. watching commercials and programmes to learn what products to buy to make a good impression on others), and such motivations to be the result of family communication structure at home (Moore and Moschis, 1981; Moschis and Moore, 1979b).

On the other hand, these studies show that concept-oriented family communication structure is positively associated with exposure to public affairs information in the mass media (e.g. Chaffee et al., 1971), which may in turn have a positive impact upon consumer knowledge and other consumer competencies (Moschis and Moore, 1978, 1979b). For example, the results of a path analysis of 301 Wisconsin adolescents suggested that a concept-oriented family communication structure leads to exposure to public affairs information in the mass media, which may subsequently lead to the learning of consumer skills. The influence does not appear to be direct, nor to be totally explained by the antecedent variables. Specifically, age and concept-oriented family communications structure were the best predictors of the adolescent's frequency of interacting with the media regarding public affairs content, that is, frequency of reading news about the economy, government and advertisements, and of viewing national and local news on television (Moschis and Moore, 1978, 1979b).

Mediating effects of family communication styles

There is evidence to suggest that family communication processes modify the effect of other socialization agents, particularly television (McLeod et al., 1982). The motivating role of family communications has also been investigated in the context of consumer socialization. The family has been found to have a particular influence over the child's consumer socialization by affecting how young consumers respond to advertising (Robertson, 1979).

Several studies have noted that the extent to which children and teenagers exhibit susceptibilities to advertising on television, for instance, is related to how often they talk with their parents about consumption matters. Families who relatively rarely talk about shopping or purchase-related matters tend to raise children who are more influenced by televised advertisements (Churchill and Moschis, 1979; Moschis and Moore, 1982).

Moschis and Moore (1982) administered questionnaires to over 200 adolescents aged 12 to 18 years. The questions were designed to address various aspects of consumer socialization, such as how often the family discussed purchasing and consumption, the extent to which the adolescent held materialistic values, and so on. The primary finding was that the effects of advertising differed depending upon whether the family discussed economic issues with their children. Advertising was associated with the development of materialist values and a traditional view of sex roles among adolescents whose parents did not discuss consumer matters with their children. Family discussion of consumer issues appeared to neutralize the effects of advertising.

Parental mediation is often the result of a child's requests for advertised products. For example, Atkin (1982) found that parents and children often discuss and argue over consumer purchase decisions that are stimulated by television advertising. Such discussions and opportunities for mediation can be attributed to high adult–child co-viewing behaviour, which has been estimated to be as high as 70 per cent for peak-time programming.

While the family's mediating role is well-documented, the nature and consequences of parental mediation are not very clear. Reviews outside the field of consumer behaviour suggest that parental mediation of television effects are either strengthened or weakened in the interpersonal context (McLeod et al., 1982). There is some evidence to suggest that the impact of outside-the-family influences such as television advertising is greater under conditions of parental restrictiveness (Atkin et al., 1979). Similarly, Hawkins and Pingree (1982) found reduced effects of television for youngsters in families that are low in conflict and parental control. These findings may be attributed to family communication patterns. For example, it has been found that protective families stress obedience and social harmony and make a conscious effort to protect the child from controversy within the home. Since parental control using restrictiveness is likely to be present in these families, parental efforts to protect the child within the home may leave the youngster unprotected from outside influences (McLeod and Chaffee, 1972). Thus, it is not surprising that studies find children from protective homes to be susceptible to the influence of external sources, such as peers and television advertising (Moore and Moschis, 1978).

The Role of Peers

Peers are also a significant source of influence upon children's consumer behaviour especially among adolescents (Campbell, 1969). Even younger (5–10 years old) children's consumer-related attitudes and values can be shaped by peer-group influence. Such influence includes *comments* which peers might make about products or brands themselves, and about the way they are advertised. There is evidence that children frequently talk with their friends about advertisements (Greenberg *et al.*, 1986). Such conversations may increase or decrease the effectiveness of advertisements to some extent. During the adolescent years, a girl or boy's need for independence from their parents leads them into establishing a dependence on peers (Coleman, 1961). Some studies have shown that adolescents' preferences for products and brands are influenced by those of their peers (e.g. Ryan, 1966; Saunders *et al.*, 1973; Vener, 1957). As adolescents interact with their peers about consumption matters, they will learn about their peers' product favourites and may take these into account in evaluating products on their own.

Some researchers have suggested that young people learn the symbolic meaning of goods from their peers (Parsons et al, 1953; Riesman and Roseborough, 1955). Research findings also indicate that peer influence may be of significance in situations involving conspicuous consumption (Saunders *et al.*, 1973). These speculations and findings support a hypothesized positive relationship between the adolescent's frequency of communication with his or her peers about consumption matters and the strength of his or her (1) social motivations for consumption and (2) materialistic attitudes.

A study of adolescent females by Brittain (1963) showed that in areas like taste in clothes, in which girls perceived their ideas to be like that of their peers, the girls tended to favour peer-suggested alternatives. Similarly, another study suggested that the typical teenager is responsive to peer opinions on topics when they perceive peers to have similar value perspectives, interests and tastes. This may be particularly true in respect of clothes and hairstyle (Remmers and Radler, 1957).

It is also likely that consumer-related cognitions learned from interacting with peers will influence the consumption of the individual's parents. Riesman and Roseborough (1955) have termed this influence as 'retroactive socialization'. Under such conditions the child may be viewed, in Stone's (1954, p. 23) terms, as an 'agent of his peers', communicating the acquired information to his parents.

Peer influence may actually start operating during fairly early childhood. McNeal (1992) reported significant peer influence on the child by age seven. Another study by Shaak, Annes and Rossiter (1975) found stronger peer influence operating among ten-year-olds than among six-year-olds, however. Unfortunately, research on learning processes through which peer influence operates is sparse. Relatively little research exists on the relative influence of the socialization agents in the child's consumer development (Adler *et al.*, 1980). There is some evidence that the child's interaction with one socialization agent affects his or her level of interaction with others. For example, the child's frequency of watching television is likely to result in a larger number of product requests of parents, as a result of seeing advertisements for products on television (Robertson, 1979). The child's interaction with others is also likely to affect his or her media-use behaviour. More will be said about the role of media in a later section.

Moschis and Churchill (1978) found that peers appear to be an important socialization agent in contributing to the learning of materialistic values and related consumer motives. Adolescents' contact with peers to discuss consumption matters centre on the social importance of goods and services, and may be a second-order consequence of learning from parents.

Adolescents may learn not only these expressive aspects of consumption from peers but also many other consumer-related skills. Overall, the findings of Moschis and Churchill suggest that interaction with peers about consumption matters may make the adolescent aware of godsend services in the marketplace and of the buying processes. This greater awareness of the consumer environment may, in turn, contribute to the adolescent's active interaction about consumption matters with other socialization agents such as the mass media, which may result in additional learning.

Sex Differences

Sex-role conceptions about family decisions naturally differ between young people. A number of researchers have suggested that power and task responsibility are built into the roles of husband and wife on the basis of cultural norms and controls (Burgess and Locke, 1960). There appears to be some degree of marital division of labour, based on gender, with respect to family decisions (Davis, 1970, 1976). There is some suggestion that sex-role ideologies are likely to start developing in early childhood and undergo formation and change throughout a person's life (Davis, 1976; Emmerich, 1973).

Research suggests, for example, that male adolescents are likely to develop 'sexist' views and more traditional attitudes than female adolescents about sexual stereotypes, career, and family roles (Angrist et al., 1977; Bayer, 1975; Hill and Aldous, 1969).

Studies have shown that females have a stronger orientation towards their peers than do males (e.g. Hamilton and Warden, 1966). Sociologists have speculated that this greater dependence on one another among females may result from the desire to clarify and boost an unsatisfactory role identification and feel more certain of their competence and achievement for future roles (Parsons, Bales and Shils, 1949), as well as to learn standards and criteria for the various elements of attractiveness that are expected to be of crucial importance in competing for husbands in the future (Sebald, 1968).

Peer groups may not be as important to boys as to girls in respect of role identification because they have more objective indices of their potential to which they can turn particularly in relation to occupation aspirations. The findings of a study of wishes of older children and adolescents appear to be in line with these speculations. Boys' wishes for personal aggrandizement and achievement exceeded those of girls, while girls' wishes about social and family relations and personal characteristics exceeded those of boys.

McNeal (1969) found sex differences in children's consumer behaviour starting at around age seven. The child's differential interaction with socialization agents also began at an early age. Apparently parents treat girls differently from boys with respect to consumer training. In an exploratory study, Cateora (1963) reported sex differences in shopping behaviour of adolescents. The same study found sex differences in the way adolescents interact with their family members. Specifically, females were found to be more likely to model after their parents than were males.

Churchill and Moschis (1979) found that male adolescents exhibited stronger expressive orientations toward consumption (materialistic attitudes and social motivations) than did female counterparts. Perhaps the adolescent's sex affects aspects of his or her social orientations other than consumption, or perhaps such orientations may be of a broader nature. It is also possible that conspicuous consumption provides the male more than the female adolescent with means for establishing his status, power and respect among peers. Children it seems have developed clear sex-role perceptions by the time they reach adolescence.

Specifically, adolescents of both sexes have accurate sex-role perceptions regarding the responsibility for decision making in traditional male or female activities. The sex of the respondents, however, did have some effect on his or her perception of spouse involvement in household decisions regarding economic, social and household activities (areas of less specialization).

Conclusion

During what may be called the child's primary consumer training period, parents may permit and model various degrees of participation in the consumer role: advice as to what to buy for a meal, choosing between two brands of a favoured product or independently seeking out foodstuff from another part of the supermarket. While in the shop, parents can and do use it as a laboratory— showing the child subtle differences between similar-looking products or explaining expiry dates. In the home, parents talk about products, often giving elaborate and complicated evaluative judgements and reasons for the purchase. Children also hear them passing judgements on magazine, radio and television advertisements.

Of course not all parents are equally conscientious in training their children in all the activities and nuances of consumer behaviour. However, parental influence in consumer socialization is mediated by parental concern and involvement. To quote researchers in this field writing 25 years apart:

> Today there is no fast line that separates the consumption patterns of the adult world from those of child except the consumption objects themselves.
>
> (Riesman et al., 1953)

> Parents are teaching their children a great deal of consumer behaviour: in fact, we might worry that parents who are ineffective consumers also are teaching their children ineffective consumer behaviour.
>
> (McNeal, 1992)

Research in this area has consistently shown the influence of parents on children's ideas and consumer patterns. Thus, Holman and Braithwaite (1982) found parental control of TV habits and attitudes toward TV usage related strongly to their children's habits of viewing and their preferences for commercials. The more pre-school age children were able to select their own programmes the more commercials they tended to watch.

Children also learn from and copy their peers but their influence appears to decline as they get older. Teachers too can be extremely influential, though in this country, unlike America, primary school teachers rarely explicitly teach consumer behaviour.

Naturally business itself attempts to act as a powerful consumer socializing agent. The attempt includes advertising, particularly on television, though this is strictly controlled by laws governing 'adult' products as well. Shops themselves try to influence parents and their children as they know loyalty to an organization (such as a bank) may last many years. Thus they may do any of the following:

- Provide rest or play facilities for children and their parents.
- Be attentive to eye-level displays for children or even specific store or age-specific credit cards.
- Provide consumer education to elementary school classes such as field trips to part of the store/factory.
- Undertake promotion efforts such as window displays particularly for children.
- Train shop assistants to be particularly responsive or helpful to children.
- Co-operate with parents in ethical dilemmas such as removing certain products or ensuring the law is observed (e.g. sale of cigarettes and alcohol to minors).

Naturally stores want business, but most realize they can only appeal to children via their parents. However, if parents are only concerned with appeasing badly behaved children, and uninterested in the children's consumer education, stores are more likely to appeal to the children directly. If, on the other hand, the store/shop notices the parents' concerns and interests they are likely to appeal to parents.

The focal point however of most concern is not the parents or teachers but rather the product itself. Consequently, the product is intermingled with so many consumption activities (pre, actual and post-purchase) that it is difficult to delineate the product's unique and special role in the consumer socialization of children. For McNeal:

Parents are practically partners with the retailers in the consumer training of children in the sense that parents provide children with much of their income (one-half or more) and then encourage the children to make independent purchase efforts at stores. Further, parents give retail stores legitimacy by visiting them often, themselves, and also by taking the children with them . . . over a period of time children make more independent purchases in a greater variety of stores when with parents than without them. Thus, the retail store, in general, is parent-blessed. This seems much less true of the advertising that concerns parents so much. Also, parents can buffer much of the influence of advertising to their children that occurs in the home, but it seems much more difficult to buffer the influence of retailers when the children are engaged in an independent purchase act with them. Thus, what children learn in their interactions with retailers is probably determined more by the retailers than by the parents, but it has at least tacit approval of the parents.

(1992, p. 168)

Children need education and protection. But whose job is it to do that: the state, the parent, both? Parents are the most efficient and effective of educators. It is they who inculcate values, beliefs and behaviour patterns into their children. It is consequently much more efficient if they regulate children's consumer (and all other) behaviour, rather than a costly, clumsy and ultimately freedom-reducing state body. McNeal has suggested five types of question about parents, children and money.

(1) Are parents aware that giving their children money to spend gives the children market power? While the money that one child receives is minor, the combined amount for all children causes children to have buying power and to be recognized as a market by some producers and retailers.
(2) Do parents really need to give their children money, particularly during pre-school years? The parents meet the children's needs already and do it better than the children can.
(3) Are parents cognizant of retailers' feelings about children being given money to spend and being encouraged to spend it? Regardless of what motives the parents have for giving their children money, by virtue of giving it to them they set in motion certain activities at the retail level, such as stocking and displaying goods. Yet parents may not know the viewpoint of retailers.
(4) Are parents giving their children money, encouraging them to spend it, but relying principally on business and elementary school to teach the children appropriate consumer behaviour? There is not much evidence that parents deliberately teach their children consumer behaviour, yet they encourage them to be consumers. Because knowing how to be a consumer is not a genetic matter, someone must or should teach them both prior to and during consumer activities.
(5) If parents insist on their children being consumers by giving them money and encouraging them to spend it, are they also giving approval to marketers to court their children as potential customers? We hear a lot of condemnation of marketers, particularly advertisers, for pursuing children as

consumers, but from a theory of business standpoint, it would be more surprising if they did not.

Thus, it seems that parents, being the most important and effective means of inculcating consumer beliefs and habits in their children, should also be a primary focus of consumer education.

3

What Do Children Consume?

Children represent a potential market for many different commodities. There are certain kinds of products and services which pre-teens and adolescents are especially likely to purchase, and others which they would rarely or never buy. We have already seen that consumer socialization begins at a very early age and is shaped by a number of important factors including parents, peers and the mass media. It has also previously been noted that child consumption is driven by different internal needs which reside within the young consumer. Satisfaction may be obtained from the purchased item and from the act of purchase.

Product Purchase Patterns

The very young child consumer demands products mostly to satisfy immediate needs, such as confectionery or sweets. With increasing age, children also like to have a degree of independence and autonomy in making purchase decisions. Early purchase habits may exhibit little consistency in terms of product preference or brand loyalty. On some occasions a purchase may be planned, while on another occasion the same item may be purchased on impulse (McNeal, 1969).

Children are introduced to the act of purchasing by their parents when still only infants. By the age of seven, many child consumers will have bought something on their own without direct parental supervision. During subsequent years child consumers will sharpen and refine their consuming skills, as their knowledge and spending power increase. During this developmental period, however, the child consumer is still mindful of parental behaviour and will often copy parents in terms of shopping mannerisms and attitudes (see Furnham, 1993). On accompanying their parents on shopping trips, young consumers may mimic parental actions.

At the same time that the child is copying parental behaviour patterns, the parents are usually trying to teach the child about purchasing procedures. Children will also copy the consumer behaviours of their peers and consult with them about consumption. This peer influence usually becomes strong at age seven. The nature of influence typically consists of recommendations about flavours and brands of sweets.

The child also learns a great deal about consumer behaviour from advertising, particularly that on television. From advertising the child learns about brands, types of stores and pricing. Even though there may be a dislike for television advertising that increases with age, children readily admit that the advertising does influence their consumer behaviour. Chapters 5 and 6 examine in more detail the role and influence of advertising among young consumers.

By the time children have reached nine or ten, they have a simple understanding of the marketing process. They can discuss the functions of stores, the sources of products and even the concept of profit. They are also able to comment in an informed way on such matters as sales and bargains. By age nine, children become more selective and discriminating in their shopping trips. The novelty of consumerism begins to wear off at this age, because most children have developed a considerable feeling of confidence and competence in shopping. However, the enthusiasm for shopping generally continues to grow.

Among younger adolescents, their own money tends to be spent on such items as sweets and snacks, magazines, records and tapes, and stationery. There is also some early evidence of saving at this stage, which is usually carried out to be spent on a major item (Mintel, 1990). What adolescents purchase for themselves with their own money is small in comparison with what parents purchase for their children. Some evidence shows a growing consumer and commercial awareness among adolescents. They know what they want to consume better than their parents. By this stage in their development, teenagers do not simply want a particular product, but a particular brand (Stewart, 1992).

As young consumers get well into their teens they begin to engage in more leisure activities which are often socially oriented, and take them out of the family home. In the early 1990s, under one in ten (8%) of pre-teens and early teenage children reportedly went to the cinema regularly (two or three times a month), but by the time they had reached their mid-teens this figure had doubled (16%) (Dunlop and Eckstein, 1995). Teenagers, of course, have a greater range of movies to choose from, given the restrictions of age-related movie certifications.

Research around the world has revealed remarkable degrees of similarity in the product purchase patterns of young people from diverse cultural environments. One international study of young consumerism found that children from Hong Kong, Taiwan and New Zealand differed little from each other or from American children in the way they spent their money. All of these children spent 60 per cent or more on things to snack on and things to play with. New Zealanders spent the most on snacks and sweets (53% of their money), while Hong Kong and American children spent about the same (38% and 35%) on this type of product. Taiwanese children spent most on play items (38%), followed by American children (31%), and then those from Hong Kong (25%) and New Zealand (18%). Children from all three Pacific Rim countries bought salty and sweet snacks. Chinese children preferred their sweet snacks less sweet than did children from New Zealand and the United States (McNeal and Yeh, 1990).

There were some purchase categories where Pacific Rim countries did differ from American children. Pacific Rim children rarely bought clothes with their own money whereas American children spent at least 12 per cent of their money on this category. However, American children usually did not buy school-related items with their own money to the extent that Pacific Rim children did. American children also spent more on entertainment items.

Favourite possessions

Do favourite possessions change over time? Kamptner (1991) carried out an extensive, open-ended questionnaire study with almost 600 southern Californian respondents in five tightly defined age groups: children of 10–11 years, adolescents of 14–18 years, young adults of 18–29 years, adults of 30–59 years, and senior citizens of over 60 years. Amongst various questions put to participants in this study, the one of most interest here concerns the possessions they most treasured and the reasons for their attachments. For toddlers and very young children, their favourite cuddly toys provide comfort and security, but are also involved in the beginning differentiation of self from the primary caretaker. The older children in Kamptner's research named stuffed animals, sports equipment and toys most often. The reasons given for their attachment by over two-thirds of the children were the enjoyment and activities afforded by these objects, and their physical properties. For the adolescents, possessions were more varied, but centred on music equipment, cars and jewellery. In addition to enjoyment, the social ties associated with these objects and the aspects of self they expressed emerged as the most common reasons. Some of these data are presented in Tables 3.1 to 3.3.

Young adults refer to the social ties that their cars, jewellery, photographs and general memorabilia symbolize, and the enjoyment they provide. As adults become older, photographs and jewellery take increasingly prominent places as favoured objects, with a growing emphasis on the social integration and networks they signify, on the positive emotions they afford and on the memories associated with them.

The main types of reason given—activity-related and pragmatic uses, emotional experiences, self-expression, symbols for interpersonal relationships, concretized personal history—correspond well with the symbolic–communicational model of the meanings of possessions for identity advanced in the previous chapter. In terms of overall development:

> the changes with age noted . . . in this study broadly suggest that with age there is a change in the 'referent' of treasured possessions from mother (in early life) to self (in middle childhood and adolescence) to others (in adulthood).
>
> (Kamptner, 1991, p. 221)

TABLE 3.1 *Most frequently named treasured possessions: relative percentage by subject grouping (N=577)*

	Total Group		Males		Females	
Middle	Stuffed animals	26	Sports equipment	28	Stuffed animals	31
childhood	Sports equipment	16	Stuffed animals	22	Dolls	15
(n=112)	Childhood toys	10	Childhood toys	20	Music	12
	Dolls	8	Small appliances	13	Jewellery	12
	Small appliances	8	Pillows/blankets	4	Books	10
Adolescence	Music	13	Music	17	Jewellery	16
(n=249)	Motor vehicles	11	Sports equipment	17	Stuffed animals	11
	Jewellery	10	Motor vehicles	11	Music	10
	Sports equipment	10	Small appliances	9	Clothing	9
	Small appliances	8	Clothing	6	Motor vehicles	6
					Small appliances	6
Early	Motor vehicles	21	Motor vehicles	33	Jewellery	22
adulthood	Jewellery	17	Music	10	Photographs	16
(n=72)	Photographs	13	Photographs	10	Motor vehicles	13
	Memorabilia	8	Jewellery	10	Pillows/blankets	9
	Stuffed animals	5	Memorabilia	7	Stuffed animals	7
	Pillows/blankets	5	Artwork	7	Music	5
Middle	Photographs	13	Photographs	18	Dishes/silverware	18
adulthood	Jewellery	13	Jewellery	15	Jewellery	12
(n=72)	Dishes/silverware	11	Books	9	Artwork	10
	Artwork	10	Sports equipment	6	Photographs	10
	Books	7	Motor vehicles	6	Memorabilia	8
	Small appliances	6	Furniture	8		
Late	Photographs	17	Small appliances	26	Jewellery	25
adulthood	Jewellery	16	Photographs	17	Dishes/silverware	19
(n=72)	Small appliances	14	Motor vehicles	11	Photographs	17
	Dishes/silverware	11	Artwork	11	Religious items	6
	Artwork	7	Sports equipment	9	Furniture	6

Note: Numbers are in percentages.
Source: Kamptner, 1991

This move from an activity-centred, pragmatic and self-concerned focus on possessions towards a greater emphasis on their symbolic features, particularly with respect to social relationships, is also reported by other researchers. Thus, information about their favourite possessions can provide a useful indication about the young consumer's economic stage of development.

TABLE 3.2 *Most frequently named meanings of treasured possessions: relative percentage by subject grouping (N=577)*

	Total Group		Males		Females	
Middle	Enjoyment	25	Enjoyment	2	Intrinsic qual.	21
childhood	Intrin. qual.	21	Activity	21	Enjoyment	19
(n=112)	Activity	16	Intrinsic qual.	20	Social	16
	Social	12	Utility value	9	Personal hist.	11
	Personal hist.	8	Social	9	Activity	11
Adolescence	Enjoyment	28	Enjoyment	40	Social	36
(n=249)	Social	22	Utility value	19	Enjoyment	17
	Utility value	16	Personal accom.	11	Utility value	14
	Personal accom.	8	Intrinsic qual.	7	Personal hist.	9
	Personal hist.	7	Social	7	Intrinsic qual.	6
Early	Social	29	Social	23	Social	34
adulthood	Enjoyment	28	Enjoyment	23	Enjoyment	32
(n=72)	Intrinsic qual.	10	Intrinsic qual.	13	Intrinsic qual.	9
	Personal accom.	7	Self-expression	10	Memories	7
	Memories	7	Personal accom.	10	Personal hist.	5
	Personal hist.	5	Personal accom.	5		
Middle	Social	42	Social	46	Social	40
adulthood	Enjoyment	21	Enjoyment	12	Enjoyment	27
(n=72)	Memories	8	Memories	6	Memories	9
	Utility value	6	Personification	6	Intrinsic qual.	9
	Intrinsic qual.	6	Utility value	6	Utility value	7
Late	Social	49	Social	34	Social	64
adulthood	Enjoyment	24	Enjoyment	34	Enjoyment	12
(n=72)	Util. value	6	Utility value	11	Memories	6
	Memories	6	Memories	6	Intrinsic qual.	6
	Personification	3	Personification	6	Self-expression	3
	Intrinsic qual.	3			Personal accom.	3
	Self-expression	3			Cult.-rel. assoc.	3

Note: Numbers are in percentages.
Source: Kamptner, 1991

Teenagers' purchasing patterns

Marketers are interested in understanding what products will sell well in the youth market. Moreover, it is important to appreciate the influence which youths exert on purchases by others, such as parents as well as peers. This secondary influence may be more significant to most marketers than is youth's role as primary purchaser of certain items (Waldrop, 1990).

TABLE 3.3 *Most frequently named 'most desired gifts': relative percentage by subject grouping (N=577)*

	Total Group		Males		Females	
Middle	Clothing	28	Childhood toys	25	Clothing	41
childhood	Childhood toys	19	Sports equipment	22	Stuffed animals	9
(n=112)	Sports equipment	12	Clothing	15	Music	9
	Money	10	Money	11	Money	9
	Stuffed animals	6	Small appliances	8	Books	9
Adolescence	Clothing	28	Money	36	Clothing	33
(n=249)	Money	26	Clothing	20	Money	19
	Jewellery	12	Motor vehicles	10	Jewellery	18
	Motor vehicles	6	Music	8	Stuffed animals	7
	Music	6	Childhood toys	5	Personal items	6
Early	Clothing	21	Money	21	Clothing	25
adulthood	Money	13	Clothing	16	Personal items	19
(n=72)	Personal items	13	Sports equipment	16	Jewellery	18
	Jewellery	12	Music	11	Money	9
	Books	6	Tools	7	Books	7
	Sports equipment	6				
	Music	6				
Middle	Clothing	22	Clothing	29	Personal items	19
adulthood	Books	12	Books	11	Artwork	17
(n=72)	Personal items	12	Money	11	Clothing	16
	Artwork	11	Sports equipment	7	Books	13
	Jewellery	9	Tools	6	Jewellery	11
Late	Clothing	29	Clothing	38	Clothing	22
adulthood	Personal items	17	Books	13	Personal items	18
(n=72)	Artwork	11	Personal items	10	Artwork	18
	Jewellery	10	Money	8	Jewellery	16
	Books	9	Tools	8	Books	6
			Memorabilia	8		

Note: Numbers are in percentages.
Source: Kamptner, 1991

How do youths spend their income? Both female and male teenagers spend most of their money on clothes, records, stereo equipment, entertainment and travel. Young women tend to spend most on cosmetics, followed by clothes, health and beauty aids, and jewellery. Young men tend to spend the most on dates and cars, followed by sporting goods, cameras, records, stereo equipment, bicycles, athletic shoes, jeans, hobby-type products, musical instruments and electronic games. As members of a highly consumption-oriented society, teenagers have become increasingly aware of new products and brands. They may spend hours shopping for themselves. Indeed, shopping often becomes a favourite social activity for young people.

In addition to their direct impact on the marketplace, youths exert secondary influence on many of their parents' product and brand choices. For example, research reveals that three out of four teens actually influence their parents' purchasing decisions. For major purchasers, teens' highest influence occurs in the initiation stage of the decision-making process and is strongest for aesthetic considerations such as style, colour, and make or model of the product but weakest for decisions such as where and when to purchase and how much money to spend (Belch *et al.*, 1985).

With the large growth in the number of families of two working parents, young people are doing more of the food shopping and other shopping for parents. For example, one study found that 50 per cent of teenagers were 'heavily involved' in family food shopping (Sellers, 1989). Kraft has recognized the importance of teenage grocery shopping (in the USA) and has advertised on TV, in network syndication, in selected teen magazines, and on contemporary hit radio, emphasizing recipes containing Kraft products. Tied in with the ad campaign is an educational kit on 'food buymanship' provided to home-economics teachers to distribute to teenagers in school.

Another factor underlining the market importance of the youth group is that this is the time when brand loyalties may be formed that could last well into adulthood (Moschis and Moore, 1981). For instance, a brand-loyalty study prepared by the Yankelovich organization for *Seventeen* magazine found that at least 30 per cent of adult women were using the same brands they first chose as teenagers. Translated into total market figures (for the USA) the findings would mean, for instance, that 6,760,000 women still are using the same brand of mascara and 8,900,000 still are eating the same kind of packaged cheese that they first bought (Fierman, 1980). A more up-to-date study by McNeal (1992) on American children showed that the products children most expect to buy when going shopping were vegetables, fruits, soft drinks and cereals among food items, and toys and clothing among non-food items (see Table 3.4).

A French study of the late 1980s showed not only what young people spent but what they spent it on. The GSI–CFRO survey (1989) of 15- to 20-year-old secondary school students in the Paris suburbs reveals other sources of income, both licit (selling used books or records) or illicit (selling stolen objects, both small ones—make-up, candy, stationery—or large ones—jackets, stereos—not to mention such things as drug dealing, rackets, etc.). One should perhaps also include money from both official and unofficial gambling. According to a 1992 study by the Institut de l'Enfant, the average monthly incomes of young people in France increased significantly between the ages of 4 and 16 (see Table 3.4).

The GSI–CFRO study (1989) showed that the proportion of young people who do not receive any allowance is twice as high (30% against 15%) in the more modest social categories as it is in the more privileged categories, and the amounts vary within the same age group from 1 to 1.7. As the child grows up, a pocket money allowance becomes linked to a contract whereby the young person must cover certain expenses him- or herself: school supplies, transport, personal-hygiene products, clothes, and so on. The amounts increased as the adolescent's day-to-day life became more autonomous. Table 3.5 gives a breakdown of the average monthly expenses of 15- to 20-year-olds.

TABLE 3.4 *Budget by age groups*

Age	Income
4–7	46 F
8–10	201 F
11–12	340 F
13–14	578 F
15–16	607 F

Note: F = francs.
Source: Institut de l'Enfant, 1992

Almost all young people have savings (see Table 3.6). Sometimes the savings are managed in a bank or savings account by the parents; sometimes it is more autonomous in a piggybank, for example. Most often, both systems coexist. The savings are meant to finance large purchases: computer, stereo system, motor scooter, driving licence, vacation.

TABLE 3.5 *Structure of the monthly consumption of 15- to 20-year-olds*

Items	Amount spent
Clothes and footwear	110 F
Records and tapes	59 F
Various outings	47,5 F
Cinema	46 F
Books and magazines	46 F
Transport	45 F
Cafes	35,5 F
Sports	31,5 F
Tobacco	30 F
Concerts	28,5 F
Hairdresser	28 F
Restaurants	24 F
Driving licence	22 F
Hygiene products and make-up	21 F

Note: F = francs.
Source: GSI–CFRO, 1989

TABLE 3.6 *Banking practices of 15- to 18-year-olds*

Bank service	15–18
Savings account	88%
Current account	34%
Credit card	23%
Cheque book	17%

Source: IPSOS, 1991

Consumer Products and Identity

To have is to be. For many western young people at the end of the twentieth century the belief 'I am what I consume and what I have' remains strong. To misquote Descartes 'I shop therefore I am'. To this extent material possessions are part of self-identity. Possessors are material symbols of identity and have numerous important functions. Dittmar (1992) points out how clothes form part of the extended sense of self. For both the wearer and the observer, clothing provides information about social and occupational standing, sex-role orientations, political beliefs, ethnicity and personal values. Thus, when people are robbed of particularly important (sentimental) possessions they may be robbed of their identity and become distraught over long periods. To give some idea of why and how possessions are important Dittmar produced a detailed classification of reasons why possessions are important to young people (see Table 3.7).

Possessions in the form of consumer goods are spontaneously described by their owners as being part of oneself and they are related to both self-esteem and well-being. This develops over time. Children often establish powerful relationship with objects (often a cuddly toy) which provides comfort and security. As they begin to understand such terms as 'mine', 'yours', etc., young children find possessions are instruments both of control and social power. Possessions can embody relationships in the world of the child because they can help dictate who is, and is not, allowed to use or play with these possessions. Further possessions can become gifts which may be symbols of affection and generosity as well as the 'love-worthiness' of the recipient.

Possessions are instruments of both control and power, whilst possessive behaviour is often motivated by the desire for security. Furby (1991) has done a great deal of research in this area. She argues that children, adolescents and adults are powerfully motivated to control their environment. Because of this force underlying human behaviour, infants' investigations and manipulations of physical objects around them are potentially universal features of human development. But such explorations of objects are bound to come into conflict with the social environment of the infant, particularly from the age of about one year onwards when physical mobility increases rapidly. Adults and older siblings

TABLE 3.7 *Coding system for reasons why possessions are important*

A. *Qualities 'intrinsic' to object*
  (1) durability, reliability, quality
  (2) economy
  (3) monetary value
  (4) uniqueness, rarity
  (5) aesthetics

B. *Instrumentality*
  (1) general utility of object
  (2) enables specific activity associated with object

C. *(Other) use-related features*
  (1) enables social contact
  (2) provides enjoyment
  (3) provides entertainment or relaxation
  (4) enhances independence, autonomy, freedom
  (5) provides financial security
  (6) provides information or knowledge
  (7) provides privacy or solitude

D. *Effort expended in acquiring/maintaining possession*

E. *Emotion-related features of possessions*
  (1) emotional attachment
  (2) mood enhancer or regulator
  (3) escapism
  (4) emotional outlet/therapy
  (5) provides comfort or emotional security
  (6) enhances self-confidence

F. *Self-expression*
  (1) self-expression per se
  (2) self-expression for others to see
  (3) individuality/differentiation from others
  (4) symbol for personal future goals
  (5) symbol for personal skills/capabilities

G. *Personal history*
  (1) link to events or places
  (2) link to past or childhood
  (3) general symbol of self-continuity
  (4) long-term association

H. *Symbolic interrelatedness*
  (1) symbol for relationship with specific person(s)
  (2) symbolic company
  (3) symbol of interrelatedness with particular group(s)

Source: Dittmar, 1992

have to prevent the child from touching and handling many objects in order to avoid damage. The result of these interactions is that children gradually learn to identify with those objects which they can explore and control and come to view them as theirs, whereas objects which occasion restriction and interference will become defined as belonging to somebody else. Possessions thus draw a boundary between what is self and what is other. The distinction between self and non-self is thus viewed as closely linked to the infant's behavioural control over certain objects. The developmental significance of possessions resides in their instrumental function as quasi-physical extensions of the self, which aid the child in controlling the environment. This means that Furby's explanation of this process emphasizes *intra-individual* rather than *social* determinants:

> an object might be considered a part of the self to the degree to which the state of the object depends on the individual's actions: that is, the degree to which there is a correlation between the child's actions and intended consequences to the object. Possessions become integrated with the child's developing concept of self because they offer a very high degree of contingent control, almost as great as the control one experiences over one's body.
>
> (Furby, 1991, p. 35)

Furby also provides a model for understanding how material possessions are related to identity (see Figure 3.1). She writes:

> The range of meanings and functions of possessions for identity can be laid out as a schematic model . . . They can be classified analytically into *instrumental* and *symbolic* ones. Instrumental purposes of possessions are their direct functional uses and the control over the environment they afford.
>
> Even such prototypically 'functional' possessions as kitchen appliances or tools may signify, for example, the social status or other attributes of the owner. Thus, a highly significant dimension of material objects is that they serve as symbolic expressions of who we are. As *categorical* symbols, they can signify status and the broad social categories we belong to, but also smaller groups we identify with. *Self-expressive* functions concern individuals' unique attitudes, goals and personal qualities. What we accumulate during our lifetime comes to represent our personal history and relationships. Moreover, possessions have a variety of *use-related* features which combine functional and symbolic elements. A car, for example, makes possible various activities, such as visiting friends, but having a car signifies the possibility of these activities at the same time. A similar argument can be put forward with respect to more emotionally-toned aspects of possessions. For example, listening to music makes hi-fi equipment a means for relaxation and mood change, but tapes and records can also become symbols of particular emotional experiences.
>
> (p. 167)

Aspects of shopping behaviour

Children have been observed in recent research to make independent visits to shops as early as the age of four or five. Surveys in the United States indicated that by 1989 this was true of 30 per cent of children. By the age of five, more than half (54%) reported going to a shop on their own and making their own purchase decisions, and by the age of seven, this figure rose to 90 per cent of youngsters (McNeal, 1992). Another trend is that as children get older they visit a wider variety of types of store. All this does not mean that children at these tender ages are often going to shops on their own. Clearly, though, as they become more independently mobile, children are allowed by parents to visit nearby stores unaccompanied.

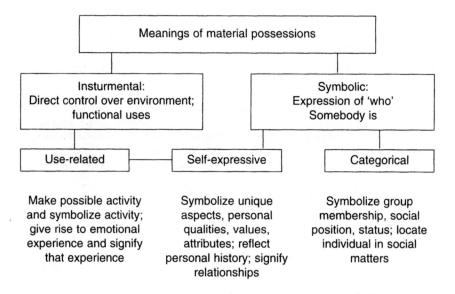

FIGURE 3.1 Meanings of material possessions for identity. Furby, 1991

The average number of independent store visits and the number of different stores visited by young children are fewer than when they are with their parents. Children remain dependent on parents to convey them to shopping locations, especially if the nearest stores are not within easy or safe walking distance. American figures show, nevertheless, that by the time children have been in school a year or so, they make around two shopping visits a week on their own and go to at least two different kinds of store (McNeal, 1992). This behaviour develops under its own steam so that by the age of ten many children have become quite accomplished shoppers.

By the time young consumers reach their teens, certain distinct shopping patterns become established. American researchers have found that teenagers do most of their shopping at weekends and relatively little during the week. With respect to the number of stores patronized, most teenage respondents indicated that they went to four or more stores for clothes and accessories (58%) and for gifts for friends and relatives (57%). In contrast to this, most (58%) patronized only one store for books and magazines. In all other product categories, other than food consumer outside the home, shopping appeared to be limited to one or two stores in the case of the majority of teenagers (Tootelian and Gaedeke, 1992).

The meaning of shopping

McNeal (1992) reported a study of what shopping meant to children. The enquiry utilized a drawing technique to elicit from children whatever came to their minds when they thought about going shopping. The children questioned were all middle-class and aged six to ten years. The kind of store thought about or drawn first and foremost was the *supermarket*. This was the most popular kind of store among the youngest children. McNeal explains this as arising out of children's earliest shopping experiences with their parents. In addition, since many of these children lived in homes where both parents worked, many were expected to help with the shopping.

The second most frequently drawn store type was the *specialty store*. The types of specialty stores illustrated were toy stores, music stores, sporting-goods stores, ice-cream stores and computer stores. These tended to be more commonly chosen by older children, aged nine and ten. In third place were department stores, with older girls being especially likely to identify with these. Some children drew a shopping mall or shopping centre rather than a single type of store. The shopping mall was seen as a good place to meet up and spend time with friends.

Turning to the types of products children thought of when they thought of going shopping, McNeal (1992) found that American six- to ten-year-olds referred to a variety of food and non-food items. The most frequently illustrated foods were not snacks and sweets, but rather vegetables (17.6% of drawings) and fruit (13.4%). McNeal noted that these foods are now often regarded as snack foods by health conscious American (middle-class) families. Even so, other more traditional snacks were also featured, such as sweets, biscuits and ice cream. Next in order of importance were soft drinks and cereal, each noted in seven per cent of children's food drawings. Meat, milk and canned vegetables were each drawn eight times (5.6%). Unexpected items were detergent (4.2%), eggs (3.5%), butter (2.8%), soup (1.7%), bottled water (0.7%) and fish (0.2%).

In addition to 142 food items, there were 129 instances of nonfood items which emerged in children's drawings. Toys were at the top of the list of nonfood drawings. These comprised stuffed animals, dolls, games, miniature cars and lorries, and robots. Other items included bicycles, skate boards, skates, books and video games. The second most popular category of nonfood item was clothing, among which various designer brands (e.g. Esprit, Guess, Calvin Klein) featured prominently. Electronic goods were popular and included home video sets, telephones, television sets, stereo sets, portable stereos and personal computers. Cosmetics and toiletries were depicted in a small number of girls' drawings. Girls also sketched jewellery (earrings, necklaces and bracelets).

TABLE 3.8 *Products children expect to buy when going shopping*

Product	Frequency	Per cent
Foods		
Vegetables	25	17.6
Fruits	19	13.4
Soft drinks	10	7.0
Cereal	10	7.0
Canned vegetables	8	5.6
Meat	8	5.6
Milk	8	5.6
Ice cream	7	4.9
Bakery foods	6	4.2
Detergent	6	4.2
Eggs	5	3.5
Peanut butter	5	3.5
Butter	4	2.8
Cookies	4	2.8
Candy	3	2.1
Chips	3	2.1
Fruit juice	3	2.1
Coffee	2	1.4
Popcorn	2	1.4
Soup	2	1.4
Bottled water	1	.7
Fish	1	.7
	142	100
Nonfoods		
Toys	30	23.3
Clothing	18	13.6
Video games	12	9.3
Cosmetics/toiletries	10	7.8
Skate boards/skates	8	6.2
Sporting goods	8	6.2
Records/cassettes	6	4.7
Stereos/jam boxes	6	4.7
Books	5	3.9
Shoes	5	3.9
Bicycles	4	3.1
Jewellery	4	3.1
Computer/software	4	3.1
Stickers	4	3.1
Television sets	3	2.4
Telephones	2	1.6
	129	100

Source: McNeal, 1992, p. 59

Further insights into what shopping might mean for young consumers resulted from a study which examined teenagers' shopping likes and dislikes (Tostelian and Gaedeke, 1992). What emerged was a strong social aspect to shopping in addition to the satisfaction of certain consumerist motives and acquisitive needs. The single largest group of teenagers (28%) indicated that being with friends was what they liked best about shopping. Looking at products (21%) and finding bargains (17%) were also mentioned by a substantial number. With respect to what teenagers disliked most about shopping, the largest group (41%) stated not finding the items they wanted to buy, while other dislikes included spending money (25%) and crowded shopping conditions (16%).

What the greatest majority of teenagers (73%) liked most about shopping was buying clothes and accessories. These products carry image connotations and may be consistent with the social function of shopping. Interestingly, the single largest group of dislikes (35%) also referred to clothes shopping. This result may be due to a variety of factors, including the multitude of product options available and the risks of making 'socially incorrect' purchases.

Store preferences

Children's exposure to consumerism begins early in their lives. The first visits to the shops occur with parents at about the same time that children are learning to walk. By the time they start school, not only have they become familiar with different shopping environments, they have already begun to form their own opinions about stores, representing personal likes and dislikes, and personal preferences. Preferred stores have certain characteristics. Children generally like and prefer stores that are child friendly, that are liked by their parents, and stock the kinds of things they want to buy, or have bought for them. It also seems that establishing a positive image with children early on may have longer term pay-offs for a store because a good impression may last into adulthood (McNeal, 1992).

Given children's product preferences, the best-liked stores tend to be convenience stores, and supermarkets, because they stock snacks and sweets, and play things. Store preferences inevitably change with age as product tastes and interests mature. Stocking well-liked products does not guarantee a positive response from children, however. If the store is not friendly towards children, this may outweigh the fact that it sells the kinds of items they want to purchase. This means that there will be stores that children readily choose to shop in and others which they will go to out of necessity. Thus conveniently located stores may be regularly visited even though low on children preference scale if there is nowhere else that they can readily go to buy the things they want.

Selectivity in shopping

As children grow up their shopping behaviour matures and they become aware of the range of products and brands that are available. Teenagers, for example, often spend hours shopping, especially on weekends. The fact that they are doing more shopping may result in their spending more money in stores they patronize. In addition, youths often have a great deal of authority in store-selection decisions, which means that stores must reach them with an effective appeal. Although there is a popular belief that young consumers buy products compulsively and are less rational than the market as a whole, surveys indicate that most young consumers in their teens compare prices and brands before buying.

One aspect of shopping selectivity is whether or not young consumers display store loyalty. The evidence for this has not been consistent with some research indicating that youngsters change the stores they patronize frequently, while other research has suggested that for certain types of products, favourite shopping locations can become established. One early study found that three-quarters of a sample of American adolescents surveyed indicated that they bought clothing at a number of different stores (Samli and Windeshausen, 1964). Lack of store loyalty among teenagers in the USA also emerged in another survey a few years later where it was found that those youngsters who paid cash for buying clothes tended to shop in a wide variety of retail outlets.

Elsewhere, however, evidence has emerged that store favourites do become established and that peer group pressure may play a particularly important role in determining which stores are fashionable and which are not, especially where shopping for clothes was concerned (Saunders *et al.*, 1973). Furthermore, peer influences would often overrule parental influences in choice of store. Mothers and daughters might frequently disagree about the best store to patronize, but daughters would only follow their mothers' advice if they were confident that same-age friends would also approve. The peer influence had a particularly strong influence upon choice of brand. Teenage girls were found to pay particular attention to peer group approval of brands when purchasing coats, blouses, dresses and scarves for school.

Research on adolescent shopping behaviour has produced the following tentative conclusions (Moore and Moschis, 1978):

- Adolescents tend to rely more on personal sources for information on products of high socio-economic and performance risk, and on most media for information on products perceived as low for such risk.
- At the product-evaluation stage of the decision process, price ("sales") and brand name are perceived as the most important evaluative criteria, with a relatively low social influence coming from parents and peers.
- As teenagers mature, they use more sources of consumer information prior to decision making, rely more on friends and less on parents for information and advice in buying, and prefer to purchase products without parental supervision.

The mall

Langman (1992) has noted that in countries that have shopping malls adolescents spend great periods of time in them, free from the observation of their parents. They are an attractive 'hangout'. She notes:

> Three major tasks of adolescence are establishing autonomy from parents, testing and consolidating one's identity(ies) and learning to cope with newly emergent sexuality. Today, automobilized mallers form distinct subcultures of consumption located in mallworlds free from the surveillance of parents or teachers. Malls become stages in which the identities gleaned in earlier socialization by parents or media are expressed and recognized. Those identities that get approval become more salient and recur. Often going to a mall on a weekend night involves elaborate preparations for transportation and, for young women, extensive rituals for make-up and costume selection to insure the proper image and impression management for group inclusion and initiating relationships that might become sexual. Males practice walks, looks and hair styles of various ranks of cool in hopes of 'scoring'—one of the primary means by which adolescent males gain self-esteem. And with the erosion of age grading—some men never grow up—teenaged malling can be considered anticipatory socialization for later life and singles-bar rituals, especially for the college-bound.
>
> These are the ages when people are most open to changes in the styles and fashions of clothes, popular culture and advanced consumer goods. This is especially the case for those trend-setting mall-jammers the marketing research people call 'alphas'. Thus many malls, especially those with theatres, video games and food courts, have become centres of social life and pseudo-community. Each region or type of store is staked out as a particular turf for the members of communities of consumption. The various subcultures of adolescence confirm not only those self-presentations constitutive of an emergent identity, but integrate the person into particular groups that affect subsequent life trajectories.
>
> (p.39)

The spreading of the American concept of the shopping mall to other industrialized countries in Europe and the Pacific Rim suggests that its influence as an environmental force moulding young people's consumer-related attitudes and behaviour will penetrate even further.

The Market Influences of Children

As any parent knows, young children frequently attempt to influence family product purchase decisions as soon as they possess the basic communication skills with which to do so. Children can play an important role in household decision-making about purchases (Hansen, 1972; Ward, 1974). They may take part in household decisions in three different ways: (1) children can be influenced by other household members in the things they wish to argue in favour of purchasing; (2) children can act as autonomous decision makers; and (3) children can influence the decisions of other family members. Children's impact on purchase decisions, however, has not always been clearly elaborated by research studies on this topic (Assael, 1981).

Older children especially are likely to participate more directly in family consumption activities. For instance, an exploratory study of family members' roles in making a decision to purchase a personal computer found that fathers were generally the most influential across most decision and information-gathering stages (e.g. selecting where and when to but it). However, children also appear to play relatively important roles when it comes to initiating interest in the new computer and the actual purchase. In contrast, mothers have been found not to be the major force when it comes to any of the decision stages or activities associated with acquiring the new family computer.

The influence that children can have on parental purchases is extensive and has been conceived by one leading child marketing scholar as principally embracing three areas:

(1) *Items for children* This group of purchases includes snacks, toys, consumer electronics, clothing, and hobby equipment and supplies.
(2) *Items for the home* Children today influence some of the purchases by their parents of furnishings, furniture, TV sets, stereo systems, and foods and beverages for meals.
(3) *Nonhousehold items for family members* These items often are major purchases and include vacations, cars, clothing, restaurant meals, and recreation things.

(McNeal, 1992, pp. 63–64)

In addition to these three categories, others were also identified which are less straightforward to classify. These include family gifts to the children's grandparents and to other relatives and neighbours, family donations to charities, licence plates for the family car (personalized number plates), and holiday homes. Children have also been observed to influence parental choice of where to shop.

The influence of children on the family decision-making process has received fairly limited research attention compared with other aspects of the child's consumerism. While a great deal of attention has been devoted to children as consumers, only a few studies have attempted to assess directly the nature and extent of a child's influence on family purchase decisions. It is important to realize that the child's own purchase behaviour is but one way in which the child interacts with the consumer society. The child can also play an important role in a great deal of purchases made by parents, since the child frequently makes purchase requests for various products. As we have seen already, the range of influence spans a variety of product types (Smith and Sweeney, 1984).

Children's influences upon parents' purchases

Children often ask their parents to buy things for them. These requests may cover both inexpensive and expensive items. Requests for the former are more likely to be granted. Even then, however, children do not always get what they want. Parents have to balance what they can afford against the cost, in terms of family harmony, of refusing to purchase the things their children wish to consume. One of the items children have been found to request parents to buy them most often is breakfast cereal. Wells and LoSciuto (1966) found that three-fifths of the American children they surveyed reportedly attempted to influence parental purchase of cereals. In more than half these cases, the child was apparently successful in obtaining the desired cereal. Ward and Wackman (1972) conducted a survey with mothers who reported that their children requested cereals more frequently than 21 other product categories. The vast majority of mothers said they usually yielded to these requests at a rate much higher than for other products.

Children are particularly likely to make purchase requests of parents at a shopping location. Atkin and Rheingold (1972) interviewed mothers after they passed through the checkout at four different supermarkets. When asked whether their children had asked them to buy any of the groceries purchased that day, almost half the mothers questioned specifically mentioned breakfast cereal. The popularity of breakfast cereals among children's purchase requests to their parents was later confirmed in another American survey (Atkin, 1975).

Children do not always have their requests granted, however. Atkin found that almost one in two of the children and one in three mothers reported that cereal requests were denied, and on some occasions this led to arguments within the family.

In addition to conducting interviews with adult and child consumers, some researchers have attempted to be less intrusive by simply observing how families behave in retail environments. In one such investigation, mother-child parents were unobtrusively observed in supermarkets, and their conversations and behaviours were noted at the cereal counter (Atkin, 1978). In two-thirds of the episodes studied, the child initiated the interaction by expressing a desire for the cereal. Approaching one in two children (46%) made a clear demand for a particular cereal, while one in five (20%) made a simple request. Mothers gave in to demands on 65 per cent of occasions and to requests on 58 per cent of occasions. Regardless of the child's approach tactic, parental purchase of the cereal occurred more than twice as often as a flat refusal, while six per cent deflected the child's initiative by suggesting another cereal. Older children got their own way more often than younger children. If a request was refused, this resulted in some kind of argument between parent and child on a substantial number of occasions.

Reasons for children's influence

The influence that children assert on family purchases has been an area of growing interest among marketers ever since the advent of popular television viewing in the 1950s. Several reasons can be highlighted as underpinning the increased attention this issue is now receiving (McNeal, 1992). First, parents are having fewer children and therefore often have more money to spend on each child. With fewer siblings, and therefore less competition, the child can also expect to have more say in what the family buys. Second, changing lifestyles and increased divorce rates have resulted in more one-parent families in which the child is expected to make a contribution towards household decision making. Third, the tendency in many homes to postpone having children until later often means that when children do arrive they are indulged more. Fourth, in many households today, both parents go to work. This means that greater participation in household chores is expected from children and this may include doing a certain amount of the household's shopping.

How much influence do children have? Children naturally turn to their parents to satisfy many of their needs. At a very early age, children are almost totally dependent upon their parents. As they grow up, they become increasingly self-reliant and self-assertive. While they may become less physically dependent upon parents in certain basic respects even quite early on in life, they remain financially dependent for much longer. Thus, although children may be perfectly able to walk to a store and make a purchase by themselves without parental escort, they are nearly always reliant on parents to supply the money needed to make the purchase.

As children grow up and attain greater independence, they are less likely to be accompanied by parents when shopping. Within the limits of their budget, young consumers acquire greater freedom to discern their own shopping habits and product purchase preferences and choices. This is a pattern which has been observed in different parts of the world, although the precise pattern of development can vary from one culture to another.

In a study of young consumers' shopping behaviour in New Zealand, Taiwan, Hong Kong and the United States, McNeal and Yeh (1990) asked parents about the extent to which their children made independent purchases when they shopped together, the extent to which children made purchase visits to stores on their own, the frequency of such visits and the types of stores in which buying took place. The ages of the children ranged from 4 to 12.

The research indicated that a larger number of Chinese children aged four made independent purchases while accompanying a parent when shopping than did children in the United States. The figures for the four countries being compared here were: Hong Kong – 67 per cent; Taiwan – 50 per cent; United States – 30 per cent; and New Zealand – 29 per cent. While the percentage for New Zealand started out fairly low, it increased with age quickly before levelling off at around 75 per cent at age 11–12. In the United States, eventually all children (100%) made their own purchases while shopping with parents. In Hong Kong and Taiwan, the percentage of children who went shopping with parents and made independent purchases actually decreased once the children were in school. In both Chinese cultures, parents (mainly mothers) tended to shop during the time the children were in school, and therefore their youngsters did not accompany them. However, parents and children sometimes shopped together at nights and on weekends.

McNeal (1992) calculated the cost of children's influence upon purchases for the United States by deriving estimates of household expenditures from various published sources in which such figures had been produced. This survey evidence was compared with official sales figures from industry sources. For each of a number of product categories, estimates were calculated of the amount of purchase by households with children. Over 62 product categories for which total product sales in the USA were $766.15 billion, it was estimated that children exerted an influence on $131.77 billion of that expenditure. It was estimated that children influenced $22.75 billion in fast-food purchases, but even more in the home consumption of food. In the case of toys, children's influence counted for the lion's share of the industry's sales—$9.4 billion out of $13.4 billion.

With increased age comes increased awareness of what delights the market holds. Children develop a keen awareness of a wide range of items they might like to possess. Indeed, so quickly does this awareness develop that the number of things children would like to own soon outstrips their capacity to use them and the parent's ability to supply. This means that young consumers must develop techniques to persuade their parents to purchase items on their behalf.

Several studies have examined the influence attempts of children and parental yielding to these attempts. Berey and Pollay (1970) found that the child-centredness of the mother was negatively related to yielding to the child's request for cereal brands while the assertiveness of the child had no effect. Ward and Wackman (1972) examined the relationship between the extent of parental yielding to children's attempts to influence purchases as a function of the demography of the household, usual patterns of parent–child interaction and the mothers' use of mass media. Results revealed that children's influence attempts tended to decrease with age, while mothers' yielding tended to increase. They also found children's requests for products and mothers' granting of these requests to be closely related to the child's involvement (interest and use) with the product. Mehotra and Torges (1976) also found variables that increased the likelihood of parental yielding to children's attempts to influence family purchases to be product specific. Finally, in an observational study of children's influence attempts and parental yielding, Atkin (1978) found that the rate of child success in obtaining the desired cereal increased with the age of the child and that slightly higher success rates were obtained by female and middle-class children.

A number of studies have made direct assessments of children's as well as parents' influence on the family decision-making process. Szybillo et al. (1977) found little difference in the family role structure over three stages of the decision process for fast-food and conventional restaurants, although there were variations within sub-decision areas. Children were generally involved in each decision stage, while sub-decisions such as those involving finances, for example, were generally made by an adult. A study by Nelson (1978) also examined the relative influence of children and parents in the family decision to eat out and generally supported the findings of Szybillo et al. Jenkins (1978) also found that the extent of children's influence varied with the product or service category and the specific sub-decision area.

Belch et al. (1985) found that family member influence varied by product, by stages of the decision-making process, and by various decision areas. The husband and wife clearly dominated the decision-making process. Observation of decision making within each stage indicated that the husband was most dominant for products such as cars and television sets, whereas the wife was dominant for household appliances, furniture, and breakfast cereal.

The influence of the teenage child in the family decision-making process was limited, with the greatest influence occurring in the initiation stage of the decision-making process. This finding suggested that teenage children may have some input in the *initial* stages, but that this involvement in the search and evaluation and *final-decision* stages was very small. This finding was understandable, since the responsibility for the shopping and purchase of most household products, and particularly for many of the durable items used in this study, lay with parents.

In general, the influence of the child was fairly limited, being strongest for aesthetic considerations such as style, colour, and make/model of the product, and was weakest for allocation decisions such as where and when to purchase, and how much money to spend. The child's influence was weakest where financial decisions were concerned.

As already noted, one way in which children may influence parents' consumer-related decisions takes the form of 'pestering' for products which they have seen advertised. Research in a number of different countries, including the United States, Britain and Japan, has indicated that children's requests for advertised products can result in conflicts within the family (Isler et al., 1987; Robertson et al., 1989) (see also Chapters 5 and 6).

A study by Adler and his colleagues (1980) asked more than 700 children aged 4 to 10 years whether they urged their mothers to buy toys they had seen advertised on television. Children who were heavy viewers of television were more likely to ask for advertised products (40%) than infrequent viewers (16%). Even these modest figures can be further reduced if children are included in purchasing decisions and if parents discuss television and advertising with them (Dorr, 1986; Feshbach, et al., 1984; Moschis and Moore, 1982). Besides, children know the difference between wanting something and asking for it. In one study, children completing a projective technique (a story completion task) about a child watching television indicated that they were aware of the large difference between *wanting* something advertised on television and asking their parents to buy the product. The children said that 90 per cent of the time the child depicted in the story would 'want' the product shown on television, but the child would only be willing to ask for it 60 per cent of the time (Sheikh and Moleski, 1977).

The degree of conflict generated by product requests is unclear. Condry (1989) has assumed that conflict is the inevitable result of product requests. Yet, Isler *et al.* (1987) report that mothers' refusal of requests rarely led to conflict. Ward and his colleagues concluded from their studies that 'the data consistently show that television advertising as a perceived influence on children's requests has little impact on mothers' responses' (Ward, Popper and Wackman, 1977, p. 57).

In a national survey, British children were asked whether they requested their parents to buy them something they had seen in an advertisement on television (Greenberg *et al.*, 1986). Here, 85 per cent said that they had, while just 15 per cent claimed not to have done. Requests were made equally by boys and girls. There were differences by age, with a drop in requests among older children: 97 per cent of 4- to 5-year-olds claimed to have made such requests of their parents, compared with 94 per cent of 6- to 7-year-olds, 86 per cent of 8- to nine-year-olds, and 71 per cent of 10- to 13-year-olds. The decline in product requests with increasing age has also been noted in other studies (e.g. Isler *et al.*, 1987). The latter researchers noted that there tended to be substantially fewer requests among children from middle-class backgrounds than from those with working-class backgrounds.

Frequently cited research on advertised food products reports that children ask for advertised products and that parents often acquiesce (Atkin, 1975; Galst and White, 1976; Stoneman and Brody, 1982). However, Young (1990) questions the validity of these studies. Typically, children watch particular commercials, following which they are given a choice from a range of snacks which include the advertised brand. According to Young:

> Under these somewhat artificial conditions researchers often, but not always, find that the advertising of brand X makes the subsequent choice of brand X by the child more likely... The results are true within the artificial universe of this kind of experimental, laboratory investigation but may not hold true in the real world.
>
> (1990, p.11)

The importance of family context in parent–child conflict is apparent in the cross-cultural study by Robertson *et al.* (1989). American, Japanese and English parents kept diaries of purchase requests and television watching. Children's requests to parents were positively correlated with television viewing, and product requests were correlated with parent–child conflict. Japanese children were significantly less demanding than British children. Japanese families were most likely to follow rules for regulating the children's behaviour.

More recently, Bennett (1991) reported a survey of British families conducted by Mintel International, *Children: The Influencing Factor 1991*. Across all social classes children were found to have the greatest influence on their parents' shopping behaviour from the age of 5 until about 11 or 12. Parents viewed their children's influence positively in many ways. Parents were concerned that their children should become consumer aware and their request behaviours indicated that they were developing their own tastes.

Factors influencing TV advertising and parent pestering

A variety of factors have been found to influence the extent to which children pester their parents to buy them things. One of the most significant stimuli is advertising, especially that seen on television. Not all children respond to television advertising in the same way. In Chapters 5 and 6 we will discuss the nature of children's awareness and understanding of advertising and the impact it has upon their consumer behaviour. It is worth examining, at this point, the evidence which has a specific bearing on the effect of advertising upon parental pestering. The factors which have particular importance in this context include the child's age, parental social class and education, cultural background, television viewing, and peers. In addition, parental pestering is often associated with particular types of product.

Most researchers have found that the most important mediating variable in relation to the effects of advertising on children purchase requests is the child's age. Galst *et al.* (1976) found that a child's purchase requests *increased* as the child grew older. Observations of shoppers in a grocery revealed that older children attempted to influence more of their mother's purchases at the supermarket than did younger children.

All the other studies that measured the relationship between the child's age and the amount of purchase request behaviour found the opposite. They indicated that children's purchase influencing attempts decreased with age. Detailed studies have been carried out with commercials for toys and child-oriented products and have invariably found greater numbers of purchase requests of parents made by younger than by older children (Robertson, 1979). Although purchase requests generally decrease among older children, the relationship between age and parental pestering is not particularly strong. There is even some evidence that it may be curvilinear with fewer requests among both the oldest and youngest children, and the greatest number occurring among middle age-range children (Robertson, 1979).

There is more mixed evidence concerning the relationship between socioeconomic class and children's purchase request behaviour. There is evidence, for instance, that children from higher socioeconomic classes, who have better-educated parents, usually make fewer purchase requests to their parents (Young, 1990). The effects of television advertising on children's purchase request behaviour can differ according to social class because of a difference in level of exposure to television advertising, with working-class children watching more television. Social class differences associated with styles of parental communication with their children can also make a difference to the nature of children's reactions to television advertising in the context of parental pestering.

Variations in children's purchase requests have also been investigated in connection with children's cultural background. Thus, Japanese children have been found to make fewer purchase requests than American or British children (Young, 1990). The reasons for these cultural differences can be attributed to a very complex set of factors which can vary greatly from country to country, and from culture to culture. Both the amount of television advertising shown and parental styles of communication with their children are probably the two most important differences (Riem, 1987).

Exposure to television may, in its own right, make a difference to the volume of children's purchase requests. Evidence has emerged that children who watch greater amounts of commercial television make more purchase requests of their parents. According to some scholars, watching television advertising may develop positive attitudes towards consumerism and product acquisition. In Britain, for example, Greenberg *et al.* (1976) reported that child viewers who watched the most ITV (commercial network) were more likely to ask their parents to buy an advertised item (especially a toy) than were light or medium viewers of the same channel. The amount of BBC-viewing (the public channel which carries no product advertising) was unrelated to reported product requests. Of course, such correlational evidence cannot conclusively prove a cause–effect relationship between exposure to televised advertising and purchase request behaviour. Indeed, the conditions under which television has any influence at all can depend upon other prevailing conditions, since there are many factors which can determine the frequency of children's purchase requests (Robertson, 1979).

A small amount of research has indicated that the extent to which children are integrated with their peer groups can make a difference to their purchase requests. This factor has been observed to play a part in particular with regard to requests for toys and games. Children who watch a great deal of television and who are poorly integrated with their peers have been observed to make the most purchase requests for toys and games. Children with equally heavy television exposure but better developed peer networks tended to make fewer purchase requests (Robertson, 1979). Among children who were relatively infrequent television viewers, peer integration made no difference to the extent of their purchase requests.

Types of products requested

The amount of purchase requests made by children differs according to the product itself. What kinds of things do children try to get their parents to buy? Various studies have indicated that the number of different items is large and include things for children themselves as well as things for the household. Most researchers agree that children are more likely to make requests for products which are frequently consumed by them, such as breakfast cereals, snacks or sweets, or for products that are of particular interest to them, such as toys or those with special offers (Galst *et al.*, 1976; Robertson, 1979).

Products which are usually requested also vary importantly according to the child's age, with requests for toys, breakfast cereals and sweets being more frequent with younger children (aged 5 to 7 years), and requests for clothing or records more frequent among children aged 11 to 12 years (Riem, 1987).

Information sources underlying purchase requests

Where do children get their ideas for purchase requests? The earlier discussion implicated advertising as a major source of influence. Advertising on television and radio, in newspapers and magazines, and on posters and billboards all play a part (McNeal, 1992). Research since the early 1970s has indicated that advertising is an important source of children's product ideas, but by no means a dominant source. One American study showed that children's main information source for gift ideas was television advertising (27% of the time), but almost equally important was friends (26%), followed closely by shops (22%) and then by catalogues (15%). Older children were more likely to mention television and less likely to mention friends as information sources compared with younger children. Older children were also more likely to cite catalogues as a gift information source. Indeed, there was evidence that with increased age, young consumers learn to use a range of mass media for purchase-related information (Caron and Ward, 1975).

Today there are more information sources, and the figures reported above are probably different, at least for certain products. For instance, in a study cited by McNeal (1992) of children's attitudes towards styles and brands of athletic shoes, it was found that their major source of information about a new style of shoe was other children, usually children older than themselves (46% of the time). Other sources were stores (25%) and catalogues (15%), with advertising accounting for only 10 per cent. These percentages were found to change, however, after the shoe style had become fashionable. Then, advertising became a somewhat more important source of information for the child.

According to McNeal:

> The fact that there are more information sources available in the '90s for young consumers than there were in the 1970s, is good for the children because they want more marketplace information. As indicated while more advertising is targeted to children, and more of it is in media other than television, children appear to be placing more importance on other commercial services relative to advertising than they once did.
>
> (1992, p. 71)

In addition to advertising media, there is the almost equally important influence of stores. In the United States, for example, it is said that a 10-year-old may visit stores 250 times a year. Each store may expose the child to hundreds of pieces of information about products and brands. Awareness amongst retailers of the possible influences they may be able to exert over young consumers within their outlets has led them to take steps to create retail environments which are young-consumer friendly. Fixtures and display racks are lowered to a child's eye level and in some cases special areas have been set aside for youngsters.

In the United States, some information about things to buy that may influence product requests from children may come along with educational materials in schools. Personnel from retail stores and banks also visit schools to present information to the children about products and services, while other stores may host school field trips to their retail locations. In addition, there are now a large number of new commercial sources of information targeted at children. These include advertisements on rental videos, product placements within movies, product samples distributed in school either in single or pack form, posters at school, television advertisements presented through classroom programming, and direct mail advertising (Pereira, 1990).

Location of children's requests

There is a general rule that governs children's requests for goods and services to parents: children are most likely to make a purchase request for an item when in the presence of a stimulus related to that item. This rule has various marketing, parenting and policy implications.

(1) A marketer who wants to direct a child's influence on parental purchases of an object should target frequent communications to the child about that object in a variety of media including the retail setting.
(2) Parents who do not want their child influenced by marketers, which in turn would produce requests from the child, should keep the child away from marketing messages.
(3) If public policy makers believe it is wrong for marketers to attempt to influence children's purchase requests or to influence them at certain times, they must limit commercial messages aimed at the children at least at certain times.

From this general rule we can expect the child to make purchase requests during or soon after watching, hearing, or reading advertisements, during visits to the shopping setting, while interacting with peers or soon afterward, and within the time zone of experiencing other marketing messages such as in the classroom, watching a movie, riding public transport, during car travel with parents, or walking to school.

Influence on parents' choice of retail outlet

Children can and do have an influence upon *where* their parents buy things. As children are exposed to the interiors and other attractions of stores by parents during the first few years of childhood, they develop likes and dislikes of particular categories of stores and of specific stores. Their store preferences are enhanced and modified by preferences of parents and peers and by actual experiences with an increasing number of outlets. According to McNeal (1992), there are two main occasions when children make retail recommendations to parents: when parents and children are going shopping together and when parents shop alone but some of the purchases are expected to be for the children.

By recommending to parents that they buy from a certain retail outlet, children are causing their parents to preselect an offering of goods and services. This has major implications for producers whose product lines could be omitted from parents' choice set depending on the store recommendations of youngsters. McNeal (1992), suggests that producers of items intended for children may wish to consider some cooperative advertising efforts with retailers. Producers of children's products may also want to investigate the images of certain retailers among children even before they begin their selling efforts to that particular store.

Parental responses to children's requests

There are almost as many kinds of responses by parents as there are kinds of purchase requests by children. In general, though, four broad types of response predominate: (1) make the purchase; (2) substitute another purchase; (3) postpone the purchase; and (4) ignore or refuse the request. It is worth looking at each of these responses in turn in more detail.

Make the purchase. As a rule, parents honour children's requests around half the time (McNeal, 1992). Most parents want to meet all their children's requests, but because of economic limits and because of impact on the welfare of the child, they do not. While parents mostly enjoy giving to their children, they can become irritated or annoyed by excessive numbers of requests, particularly if they perceive the product to be bad for the child's health or welfare. Parents are more likely to fulfil purchase requests made in the retail environment than one made at home. Requests at home can be delayed or conveniently forgotten about before shopping takes place. The opportunity for purchase is more immediate in the store and the wish to avoid a scene upon refusal of the child's request often preys on the parent's mind.

Substitute another purchase. Parents may feel that a certain brand or type of product requested is too expensive, of poor quality, or inappropriate for their child, and offer a substitute. This may cause conflict within the family and be less satisfying for the child, as well as being a lost sale for the child's preferred manufacturer or retailer.

Postpone the purchase. Requests made at home can more readily be postponed than ones made in the store. The parent can expect the request to come again. The hope that with delay the child will forget does not always come true. A purchase may therefore eventually be made, but not as quickly as the marketer might like. Middle-class parents are also likely to believe in the importance of the postponement of gratification.

Ignore or refuse the request. This happens often, but children may have trouble with these responses. Confrontations may result, with arguments, loss of temper and tantrums. All these things can be embarrassing for all parties. Different styles of parenting have varying methods for dealing with these occasions.

Not all parents respond in the same way to children's purchase requests. While differences may be attributed to the economic conditions of the household, parenting style is often a significant part of the explanation. Parental style refers here to the patterns of child-rearing and disciplinary practices adopted by parents. While parents cannot be exclusively grouped into a specific type of parenting style, they do tend to follow or subscribe to certain defined patterns (Carlson and Grossbart, 1988). As noted earlier, there are *authoritarian* parents who discourage independence in their children and usually make all decisions for the children. At the other extreme are the *permissive* parents who avoid exercising any control over their children. Far from being disciplinarians, these parents are more like friends to their children. In the middle, so to speak, are the parents who can be described as *authoritative* who clearly are in charge but have flexible boundaries for their children that encourage autonomy for them. Finally, there are *neglecting* parents who, for whatever reasons, show little concern for their children's development. All of these parents probably honour many of their children's purchase requests, but logically we might expect the authoritarian parent to discourage such requests, the permissive and the authoritative to encourage such requests, although for different reasons, and the neglecting parent not to respond to them.

Research has also indicated that parental yielding to children's purchase requests can depend upon the type of product, and on the question of whether the product requested was primarily for the child's consumption. Consequently, it has been observed that mothers (or fathers) were most likely to yield to requests for food products. A study by Ward and Wackman (1972) showed the following products exhibited varying percentage rates of success: cereals (87% of requests successful), snack foods (63%), games and toys (54%), sweets or candy (42%), toothpaste (39%), shampoo (16%) and pet food (7%). Other studies have found different absolute figures, but have indicated similar relative differences between products. In general, parents tend to yield to children's requests for breakfast cereals or snacks more than any other product type (Galst *et al.*, 1976).

Some evidence has indicated that parents may be more likely to purchase an item when they feel that the request has originated through non-media influence (such as having tried the product somewhere else before) than when the request appears to have been based on media-influences. The reason behind this seems to be that for the kind of requests that were not based on television advertisement alone, parents feel more secure that the child has made a definite choice (Smith, 1984).

4

Children's Use and Understanding of Money

The Economic Socialization of Children

Socialization is generally defined as a process through which individuals learn to interact in society. So far, comparatively little research has been done on economic socialization than on other aspects of social development (e.g. moral development). Still less has been done on how economic knowledge and beliefs are acquired as opposed to the content of the knowledge base (Berti and Bombi, 1988; Haste and Torney-Purta, 1992). Furthermore it has not been until comparatively recently that researchers have looked at young people's reasoning and understanding about economic issues.

A detailed examination of the economic and political socialization of children and adolescents is of both academic and applied interest. In 1990 in Great Britain, 14- to 16-year-olds had nearly £10 per week in disposable cash. In 1988 in Germany 7- to 15-year-olds received 7.5 billion DM of pocket money and monetary gifts and the total spending power of 12- to 21-year-olds amounted to 33 billion DM annually. And of course in most western democratic countries teenagers of 18 years are allowed to vote in local municipal and national elections. Young people have both political and economic power.

There also appears to be a relative paucity of research on adolescent economic beliefs and values. This is perhaps surprising as there are both practical and theoretical reasons for wanting to know what adolescents know of, and think about, the working of the economy, as well as how to earn, save and spend money. Two 'practical' reasons seem obvious: first, adolescents have considerable buying power. For instance, in America children spend over $4 billion annually and teenagers spent over $40 billion in 1980, while British 5- to 16-year-olds had an estimated £780 million to spend in the early 1980s on preferred goods and services (and it is of considerable interest to people in trade how, where and why that money is spent). Secondly, teachers of economics are clearly interested in the way economic concepts are acquired so that they may teach them more effectively at the appropriate age (Kourilsky, 1977; O'Brien and Ingels, 1985, 1987). There are also many interesting theoretical questions concerning adolescent understanding and beliefs about the economy (trade, work, consumption, advertising), such as at what age various sophisticated economic concepts are grasped and what socialization experiences determine the extent and structure of economic beliefs. Economic beliefs may influence further education and career choice as well as how young people vote. McNeal (1987) also noted the number of agents in the socialization process whereby children and adolescents learn to become consumers: parents, peers, teachers and business. Visits to stores, advertising, features, functions and packaging for young people's products are all important factors in their understanding of how the economy works.

Many different aspects of young people's understanding and perception of the economic and political world, their attitudes towards money and possessions, their spending and consumption habits are relevant to the teaching of economic principles in schools as well as to the research of psychologists, educationists, marketing people and even to economists (Furnham and Stacey, 1991).

The Development of Economic and Political Ideas in the Child

Stages

What do children know about money, work and economics? How and at what age do they acquire their knowledge? To what extent are there differences of knowledge and belief regarding gender, age, nationality, socioeconomic background and experience with money? These are some of the early questions researchers concentrated on in studies examining children's and adolescents' cognitive development related to economics and to a lesser extent politics. For many years research was predominately concerned with attempting to describe the stages children went through in the development of specific concepts. Stage-wise theories are currently out of fashion but often retained for heuristic purposes to help describe the different types of thinking about the economy that young people exhibit.

Strauss (1952) was among the first to examine the development of money-related concepts. In his 1952 study he interviewed 66 children of both sexes between 4½ and 11½ years and classified the answers into *nine* different developmental stages that reinforced the Piagetian idea of the child's advancement by stages rather than by continuum. For Strauss, the content of the child's concepts undergoes systematic change as it moves from one level to the next, which depends on his having understood the respective prerequisite notions. Each level of conception though does not only signify a different degree of intellectual maturity but also a different level of experience, perception and values. Thirty years later Danziger (1958) asked 41 children between 5 and 8 years questions about money, the rich and the poor and the 'boss', in order to examine whether the development of social concepts in the child could be applied to Piaget's theoretical model of cognitive development.

From the results he drew up *four* different stages in the development of economic concepts:

(a) An initial pre-categorical stage occurs when the child lacks economic categories of thought altogether. There is no special realm of economic concepts differentiated from social concepts in general. (b) At the second, or categorical stage the child's concepts appear to represent a reality in terms of isolated acts which are explained by a moral or voluntaristic imperative. (c) At the third stage the child becomes able to conceptualize relationships as such, by virtue of the fact that a reciprocity is established between previously isolated acts. But these relations are in their turn isolated and cannot be explained in terms of other relationships. (d) Finally, the isolated relationships become linked to each other so as to form a system of relations. We then have a conceptualization of a totality wherein each part derives its significance from its position in the whole. At this point a purely rational explanation becomes possible.

(Danziger, 1958, pp. 239–240)

Danziger believed that first-hand experience enhances the advancement onto the next level of conception. The children in his study appeared to be at a higher level in their understanding of economic exchange than in production and he attributed this to the fact that they had experience of buying but not of work.

Sutton (1962) interviewed 85 children between 6 and 13 on money and the accumulation of capital. Irrespective of age, intelligence and socioeconomic background the majority of replies were in the beginning stages of conceptualization, thus emphasizing the importance of first-hand experience in the development of economic concepts (63% of the answers were to be found in the second of the six stages she codified from the 1020 replies). Sutton maintained that theory and research on the attainment of economic concepts have attempted to answer five questions:

(1) How do children achieve information necessary for isolating and learning a concept?
(2) How do children retain the information from encounters so that it may be useful later?
(3) How is the retained information transformed so that it may be rendered useful for testing an hypothesis still unformed at the moment of first encountering new information?
(4) What are the general features in the growth of economic concepts?
(5) To what extent are the concepts of children a cultural product of the environment?

In his study Sutton asked 85 children, randomly chosen from the first to the sixth grade, 12 questions such as 'How do people get money?', 'What is a bank?', 'Why do people save?', etc. The 1020 replies were arranged into six (developmental) categories:

(1) No replies (1%).

(2) Pre-categorical stage where objects are named but with little understanding of economic meaning (63%).
(3) A category of moral value judgements (good/bad, right/wrong) irrespective of economic function (18%).
(4) Two isolated acts/factors that are economically significant (people save just to be saving) (12%).
(5) Two acts involving a reciprocity which cannot be explained by other economic relationships (if you put money in a bank you get more back) (5%).
(6) The subjective explanation gives rise to the objective; the single act derives its significance from its position in a system of relationships that is no longer conceived in an isolated way.

Jahoda (1979) conducted a study that comprised a role play in which 120 working-class Scottish children aged between 6 and 12 played the role of the shopkeeper while the interviewer acted as customer and supplier. Answers were grouped into notion (of profit) absent, transitional and notion present according to whether the difference between buying and selling price had been realized. The results suggested that most children did not begin to understand the concept of profit until about the age of 11. The interview that followed showed that the development of the understanding of the concept of profit passed through three stages: (1) no grasp of any system—transactions conceived of as simply an observed ritual; (2) two unconnected systems—shop owner buys and sells at the same price; (3) two integrated systems—awareness of the difference between buying and selling price.

Burris (1983) found, from the answers of 32 children at each distinct stage (preoperational, concrete operations, and formal operations), general compatibility with the Piagetian view that knowledge develops through a sequence of qualitative cognitive stages. Leiser (1983), Schug and Birkey (1985), Sevon and Weckstrom (1989) supported these findings. Schug and Birkey, like Danziger, also stressed that children's economic understanding varies somewhat depending upon their own economic experiences though the quality of the evidence they acquired is debatable. Sevon and Weckstrom characterized younger children's perception of the economy as from the viewpoint of homo sociologicus (driven by moral and social norms) and the one of older children more as of homo economicus (striving for personal hedonistic satisfaction). Of the three age groups, 8, 11 and 14, the youngest group when asked about the thinking and acting of economic agents first felt the need to decide whether these agents would become happy or unhappy before thinking about why this was the case (e.g. 'The shoe retailer would be happy about the reduction in shoe prices because "people can save their money"'...). The answers of the younger children thus described *moral* or 'Christian' concern (other people's approval or disapproval of own behaviour as important) rather than *economic* thinking (other people as means, constraints or obstacles to personal satisfaction). Some of the older children, however, saw the economy more as an instrument and the action of the individual as being led by the search for an opportunity to increase his or her own wealth. This was partly due to their increased ability to think abstractly. However, as adults also sometimes argue from a moral viewpoint, intellectual sophistication cannot be the only explanation, with family values and socialization clearly also playing a part.

There were differences between age groups in the answers given to some of these questions. For example, in response to a question about what would happen if most taxes were abolished, children aged 8 and 11 years were more likely than those aged 14 to think that this would be a good thing because people would have more money. The 14-year-olds, on the other hand, were more likely than the younger children to acknowledge that there could be bad as well as good effects.

Although most researchers largely agree on the Piagetian view about the development of economic concepts in the child they apparently have found different numbers of stages. This might be due to several reasons: the age ranges of the subjects were different; the number of subjects in each study were different (sometime perhaps too small to be representative); each researcher's precision in the definition of where one stage ends and the next starts. Thus, the assignments of the subjects to the respective stages vary, the methodologies used are different in precision, etc. These are possible explanations although they do not all necessarily have to be true for every single study (see Table 4.1).

TABLE 4.1 *Studies of economic socialization*

Researcher	Year	Subjects	Age range	Stages
Strauss	1952	66	4.8–11.6	9
Danzinger	1958	41	5–8	4
Sutton	1962	85	Grades 1–6	6
Jahoda	1979	120	6–12	3
Burris	1983	96	4–5, 7–8, 10–12	3
Leiser	1983	89	7–17	3

Table 4.1 shows that there is disagreement about the number of stages, points of transition and content of understanding at each respective stage. The trend among the more recent studies though seems to be that the number of (sub)-stages are summarized and three broad main phases are defined: (1) no understanding; (2) understanding of some isolated concepts; and (3) linking of isolated concepts to full understanding. By no means do these stages suggest though that the child's understanding of different economic concepts always advances at the same rate. As Danziger (1958) stressed, children's understanding of buying and selling may be more advanced than their understanding of work, as they might have had experience of the former but not of the latter. It is important to further investigate if and what other factors (e.g. parental practices,

social class) actually tend to speed up or perhaps slow down the transition from one stage to the next.

Nearly all the relevant research consists of self-report studies using interviews. Most Piagetian work is task-based (role play, games, etc) and it may well be that experimental studies on economic concepts would yield clearer, more interesting results. Also, most of these studies have been conducted in western, industrialized, capitalist countries and, if economic education and experiences are relevant to the understanding of economic concepts, studies also need to be done in developing-world and socialist countries.

Furnham and Stacey (1992) concluded:

> Frequently rather different stage-wise models compete in the description of a phenomena. Yet there are a number of characteristics common to all stage-wise theories:
> ● A stage is a structured whole in a state of equilibrium.
> ● Each stage derives from the previous stage, incorporates but transforms the previous one and prepares for the next.
> ● Stages follow in an invariant sequence.
> ● Stages are universal to all humans at all times in all the countries.
> ● Each stage has a stage from coming-into-being, to being.
>
> All stage-wise theories appear to have a number of implicit assumptions; *that the sequence of development is fixed that there is an ideal end-of-state towards which the child and adolescent inevitably progresses* and that some behaviours are sufficiently different from previous abilities that we can identify a child or adolescence as being in or out of a stage. Non-stage theories do not see people progressing inevitably to a single final stage since environmental forces are given more power to create a diversity of developmental responses. At the one end of the stage-non-stage continuum is the view that most of a young person's time is spent in one of several specific stages with short, relatively abrupt transitions between stages. As the length of time spent in a stage is perceived to be shortened and the time in transition is lengthened, one moves along the continuum until all the time is seen as spent in transition, and development is seen as continuous and non-stage. Since a non-stage theory does not necessarily dictate any specific end of state of singly developmental sequence, the study of individual differences assumes more importance.
>
> However, rather than portray the stage-non-stage approach to development as another manifestation of the famous heredity-environment, nature-nurture maturation learning debate, most would argue that this is a false dichotomy and a non-issue. Most researchers would be interactionists, at an intermediate point on the extreme or strict stage vs. non-stage (or process) approach. A second assumption that most would agree with is that the young play an active part in their own development. That is young people construct an interpretation of the information that they selectively attend to, based on their previous experience, maturation and indeed momentary needs. The moderate novelty principle applies here which states that young people attend to and learn most from events that are mildly discrepant from (as opposed to very different from or identical to) their current level of conception about the social world.
>
> (pp. 192–193)

Webley (1983) and others have criticized the application of the standard Piagetian approach and argued in favour of looking for what is distinct about economic concepts instead of treating economic cognition as just another area where general principles of cognitive development apply. He reproached researchers for their use of a static standard approach towards the investigation into children's development of economic thinking and regretted that no attempts have been made to 'produce a characterization of the environment which might allow variations in the development of economic thought apart from social class distinction'. What is special about economic factors (e.g. property) is that they form the basis of power in society and interpersonal relations and the concepts/ideology a child develops are therefore of vital concern to the possessing. The need to relate to the economic structure of the society—an idea more radically expressed by Cummings and Taebel (1978)—and the importance of characterizing a child's environment (e.g. exposure to own economic experience) are therefore aspects that might distinguish the development of economic concepts from others. In this sense the understanding of economics, history and politics is different from that of physics, chemistry and say meteorology. Social values and ideology are intricately bound up with the latter and not the former and can influence understanding profoundly.

Researchers are generally agreed that changes in economic reasoning occur as children get older. But not all agree what these changes are or how much of the following factors, that co-vary with age, are the major influence on economic understanding: (1) an accumulation of knowledge and experience from primary and secondary socialization and education; (2) an increase in general ability of complex reasoning; (3) a diminishing of egocentrism; (4) changing role behaviour—with increasing age children assume more of the adult behaviour in the economy, etc. It is impossible to compute how much cognitive development can be attributed to each process (and others) as they are interdependent and vary with each individual.

Research on the Development of Economic Thinking

Although numerous studies of children's understanding of different aspects of the economic world have been carried out, they have tended to concentrate on certain topics (Berti and Bombi, 1988). Relatively few studies exist on young people's knowledge of betting, taxes, interest rates, the ups and downs of the economy (boom, recession, depression, recovery etc.) or inflation. This might be because these concepts are considered to be too difficult for children to understand. A study in Yugoslavia by Zabukovec and Polic (1990), however, showed that economic awareness clearly reflected aspects (e.g. inflation) of the then current economic situation. There is, however, little detailed research on topics like possession and ownership, wealth and poverty, entrepreneurship, prices, wages, money, buying and selling, profit and the bank. Yet the common denominator to all economic interactions in the Western World is money and therefore understanding about money is a prerequisite for understanding of other key economic concepts.

Money

As money is the basis to almost all economic actions today, a full understanding of it clearly is a prerequisite for the understanding of other, more abstract concepts (e.g. credit or profit). Children's first contact with money happens at a quite early age (watching parents buying or selling things, receiving pocket money, etc.) but research has shown that although children use money themselves they do not necessarily fully understand its meaning and significance. For very young children, giving money to a salesperson constitutes a mere ritual. They are not aware of the different values of coins and the purpose of change, let alone the origin of money. Children thus need to understand the nature and role of money before being able to master more abstract concepts.

To investigate children's ideas about the payment for work Berti and Bombi (1979) interviewed 100 children from three to eight years (20 from each age level) on where they thought money came from. *Four* categories of response, or stages, emerged. At stage 1, children had no idea of its origin: the parent simply takes the money from a pocket. At stage 2, children saw the origin as independent of work: somebody, such as a bank, gives it to everybody who asks for it. At stage 3, the subjects named the change given by tradesmen when buying as the origin of money. Only at stage 4 did children name work as the source. Most of the three- and four-year-olds' answers were at stage 1, whereas most of the six- to seven- and seven- to eight-year-olds were at stage 4. The idea of payment for work (stage 4) thus develops out of various spontaneous and erroneous beliefs at stages 2 and 3, where children do not yet understand the concept of work, which is a prerequisite for understanding the origin of money. Although at that those stages they did notice occasionally that their parents took part in extra-domestic activities, children did not call it work or even see a need for it. Two years later Berti and Bombi (1981) undertook another investigation (80 subjects between three and eight years old) into the concept of money and its value. Building on the work of Strauss (1952) and others they singled out *six* stages: stage 1—no awareness of payment; stage 2—obligatory payment (no distinction between different kinds of money, and money can buy anything); stage 3—distinction between types of money (not all money is equivalent any more); stage 4—realization that money can be insufficient; stage 5—strict correspondence between money and objects (correct amount has to be given); stage 6—correct use of change.

The first four stages clearly are to be found in the preoperational period whereas in the last two, arithmetic operations are successfully applied. Strauss (1952) had found *nine* stages in the child's understanding about money, ranging from the first stage where the child believes that any coin can buy any object to the last where correct understanding is achieved.

Pollio and Gray (1973) conducted a more 'practical' study with 100 subjects, grouped at the ages of 7, 9, 11, 13 and college-age, on 'change-making strategies'. They found that it wasn't until the age of 13 that an entire age group was able to give correct change. The younger subjects showed a preference for small value coins (with which they were more familiar) when giving change, whereas the older ones used all coins available. More recent studies have looked at such things as children's actual monetary behaviour. For instance, Abramovitch *et al.* (1991) found that Canadian children aged 6 to 10 years who got allowances seemed more sophisticated about money than those who did not get an allowance. Clearly understanding of the origin, function and meaning of money in young people will attract a great deal of further research as it remains unclear what factors influence these various cognitions (Furnham and Argyle, 1997).

Prices and profit

Buying is one of the earliest economic activities a child can engage in. There are a number of prerequisites for being able to understand buying and selling, and therefore prices and profit: a child has to know about the functions and origins of money, change, ownership, payment of wages to employees, shop expenses and shop owner's need for income/private money. As this list indicates, the simple act of buying and selling is in fact rather complex. Furth (1980) pointed to *four* stages during the acquisition of this concept: stage 1—no understanding of payment; stage 2—understanding of payment of customer but not of the shopkeeper; stage 3—understanding and relating of both the customers' and shopkeeper's payment; stage 4—understanding of all these things.

In Furth's first stage children exhibit little understanding about the basic functions of money, how it is obtained or how it relates to the purchase of commodities. In the second stage of development, primitive understanding starts to emerge, mostly as a result of transactions they observe between others. In the third stage, a more elaborate set of concepts develops about the mechanism of buying and selling and the significance of having a paid job. So children at this stage know, for instance, that if you go into a shop you pay money and receive goods in return. However, they have little higher level understanding of the shopkeeper's need to make a profit. In stage 4, a broader understanding of the role of money in society becomes more firmly established, with links being made between government actions, the state of the economy and personal financial position.

Jahoda (1979), using a role play where the child had to buy goods from a supplier and sell to a customer, defined *three* stages: (1) no understanding of profit—both prices were consistently identical; (2) transitional—mixture of responses; (3) understanding of profit—selling price consistently higher than buying price. The fact that in this study there is one stage fewer than in Furth's may to due to the fact that it concentrated only on the ideas of profit and whether children understand the concept. Jahoda inferred understanding from behaviour.

Supporting the idea of gradually integrating sub-systems, Berti, Bombi and de Beni (1986) pointed out that the concepts about shop and factory profit in 8-

year-olds were not compatible. Despite improving their understanding of shop profit after receiving training, the children were not able to transfer this knowledge when considering factory profit, thinking that prices were set arbitrarily.

Berti, Bombi and de Beni (1986) showed that with training, children's understanding of profit could be enhanced. Both critical training sessions stimulating the child to puzzle out solutions to contradictions between their own forecasts and the actual outcomes and ordinary, tutorial training sessions (information given to children) that consisted of similar games of buying and selling proved to be effective. However, the results of the post-tests also showed that neither kind of experience was sufficient in itself to lead children to a correct notion of profit, partly due to lack of arithmetical abilities involving the addition and subtraction of small numbers. Nevertheless the authors suggested that although arithmetical abilities are essential, 'making children talk about economic topics they have not yet mastered, far from being an obstacle to learning may contribute to their progress, constituting in itself a kind of training, as Jahoda (1981) also found in different circumstances' (p. 28).

In a study of 11- to 16-year-olds, Furnham and Cleare (1988) also found differences in understanding shop and factory profit. 'Of 11–12 years olds, 7% understood profit in shops, yet 69% mentioned profit as a motive for starting a factory today, and 20% mentioned profit as an explanation for why factories had been started.' (p. 475). The understanding of the abstract concept of profit, which depends on the previous understanding of the basic concept of buying and selling, grows through different phases. Young children (6–8 years) seem to have no grasp of any system and conceive of transactions as 'simply an observed ritual without further purpose' (Furth *et al.*, 1976, p. 365). Older children (8–10 years) realize that the shop owner previously had to buy (pay for) the goods before he can sell them. Nevertheless, they do not always understand that the money for this comes from the customers and that buying prices have to be lower than selling prices. They thus perceive of buying and selling as two unconnected systems. Not until the age of 10–11 are children able to integrate these two systems and understand the difference between buying and selling prices. Of course, these age bands may vary slightly among children (or cultures) as experiential factors play a part in the understanding of economic concepts. Because of the obvious political implications of the ideas of profit and pricing it would be particularly interesting to see not only when (and how) young people come to understand the concepts but also how they reason with them in such areas as the nationalization or privatization of state assets.

Banking

Jahoda (1981) interviewed 32 subjects at each of the ages 12, 14, and 16 about how banks make profits. He tried to determine whether children know that more interest is paid on a loan than is received in interest on deposits. He asked whether one gets back more, less or the same as the original sum deposited and whether one has to pay back more, less or the same as the original sum borrowed. From this basis he drew up six stages:

(1) No knowledge of interest (get/pay back same amount).
(2) Interest on deposits only (get back more, pay back the same).
(3) Interest on both, but more on deposit (deposit interest higher than loan interest).
(4) Interest same on deposits and loans.
(5) Interest higher for loans—no evidence for understanding.
(6) Interest more for loans—correctly understood.

Although most of these children had fully understood the concept of shop profit, many did not perceive the bank as a profit-making enterprise (only one in four of the 14- and 16-year-olds understood bank profit). 'They viewed the principles governing a bank as akin to those underlying the transactions between friends: if you borrow something, you return the same, no more and no less— anything else would be "unfair"' (p. 70).

Ng (1983) replicated the same study in Hong Kong and found the same developmental trend. The Chinese children however were more precocious than the Scots, showing a full understanding of the bank's profit at the age of 10. From the same study he discovered two more stages (stage 0—funny idea stage; stage 2b—interest on loans only, unrelated to profit) in addition to Jahoda's original six. A study in New Zealand by the same author (Ng, 1985) confirmed these additional two stages and proved the New Zealand children to 'lag' behind Hong Kong by about two years. Ng attributes this to Hong Kong's 'high level of economic socialization and customer activity, and the business ethos of the society at large . . . Their maturity represents, in short, a case of socioeconomic reality shaping (partly at least) socioeconomic understanding' (pp. 220–1). This comparison demonstrates that developmental trends are not necessarily *always* similar throughout different countries, because the trends are the same but some groups appear to move faster than others. A decisive factor seems to be the extent to which children are sheltered from, exposed to, or in some cases even take part in, economic activity. In order to evaluate the impact of the latter it would be necessary to examine exactly what kind of experiences influence the understanding of which economic concepts at what age. This means that there sometimes may even be greater differences within the same country than between different countries, depending on the way parents raise their children, and explain and show them how banks operate. Furthermore, different banking procedures and laws (for instance in Muslim countries) could also easily account for these differences.

Possession and ownership

The topic of possession and ownership is clearly related both to politics and economics but has been investigated mainly through the work of psychologists interested in economic understanding. Berti, Bombi and Lis (1982) conducted research into children's conceptions about means of production and their owners. They interviewed 120 children of ages 4–13 on three areas to find out children's knowledge about (1) ownership of means of production; (2) ownership of products (industrial and agricultural); and (3) product use. From the answers they were able to derive five levels:

1 (a) Owner of means of production is person found in spatial contact with it (bus owned by passengers).
   (b) Industrial and agricultural products not owned by anybody; anybody can take possession of them.
2 (a) Owner is the person who exercises an appropriate use of or direct control over object (factory owned by workers).
   (b) Owner is person closest to or using/constructing object.
3 (a) Owner uses producing means and controls their use by others ('the boss').
   (b) Product ownership explained through ownership of producing means (boss must share produce with employees).
4 (a) Differentiation between owner (giving orders) and employees.
   (b) Product belongs to boss.
5 (a) Distinction between owner (top of hierarchy) and boss (between owner and worker).
   (b) Products belong to owner of means of production; employees are compensated by salary.

Children's ideas about differential ownership of means of production develop through the same sequences but at different speeds. The notion of a 'boss–owner' for instance seem to occur at 8 to 9 years for the factory, 10 to 11 years for the bus, and 12 to 13 years for the countryside, perhaps due to the fact that 85 per cent of the subjects in the study had had no direct experience of country life. Although very few had had direct experience of the father's working environment, they heard him talk a lot about his work and thus acquired their information. Cram and Ng (1989) in New Zealand examined children's understanding of private ownership (172 subjects of three different age groups: 5–6, 8–9, 11–12 years) by noting the attributes the subjects used to endorse ownership. The older the child the greater the endorsement of higher-level (i.e. contractual) attributes and rejection of lower-level (i.e. physical) attributes, but there was only a tendency in the direction. Already 89 per cent of the youngest group rejected 'liking' as a reason for possessing, which increased to 98 per cent in the middle and oldest group, whereas the differences on the other two levels were more distinct. This indicates surprisingly that 5- to 6-year-olds are mainly aware of the distinction between personal desires and ownership. This does not necessarily contradict earlier work but makes it necessary to interview children younger than the ones in this study to find out whether and at what age egocentric ownership attributes are endorsed during earlier stages of development.

Furnham and Jones (1987) studied children's views regarding possessions and their theft. They asked 102 subjects aged 7–8, 9–10, 12–13 and 16–17 years to fill out a questionnaire based on work by Furby (1980a, b) and Irving and Siegal (1983). Results indicated that, as hypothesized, views about possessions become more sophisticated and 'realistic' with age.

The type of favourite possessions proved to be age-dependent, varying from toys, to sound and sports equipment, to computers and clothes. The younger groups showed no preference for the means of acquisition of an object whereas the older groups attached great importance to self-bought and individually owned objects motivated by a desire to affect and control their environment. As with increasing age the child's self-concept gradually depends more and more on his or her possessions, reactions towards theft become more punitive and empathy with the victim increases, even under mitigating circumstances. Most of the younger subjects simply demanded a return of the stolen object, creating mitigating circumstances (i.e. poverty or unhappiness) even where there were none, whereas older subjects demanded conditional discharge or prison sentences of different durations as a punishment. Although the oldest group was relatively stringent in their actual demands for punishment, in moral terms they were rather lenient. In other words, whilst they did not see the acts as morally wrong, they did demand some legal retribution. This is understood as a pragmatic acceptance of the need for law and order to provide general safety.

For children of all ages the element of control over their environment seems to be the most important characteristic of possessions. For older children who are more active consumers themselves, possessions often imply power and status and an enhancement of personal freedom and security. This suggests that in societies or group situations (as in a Kibbutz) where ownership is shared, young people acquire the understanding about possessing in a quite different way.

Concepts relating to means of production seem to develop similarly to those of buying and selling. They also advance through phases of no grasp of any system, to a grasp of unconnected systems (knowledge that the owner of the means of production sells products but no understanding of how he gets the money to pay his worker), to a grasp of integrated systems (linking worker's payment and sales proceeds), depending on the respective logical-arithmetical competence of the child. Although these concepts seem to follow the same developmental sequence, it cannot be said whether, to what extent and how the same factors (experimental, maturation, educational) contribute equally to the development of each concept.

Poverty and wealth

In 1975 Zinser, Perry and Edgar conducted a study to determine the importance of the affluence of the recipient in pre-school children's sharing behaviour. Most of the children favoured sharing with poor rather than rich recipients. They were also more generous with low than with high value items. These findings were consistent over all three ages (four, five and six years). There are two possible explanations for this behaviour: (1) societal values—society already has communicated to these young children that poor people are more deserving as recipients of sharing than rich people; or (2) empathy—perceived need arouses affective reactions in the children that motivate sharing, which in turn reduces affective reactions.

Winocur and Siegal (1982) asked 96 adolescents (aged 12–13 and 16–18 years) to allocate rewards between male and female workers in four different cases of family constellations and the results indicated that the focus on need decreased with age. Older subjects preferred to distribute rewards on an equal-pay-for-equal-work basis whereas younger subjects supported the idea that family needs should be reflected in pay. There were no sex differences in the perception of economic arrangements. This confirms Sevon and Weckstrom's (1989) suggestions that younger children judge from a homo sociologicus and older children from a homo economicus point of view.

Leahy (1981) asked 720 children and adolescents of four age groups (5–7, 9–11, 13–15, and 16–18 years) and four social classes to describe rich and poor people and to point out the differences and similarities between them. The answers were grouped into different descriptive categories: (1) personal peripheral—possessions, appearances, behaviour; (2) personal central—traits and thoughts; and (3) sociological—life chances and class consciousness. The use of peripheral characteristics in descriptions decreased considerably with age and thus adolescents emphasized central and sociological categories more than younger children. To explain these findings two theoretical models are conceivable: (1) a cognitive developmental model, suggesting that later adolescence is marked by an increased awareness of the nature of complex social systems; and (2) a general functionalist model, suggesting the socialization results in uniformity of views among classes and races as to the nature of the social class system and thus retains stability in social institutions. As there has been no research on that topic in other societies in other historical periods, it is not possible to exclude the second model although the way studies have been conducted and interpreted so far (with the understanding of all concepts reached through gradual advancement by stages) incline to favour the cognitive–developmental model of class.

Following Furnham (1981), Stacey and Singer (1985) had 325 teenagers of 14 1/2 and 17 years from a working-class background complete a questionnaire, probing their perceptions of the attributes and consequences of poverty and wealth. Regardless of age and sex all respondent groups rated familial circumstances as most important and luck as least important in explaining poverty and wealth. With internal and external attributions for poverty and wealth rating moderately important, these findings differ slightly from those of Leahy's (1981) results, as here adolescents clearly thought sociocentric categories to be more important than the other two. A reason for this might be that here all subjects were from a working-class background, and Furnham (1982) found subjects from a lower socioeconomic background tend to attach more importance to societal explanations than subjects from a higher socioeconomic background, who tend to offer more individualistic (e.g. lack of thrift and proper money management) explanations for poverty.

Most of the studies in this field have tried to describe the levels which children go through in their development of certain economic notions. The occasional disagreement as to the number of levels and points of transitions is probably mostly a matter of methodology. Results have been interpreted within the Piagetian developmental idea, but whether this is justified or not remains to be debated. Webley (1983), for instance, questions whether the Piagetian approach is applicable for economic concepts, and favours a social learning model. Furthermore most of the researchers already agree that external stimuli (socioeconomic environment, personal experience with money, formal teaching, parental practices) have great influence on the child's development of economic thinking and may contribute to premature knowledge. For instance, Wosinski and Pietras (1990) discovered in a study with 87 Polish subjects of ages 8, 11 and 14 that for some aspects of economic understanding such as the definition of salary, the possibility of getting the same salary for everybody, the possibility of starting a factory, the youngest had a better economic knowledge than the other groups. They attributed this to the fact that these children were born and had been living under conditions of an economic crisis in Poland since the second world war. They had experienced conditions of shortage, increases in prices and inflation, and had heard their family and TV programmes discuss these matters. This, too, represents 'a case of socioeconomic reality shaping (partly at least) socioeconomic understanding' (Ng, 1983, p. 220–1). It therefore seems to be that up to a certain extent the development of economic notions can be accelerated through experimental and educational factors. This still merits further study.

Economic relations and justice

A few studies have been done attempting to understand how children perceive and understand political and economic relationships. For instance Miller and Horn (1955) were interested in children's perceptions of debt. They chose 20 actual court cases involving debt that would be interesting and easy for children to interpret as well as being representative of a broad area of debt, credit, promises and related contracts. These were given to a panel of adults closely associated with debt or ethics to obtain their opinions concerning the 'best' ethical responses to these cases. They were also shown to 1297 children, ranging in age from 10 to 18 years.

One of the major findings was the lack of agreement between the consultants and the children on 47 of the 129 items. The children of varying ages sexes and socioeconomic backgrounds tended to disagree with the ethical consultants on the following points which they and the courts had accepted:

(1) Debtors ought not to be jailed or forced to labour because of their debt.
(2) All acts of the courts should be upheld and respected, despite personal or contingent circumstances.
(3) Gambling losses do not constitute legally enforceable obligations.
(4) Using credit in making purchases is not morally wrong.
(5) Warranties of quality are implied in sales on the open market.
(6) Banks and depositors have well-established responsibilities towards one another.

Predictably they found evidence of age differences. Those of 14 and above showed greater tolerance and an ability to differentiate between various kinds of promises in respect of their cruciality and seriousness. In contrast the younger children (10- and 12-year-olds) strongly believed that performance of promises should be enforced, and debt-evasion should be punished. Involuntary bankruptcy was also viewed as a legitimate means of collecting debts. The authors concluded that children should be explicitly taught elements of debt, credit, promises and simple contract in school.

Irving and Siegal (1983) were interested in children's perception of justice in relation to crimes of assault, arson and treason, each with the respective mitigating circumstances of brain damage, passion and economic need. Children aged 7 to 17 were asked to judge the appropriate punishment to be given in each of these various cases. Although younger children were harsher in their judgement than older children, their leniency and acceptance of mitigating circumstances were more highly dependent on the situation.

Saving

A topic that has only recently received empirical attention is that of children's saving (Sonuga-Barke and Webley, 1993; Webley et al., 1991). Sonuga-Barke and Webley (1991) chose an experimental approach and a degree of abstraction in the use of 'play economy' in their study of economic socialization. This play economy had a common format through a series of experiments. Children took part in a board game using tokens which they had previously earned. The board game was structured to operationalize aspects of temptation to spend and the threat of losing savings. The details of the board game varied from study to study, but all had a toy shop (containing the long-term object the children were saving for), a sweet shop (a temptation), and a bank that paid interest.

The major improvements in economic performance occurred between the ages of six and nine. At age four, the use of the bank was essentially random. To the six-year-olds, it appeared that money saved was money lost. Yet they did save, as they believed it was something they ought to do. In contrast, the nine-year-olds viewed saving strategically and were aware that savings could be used for expenditure in the future and that savings and expenditure are related, not distinct activities.

In a different study Webley, Levine and Lewis (1991) had 30 children, 10 each aged 6, 9 and 12, take part in a 'play economy' which consisted of four adjoining rooms representing opportunities to save (one room was a 'bank') or a temptation to spend (another room contained a sweet shop with real sweets). Children were given 90 tokens over the duration of the game and had to save 70 in order to purchase a desired toy which had been chosen at the outset. While the results showed a predictable pattern of increased understanding of savings (especially institutional saving) and improved savings 'success' rates with increasing age, the information gathered from the accounts showed that younger children developed 'rational' strategies which were not necessarily inferior when viewed in a wider social context.

They concluded:

> ... studies such as the present one are of some interest to economists who are concerned with the development of economic preferences and, at a practical level, to marketing personnel searching for the best ways of increasing institutional saving. More fundamentally perhaps, the current paper is a small contribution to the re-psychologizing of the study of saving. The early economists made extensive use of psychological concepts in devising an 'impatience' model of saving but since Keynes such ideas have played little part. In the dominant economic model of saving of today, the life-cycle hypothesis, there is no psychology; even concept is economic or demographic or is translated into such terms. We believe that stripping out psychology in this way is a mistake and that an improved model of saving should utilize insights from psychology and sociology.
>
> (Webley, Levine and Lewis, 1991, p. 145)

Entrepreneurship

For economists, sociologists and informed lay people the entrepreneur is a risk-taking individual, who seeks new markets, promotes new methods of production, has a future time orientation, and is able to fill gaps in services or demands. Though nice distinctions may be made between 'real' craftspeople and 'quasi'-opportunistic entrepreneurs, there is no doubt both that adults recognize the qualities of an entrepreneur and that entrepreneurship is one prerequisite for economic growth. Kourilsky and Campbell (1984) set out to determine children's (938 8- to 12-year-olds) beliefs about entrepreneurship before participation in an instruction system designed to encourage economic success, risk-taking and entrepreneurial persistence. They were also very interested in sex differences. Results indicated that the stereotypic entrepreneur was male, but the effect of the instruction and role-playing exercises was to encourage girls to be more interested. Perhaps the most important aspect of this study was however the demonstration that various entrepreneurial behaviours could be taught and measured. Economic success was measured by profit made in a mini-business; risk-taking was measured by exposure to loss and disadvantages; and persistence as the tendency to stick to a task till completed. In a study of British 10- to 19-year-olds, Bonnett and Furnham (1991) attempted to establish which factors discriminated between those who chose to go or not to go on a British Youth Enterprise scheme. Budding entrepreneurs had a more internal locus of control and a stronger work ethic as predicted but did not differ in their need for achievement. There were no differences in parenting style or demography of these groups. This suggests entrepreneurial beliefs may be self-fulfilling. Most young people seem to realize that hard work and self-reliance are key factors in being successful in business.

Economic Socialization: Pocket Money

The paucity in the literature on children's understanding of the social world is matched by a dearth of reviews of economic socialization. In a review of this literature Stacey (1982) has divided the research into four different areas: money, possessions, social differentiation and inequality, and socioeconomic understanding. He concludes thus:

> The most early experience of economic socialization appears to revolve around possessions which take on social characteristics involving inter-personal control and power over possessions. Between the ages of four and six children acquire monetary understanding, by associating money with buying, but it is not until the age of about ten that the numerical value of money, and the functional understanding of money transactions, is developed.
>
> (p.172)

At about the same time children begin to develop ideas of poverty, wealth, income, property and class differences. In early adolescence, teenagers are able to give 'near-adult' explanations of economic events and relationships. Finally the literature led Stacey to conclude that:

> In the first decade of life, the economic socialization of children does not appear to be strongly influenced by their own social backgrounds, with the exception of the children of the very rich and possibly of the very poor. In the second decade of life, social differences in the development appear to be more pronounced.
>
> (p. 172)

Perhaps the most important way in which parents socialize their children in monetary and economic matters is through their pocket money—a weekly or monthly allowance given either unconditionally or for some work. Almost no research has been done in this area although market research over an eight-year period in Britain has attempted to determine changes in pocket money patterns. On average in 1982, 5- to 7-year-olds got 64p, 8- to 10-year-olds 74p, and 11- to 13-year-olds 113 1/2p. Girls tended to get less than boys at all ages, and pocket money was often supplemented by part-time jobs, as well as gifts. It is also noted that children's spending power is almost £640 million a year on pocket money alone, and in excess of £780 million if earnings from jobs and gifts from relatives are included. However, as is the case with most opinion-poll studies, no effort is made to analyse the cause or consequences of these differences, which are presented simply in terms of percentages (Walls, 1983).

On the other hand, books and articles have been written to guide parents in the economic socialization of their children. Rarely, if ever, do they present data but are nearly always forceful, moralistic and middle-class in their advice:

> The allowance should be paid weekly—on the same day each week—to younger children, and monthly to kids as they approach their teens. The shift to a monthly payment is not for your convenience but is for the purpose of encouraging more careful attention to budgeting and planning ahead on the part of your teenager. The important thing is that the payment should represent a predictable source of income that the child can count on.
>
> (Furnham and Thomas, 1984)

However, much less work has been done on how children come to acquire these various economic concepts. Fox (1978) has argued that even by the time children enter school they already have experience of working, buying, trading, owning, saving, etc.: 'Research on children's informal economic learning indicates that early economic instruction in the classroom needs to take into account these unprocessed experiences, economic attitudes and children's cognitive capacities' (p. 137).

Through primary and secondary socialization children acquire knowledge of money and economic concepts. Marshall and Magruder's (1960) study appears to be one of the few studies specifically investigating the relationship between parents' money education practices and children's knowledge and use of money. Amongst the many hypotheses examined were: 'Children will have more knowledge of money use if their parents give them an allowance' and 'Children will have more knowledge of the use of money if they save money'. They found as predicted that children's knowledge of money is directly related to the extensiveness of their experience of money—whether they are given money to spend; if they are given opportunities to earn and save money; and their parents' attitudes to, and habits of money spending. Thus it seems that socialization and education would have important consequences on a child's or adolescent's understanding of economic affairs. However, they did *not* find any evidence for a number of their hypotheses. These were: children will have more knowledge of money-use if their parents give them an allowance: if children are given allowances, less of the family's money, rather than more, will be taken for children's spending money; if children are given opportunities to earn money, they will have more knowledge of money-use than children lacking this experience; children will have less knowledge of money-use if money is used to reward or punish their behaviour; and children will have the attitudes about the importance of money and material things that are expressed by their parents.

In an extensive study of over 700 seven-year-olds Newson and Newson (1976) collected data on children's pocket money. They found that most of their sample could count on a basic sum of pocket money, sometimes calculated on a complicated incentive system. Some children appear to be given money which is instituted for the express purpose of allowing the possibility of fining (confiscating); others are given money as a substitute for wages; while some have to 'work' for it. Over 50 per cent of the sample earned money from their parents beyond their regular income but there were no sex or social class differences in this practice.

This means that it is difficult to determine how much money children received each week. Newson and Newson (1976) did however find social-class differences in children's unearned income and savings. Middle-class children received less (18p vs. 30p) than working-class children, and saved more (90% vs. 48%). That is 52 per cent of class V children *always* spent their money within the week, whereas only 10 per cent of class I or II children did so. The authors concluded: 'Having cash in hand is equated with enjoying the good life: the relationship between money and enjoyment is specific and direct . . . the working-class child already begins to fall into this traditional pattern of life in his use of pocket money' (p. 244).

Furnham and Thomas (1984) set out to determine age, sex and class differences in the distribution and use of pocket money. They predicted age differences: older children would receive more money and take part in more 'economic activities' such as saving, borrowing, lending; and class differences: working-class children would receive more but save less than middle-class children. They tested over 400 7- to 12-year-old British children and confirmed many of their hypotheses. Table 4.3 shows that there were many more age, than sex or class differences. Older children received more money, saved more and were more likely to go shopping than younger children.

More middle-class than working-class children reported that they had to work around the house for their pocket money and that they tended to let their parents look after the pocket money that they had saved. Overall, however, there were surprisingly few class differences. The authors point out that the questions that did not reveal significant differences are as interesting as those that did.

Fox (1978) has drawn a number of conclusions from her review of studies on economic education: 'For example, we might consider the optimal timing for instruction in economics . . . Second, we might try to determine what economic misconceptions are corrected by maturation and life experience and which ones tend to persist' (p. 480).

Gender differences most probably may be attributed to children's different upbringing and the role women play in society. If one parent stays at home or works only part-time it is most commonly the mother. The father is most often seen as the source of money by young children ('brings it home from work'). Virtually all persons that are thought of as important by the child are men (e.g. presidents, 'bosses', headmasters and priests). Children, therefore, already perceive men and women in different roles whilst growing up. This may again be more or less obvious in different countries. Wosinski and Pietras (1990) for instance clearly attribute the gender differences they found in their study to traditional sex socialization, as in Poland economic problems are traditionally left to males rather than females.

Economic Values

The determinants and structure of adolescents' beliefs about the economy were the subject of research by Furnham (1987). This work examined the determinants of economic values in 86 adolescents aged 16 to 17 and the second looked at the economic preferences and knowledge of 150 subjects aged 18 to 19. Based on a questionnaire (Economics Values Inventory) by O'Brien and Ingels (1985) the determinants of economic values turned out to be more closely associated with the subject's political belief than with gender, religion or personal economic experience. Those subjects that stated they would not vote believed more in economic alienation and powerlessness than the others.

O'Brien and Ingels (1987) previously had conducted the first study in the US. Their findings, and those of Furnham, suggested socioeconomic status as the strongest predictor of economic values. Possible reasons for this could be the much weaker political interest in the US (a far lower percentage of American citizens votes), different political traditions (strong trade unions in Britain) or less pronounced economical differences between socioeconomic status and political belief anyway (working class—'left'; middle class—'conservative') and therefore, if examined, it might be the case that subjects who had a 'conservative' political opinion are predominantly from a middle-class background, which would then be in accordance with the American study.

Furnham's studies showed a close affinity between political and economic beliefs and found that the latter is governed by the former. The way political parties publicly compare their agendas, and families possibly discuss their present and future situation (e.g. jobs, education, health, finances, etc.) at home may arouse political awareness. Being in favour of certain political ideas implies having economic priorities, as a lot of the differences between political parties are in their respective budgets. A possible reason for this may be that the economic topics covered were all macro-economic topics of popular debate that were on the political parties' agenda, which suggests that there may also be 'less political' topics. As only beliefs were tested (and not knowledge) the subjects

TABLE 4.3 *Amount (in pence) of pocket money received by the three age groups*

	Years		
	7–8	*9–10*	*11–12*
(1) How much pocket money do you get each week?	57.32	76.43	97.93
(2) How much money do you get at birthdays?	353.86	712.72	1417.95
Christmas?	257.69	480.88	940.97
(3) How much have you already saved?	1498.60	2320.41	3845.13

Source: Furnham and Thomas,1984

Furnham and Thomas (1984) investigated adults' perceptions of the economic socialization of children through pocket money. Over 200 British adults completed a questionnaire on their beliefs concerning, for instance, how much and how often children should be given pocket money, as well as such things as whether they should be encouraged to work for it, save it, etc. There were a number of differences based on sex, age, social class and children (i.e. whether the subjects did or did not have children). Sex differences that existed showed females more in favour of agreeing with children in advance on the kinds of items pocket money should cover, more in favour of giving older children pocket money monthly, and also more in favour of an annual review of a child's pocket money, than males. Thus, all of these differences show females more willing to treat children as responsible individuals. It is possible that this is due to the tendency for women, both at work and in the home, to have greater contact with children and therefore a better understanding of their capabilities.

The age differences showed, as expected, that older adults were more likely to expect children to spend less on entertainment and more on reading materials, than younger adults. Further, as expected, older adults disagreed less than younger adults that boys should be given a little more pocket money than girls. Younger adults were also more in favour of pocket money being linked to the performance of household chores. Younger adults tend to view pocket money more as a contractual arrangement between adult and child than older adults. Middle-class adults were more in favour of giving children pocket money and of starting to give pocket money at an earlier age than working-class adults. Over 90 per cent of the middle-class adults believed that by the age of 8 years children should receive pocket money, while just over 70 per cent of working-class adults believed that children of 8 should receive pocket money. All middle-class adults believed that by the age of 10 the pocket-money system should be introduced, yet only 84 per cent of working-class adults agreed. Indeed, some working-class respondents did not believe in the system of pocket money at all. A similar class difference was revealed in the question concerning when children should receive their pocket money. Whereas 91 per cent of the middle-class believed children should receive it weekly (and 4% when they need it) only 79 per cent of working-class adults believed children should receive their pocket money weekly (and 16% when they need it). Furthermore, significantly more working-class adults believed that boys should receive more pocket money than girls.

These class-difference findings are in line with previous studies on childhood socialization (Newson and Newson, 1976) and with figures on class differences in general. That is, working-class adults introduce pocket money later and more erratically than middle-class parents. However the study of Furnham and Thomas (1984a) revealed far fewer class differences which may be the result of the fact that a greater range of ages were considered in that study.

Certainly investigations of pocket money or allowances seem a most fruitful avenue for research, especially as so many researchers have reported that experience plays such an important part in the understanding of the economic world in children and adolescents.

However, Davis and Taylor (1979), writing for American parents, are clear about the benefits of children working and the pocket-money rules. As regards the benefits of work they state:

(1) Once they get a job, they have to show up on time. In order to keep most jobs, they are forced to develop promptness and dependability. The principal skill they will acquire is that of planning their time.

(2) They will find that the world is competitive. This will be an important discovery in terms of their future ability to understand the adult world. The degree of competition they encounter will, of course, depend upon the job and their age. There may be no competition to run errands for a neighbour at age eight. There will be plenty of competition for a job at McDonald's. Your hope is that they will acquire the ability to compete effectively in the business and job world.

(3) Depending on what approach they use to make their money, they might discover that a lot of money can be made with the right idea. This discovery can have a very positive effect on their attitude and stimulate their creativity as they search for even better job ideas in the future. If they can acquire the ability to apply their imagination to the practical problems they will confront later on, they will have a substantial head start on their contemporaries.

(4) They'll find that they must make choices—that they cannot do and have everything all at once. Youngsters typically want to make their own decisions. At least they think they want to until they have to make the difficult ones. Then they probably expect you to make those for them. If you are able to hold back and force them to decide things for themselves, they will develop decisiveness. The ability to choose between alternatives is something that many adults have never quite mastered.

(5) With some help from you, they can find that failures along the way are normal, expected events and should be viewed as lessons rather than disasters. If this lesson can be learned and accepted, they will never lack courage to attempt something for fear they will fail, and they will develop the determination to succeed at whatever they try. If, rather than giving up, they acquire the ability to analyse their mistakes, see what went wrong and why, they will be able to avoid those mistakes in the future.

(6) A job can expand their horizons. It's very easy for any kid to assume that the whole world is just like the one he knows if he has had no experience outside that world. Many of the jobs kids can do will bring them into contact with a wide range of people, people who live differently from the way they were raised and who have different backgrounds and interests.

(pp. 157–158)

They also have clear suggestions about how pocket money/allowance systems should be run. They offer 13 rules, though it should be said that it is personal experience and not research that 'backs-up' their suggestions.

(1) The system you will use should be explained to the child at the time it is started.
(2) The allowance is initiated at around 6 or 7.
(3) The amount should be a reasonable one, and increased as the child grows older when it is expected to cover a wider range of the child's expenses.
(4) The parent and child should agree in advance on the kinds of expenses the allowance will cover.
(5) The allowance should be paid weekly on the same day each week to younger children, and monthly to kids in their mid teens.
(6) The allowance should always be paid and should not be based upon performance of chores. It should never be withheld as discipline or to influence the child's behaviour.
(7) Once the amount of the allowance has been established, the child should not be given more money just because he has spent all he had.
(8) The child should be allowed to make his own spending decisions.
(9) The child should be assigned an agreed-upon chore (or chores), which he will be responsible to do for the benefit of the entire family.
(10 No pay is to be expected or received for doing the job.
(11) Failure to do the assigned chore must not result in reduction or elimination of the allowance.
(12) Parents who are able to pay their kids for doing extra jobs around the house should do so.
(13) An annual review should be held yearly on the child's birthday to set the allowance and chores for the coming year.

(p. 50)

Cross-cultural, Social and Gender Differences

Various studies in different (mainly western) countries have been undertaken but few that investigate specifically cross-cultural differences. Furby (1978, 1980a,b) compared American and Israeli (kibbutz and city) children's attitudes towards possessions and found rather more differences between American and Israeli subjects than between kibbutz and all others.

In a recent cross-cultural project initiated by Leiser *et al.* (1990), entitled the 'Naive Economics Project', he tested 90 children aged 8, 11 and 14 from 10 countries: Algeria, Australia, Denmark, Finland, France, Israel (town and kibbutz), Norway, Poland, West Germany and Yugoslavia. Topics covered were: (a) understanding—who decides what, how and why (prices, salary, savings and investment, the mint); (b) reasoning—how well do children appreciate the consequences of economic events of national dimensions; (c) beliefs—how do they account for the economic fate of individuals. In accordance with previous investigations in various countries there was an obvious progression with age. However, there were some differences in answers between the participating countries. These could be due to the different contemporary political and economic systems and the prosperity of the whole country. The dominance of the government as a visible economic factor was reflected by the frequency with which it appeared in children's answers. The differences in each society's values and attitudes (such as more individualistic attitudes in western democracies, religion, the work ethic, different moral standards in Christian than in Atheist or Moslem countries etc.) and slight differences in the conditions of the interview are all possible reasons for the disparity in country responses. Furthermore, the size of the sample (90 subjects from each country) may not have been large enough to provide for representative cross-cultural comparisons. The differences, however, show that the child's understanding of how economic systems work is influenced by various factors in the child's environment as suggested by the social learning model.

In a smaller study in West Germany, Burgard, Cheyne and Jahoda (1989) replicated a Scottish study by Emler and Dickinson (1985) that had asked 140 children of 8, 10 and 12 years from middle- and working-class backgrounds and 67 parents to estimate occupational incomes of a doctor, a teacher, a bus driver and a road sweeper—and the cost of some consumer goods. Emler and Dickinson (1985) had found substantial social-class but no age differences in their Scottish sample. In West Germany, however, there were significant age but virtually no social-class differences found, among both parents and children. One explanation might be that socioeconomic differences in West-German society are less pronounced than in the UK. Furthermore there was no relationship between parents' and childrens' income estimates. This, according to the authors, throws considerable doubt on ' . . . Emler and Dickinson's (1985) contention that class-tied social representations outweigh developmental changes' (p. 285).

Similarly, gender differences have been reported through several studies. While some authors have set out quite specifically to measure these phenomena, Kourilsky and Campbell (1984) set up a study ' . . . (1) to measure sex differences in children's perceptions of entrepreneurship and occupational sex-stereotyping and (2) to assess differences in children's risk taking, persistence, and economic success' (p. 53). A total of 938 subjects aged 8 to 12 took part in an economics education instructional programme over 10 weeks. Prior to the study of 'Mini-Society', entrepreneurship was perceived as a predominantly male domain. After Mini-Society, boys still possessed a somewhat stereotyped picture of the entrepreneur. This trend was also observable at occupational sex-stereotyping. In the Mini-Society, girls were more likely to increase the number of occupations they thought appropriate for women. As to ratings in success (profit made in a mini-business), persistence (sticking to a task until completed) and risk-taking (exposure to loss and disadvantages) boys and girls achieved similar results, girls even being slightly in the lead in the first two categories. In this study at ages 8 to 12 there were no sex differences in the major characteristics that are associated with successful entrepreneurship. The fact that in reality there are few females entrepreneurs though must therefore have different causes (e.g. traditional sex socialization).

Gender differences most probably may be attributed to children's different upbringing and the role women play in society. If one parent stays at home or works only part-time it is most commonly the mother. The father is most often seen as the source of money by young children ('brings it home from work'). Virtually all persons that are thought of as important by the child are men (e.g. presidents, 'bosses', headmasters and priests). Children, therefore, already perceive men and women in different roles whilst growing up. This may again be more or less obvious in different countries. Wosinski and Pietras (1990) for instance clearly attribute the gender differences they found in their study to traditional sex socialization, as in Poland economic problems are traditionally left to males rather than females.

Economic Values

The determinants and structure of adolescents' beliefs about the economy were the subject of research by Furnham (1987). This work examined the determinants of economic values in 86 adolescents aged 16 to 17 and the second looked at the economic preferences and knowledge of 150 subjects aged 18 to 19. Based on a questionnaire (Economics Values Inventory) by O'Brien and Ingels (1985) the determinants of economic values turned out to be more closely associated with the subject's political belief than with gender, religion or personal economic experience. Those subjects that stated they would not vote believed more in economic alienation and powerlessness than the others.

O'Brien and Ingels (1987) previously had conducted the first study in the US. Their findings, and those of Furnham, suggested socioeconomic status as the strongest predictor of economic values. Possible reasons for this could be the much weaker political interest in the US (a far lower percentage of American citizens votes), different political traditions (strong trade unions in Britain) or less pronounced economical differences between socioeconomic status and political belief anyway (working class—'left'; middle class—'conservative') and therefore, if examined, it might be the case that subjects who had a 'conservative' political opinion are predominantly from a middle-class background, which would then be in accordance with the American study.

Furnham's studies showed a close affinity between political and economic beliefs and found that the latter is governed by the former. The way political parties publicly compare their agendas, and families possibly discuss their present and future situation (e.g. jobs, education, health, finances, etc.) at home may arouse political awareness. Being in favour of certain political ideas implies having economic priorities, as a lot of the differences between political parties are in their respective budgets. A possible reason for this may be that the economic topics covered were all macro-economic topics of popular debate that were on the political parties' agenda, which suggests that there may also be 'less political' topics. As only beliefs were tested (and not knowledge) the subjects only needed to 'have an opinion'. Opinions are shaped through debate, which again is a political process.

So far the majority of studies have concentrated on children's understanding of certain economic concepts, mainly in industrial societies. The reason for neglecting other concepts might be that children are not expected to understand them, perhaps because not many adults are expected to understand them either (e.g. exchange rates between currencies, macro-economic situations such as boom–recession etc.). Studies like those of Wosinski and Pietras (1990), Ng (1983) and Kourilsky (1984) have shown that children sometimes have been underestimated and that they were able to understand concepts that they were not expected to understand at that age; being exposed to certain external stimuli (instruction, experience, economic crisis, etc.) helped speed up their understanding.

More studies examining developing-world countries would show how entirely different external stimuli contribute to cross-national differences. However, although it would be fascinating to investigate cross-national differences, one always has to bear in mind the difficulties associated with obtaining equivalent samples and asking equivalent questions.

Economic Education

Formal instruction is one means by which young people acquire an understanding of the economic and political world. Much more research has gone into economic than political education however.

The effect of instruction in economics

Whitehead (1986) investigated the eventual change in students' attitudes to economic issues as a result of exposure to a two-year 'A' level economics course. The 16- to 18-year-old subjects were divided into a test group of 523 and a control group of 483. The questionnaires did not test economic knowledge but economic attitudes (e.g. dis/agreement about private enterprise as the most efficient economic system; 'Capitalism is immoral because it exploits the worker by failing to give him full value for his productive labour'). In absolute terms, considerable correspondence existed between the responses of experimental and control groups with respect to those items where a large majority expressed either conservative or radical attitudes. On the whole, the experimental and control groups held differing views only on most items suggesting that economics education was *not* a powerful shaper of politicoeconomic attitudes.

In a similar study O'Brien and Ingels (1987), who developed the Economics Values Inventory (EVI), an instrument aimed at measuring young people's values and attitudes regarding economic matters, had their hypothesis confirmed that formal education in economics influences students' economic attitudes. Those who studied economics developed stronger beliefs in the free-enterprise system and trust in business with concomitant beliefs in a reduced government role in social welfare and price setting. The teaching of economics therefore not only increases children's understanding of certain economics contexts but also may help them review their values and attitudes which are mostly influenced by or even taken over from their parents.

Economics instruction in primary grades

In most countries, economics is not taught before age 16. The majority of adolescents who complete secondary education, still never receive formal economics instruction. As macro-economic knowledge cannot be learned by observation there is obviously a need for the teaching of economics.

Kourilsky (1977) showed, however, that even kindergarten is not too soon to start educating economically literate citizens. In the 'Kinder-Economy', an education programme, children became acquainted with the concepts of scarcity, decision-making, production, specialization, consumption, distribution, demand/supply, business, money and barter. Her study examining 96 subjects age five to six years was supposed to answer four questions:

(1) Is the child's success in economic decision making and analysis related to instructional intervention or to increased maturity inherent in the passage of time?
(2) To what extent and degree, through intervention, are children able to master concepts that, psychologically they are considered too young to learn?
(3) What type of school, home and personality variables are predictors of success in economic decision making and analysis?
(4) What are the parents' attitudes toward the teaching of economic decision making and analytical principles as a part of early childhood education?

The examination of the first issue of economic decision making showed a significant difference between the scores of the subjects in the Kinder-Economy and in the control group which proved that significant progress was induced by instruction. The study showed that children are in fact able to learn concepts which developmentally they are considered to be too young to learn. To answer the third question, six predictor variables were examined: parent report, verbal ability, maturation level, general ability, social ability and initiative. The first three proved to be the best predictors of success in economic decision making, the strongest, parent report, accounting for 62 per cent of the total variance. Parents' attitudes towards the teaching of economics in kindergarten turned out to be positive: 96.7 per cent of the parents were in favour and 91.3 per cent thought that an economics programme should be continued throughout the rest of the grades. Some even mentioned that they were embarrassed to find that their children knew more about economics than they did, encouraging them to increase their own knowledge. These findings and the general ignorance of children and adults concerning economic interdependencies and contexts seem to give clear evidence for the importance of economic education as early as possible.

Fox (1978), however, challenged Bruner's view that 'any topic can be taught effectively in some intellectually honest form at any stage of development'. She cited three things that children already possess when going to school: economic attitudes, unprocessed direct experience (e.g. shopping trips) and cognitive capacities (level of cognitive development). Considering that children at the preoperational level are not able to think abstractly, Fox saw difficulties in formal teaching of economic concepts to children who are, for instance, unable to understand the transaction of economic exchange in a shop. She warned that 'the fact that kinder-garten children can learn economic terms is not compelling evidence that the concepts underlying those terms are in fact understood'. Instead she pleaded for using direct experience as a basis for economic education in primary school and suggested that teachers use everyday situations of economic behaviour in the classroom to help children make sense of what they already know, always considering the level of the child's cognitive abilities. This contradicts Kourilsky's findings that children are to some extent able to master concepts that psychologically they are considered too young to learn. This contradiction might be an indication that Piaget's stages of general cognitive development, originally 'trying to explain the way that the individual represents physical reality' can simply be transferred into economics without any alteration.

Webley (1983) pointed out that 'since we learn about some aspects of the economic world mainly by actually engaging in the behaviour and not, as with the physical world, in two ways—both directly and didactically via the mediation of other—the nature of the construction may be different'.

In the *Journal of Economic Education*, solely dedicated to research into the teaching of economics, Davidson and Kilgore (1971) presented a model for evaluating the effectiveness of economic education in primary grades. They had tested 504 second grade pupils in 24 classes from different socioeconomic backgrounds, in one control and two different experimental groups. Pupils in the control group were taught their regular social studies curriculum, the first experimental group was taught with 'The Child's World of Choices' materials and the teachers in the second experimental group additionally received in-service training in teaching that programme. Analysis showed that both experimental groups scored significantly higher on the post Primary Test of Economic Understanding (PTEU) than the control group, but no experimental method proved to be superior to the other. Pupils from lower socioeconomic backgrounds scored significantly lower on both PTEU pre and post tests than pupils from a higher socioeconomic background. It could thus be concluded that elementary grade children can be taught basic economic concepts, and growth in understanding them can be measured. Specially designed material prompted the pupils' growth in understanding but an additional full-scale program in economic education for teachers did not have any significant effects on pupils' advancement. As to the 'how' of teaching of economics concepts to children Waite (1988) suggested that the child must be the centre of activity, as case studies have shown that the acceleration of children's conceptual understanding can be achieved using a number of different strategies. Since the child's economic awareness is acquired through information channels outside the classroom, case studies seem to be a good way of teaching children about the economy. Ramsett (1972) also suggested staying away from the traditional lecture approach and using daily life classroom events (which are either directly or indirectly relevant to economics) as a basis for further discussion and explanation (e.g. if a pupil's family has to move away because his mother/father has accepted a new job, the teacher could take this opportunity to discuss employment, incomes, dependencies, etc.).

More recently, Chizmar and Halinski (1983) described the impact of 'Trade-offs', a special series of television/film programmes designed to teach economics in elementary school, on students' performance in the Basic Economic Test (BET). The results indicated that (1) as the number of weeks of instruction increased, the rate of increase in students' scores was significantly greater for students using 'Trade-offs'; (2) there were no sex differences in scores for students using 'Trade-offs' whereas for those being instructed traditionally gender was a statistically significant predictor of student score (girls out-performing boys). Furthermore, the grade-level and teacher training (McKenzie, 1971; Walstad, 1979; Walstad and Watts, 1985) in economics were significant positive determinants of BET performance. These findings may indicate that gender differences here could possibly be attributed to the way instruction was given, as boys performed better under 'Trade-offs' than under traditional instruction. Taking this premise it would be interesting to examine how sex differences found in other studies possibly could have been caused.

Hansen (1985), acknowledging that the teaching of economics to elementary school children has proved effective, suggested that this subject should be included in the curriculum of the primary grades. He briefly summarized the basic knowledge about children and economic education which is as follows: What happens in a child's early years—before the end of the primary years—has lasting effects into adulthood; children enter kindergarten possessing an experience-based economic literacy; children can acquire economic concepts and can do so earlier than previously thought; a variety of economic materials and teaching approaches are both available and effective; evaluation procedures are available, and new ones are being established even though they need continued refinement; economic education programs show greater student gains where teachers are well versed in economics.

The apparent opportunity cost of introducing economics into primary schools is still deemed to be too high. If economics was not considered as a subject to be studied on its own, competing with other subjects in the curriculum, but rather being taught in connection with already existing subjects such as mathematics (case studies), this problem could be avoided. In other words, the teaching of economics to primary school children could be integrated with other subjects such as mathematics. However, as long as it is seen as a specialist discipline for secondary schools, it is unlikely that it will appear in any national curriculum.

Reasons for goals and economic education

In order to decide what should be taught in a economics course and how such economics instruction should take place, explicit goals need to be defined. Horton and Weidenaar (1975) tried to do this and interviewed more than 200 economic educators, economists, other social scientists, trainers of social studies teachers, businessmen and others for their views. Three goals were singled out:

(1) To help us to be more capable as direct participants in the economy—that is, as consumers, workers, business people or investors.
(2) To 'improve' decisions when we act in our society as citizens.
(3) To improve our understanding of the world in which we live.

All three goals appear to be of equal importance and probably cannot be separated completely from one another anyway. Still, depending on the emphasis that is put on each goal, an economics course would probably touch slightly different topics. The authors suggest that for the third goal an economics course might cover such concrete questions 'as why automobile mechanics often earn more than English teachers; why teenagers, females and non-whites are disproportionately unemployed; and why more money for each of us would do so little to meet our fundamental economic problem of relative scarcity' (p. 43).

Possessing a better knowledge of the economic aspects of our environment makes us better prepared to analyse and interpret the situations and problems we face. As with any knowledge this gives us a greater and better choice of possible solutions and, considering the widespread ignorance about economic topics in both children and adults, economics instruction seems necessary. As early as 1961 in America a task force made 12 specific recommendations about economic education (see Table 4.4).

More recently the Americans believe there are very specific concepts to be taught which are divided into six broad areas. These are shown in Table 4.5.

According to Saunders (1994) however this can be boiled down to seven crucially important concepts learnt by all 15-year-olds:

TABLE 4.4 *Recommendations of the 1961 national task force on economic education*

Increase instruction
(1) We recommend that more time be devoted in high school curricula to the development of economic understanding.
(2) We recommend that wherever feasible students take a high school course in economics or its equivalent under another title (such as Problems of American Democracy); and that in all high schools of substantial size there be at least an elective senior-year course in economics.
(3) We recommend that courses in problems of American democracy (now taken by perhaps half of all high school students) devote a substantial portion of their time to development of economic understanding of the kind outlined.
(4) We recommend that more economic analysis be included in history courses.
(5) We recommend that all business education curricula include a required course in economics.
(6) We recommend that economic understanding be emphasized at several other points in the entire school curriculum.

Content revision
(7) We recommend central emphasis on the rational way of thinking presented in Chapter II should be a prime objective of the teaching of economics.
(8) We recommend that examination of controversial issues should be included, where appropriate, in teaching economics.

Teacher education
(9) To improve the ability of teachers, we recommend several steps.
　(a) We recommend that teacher certification requirements in all states require a minimum of one full year (6 unit) course in college economics for all social studies and business education teachers.
　(b) We recommend that school boards and administrators consider these certification standards as minimum requirements, and they take steps to enforce higher standards wherever feasible.
　(c) To help present teachers improve their economic competence, we recommend increased use of summer workshops, teacher participation in a nationwide television economics course planned for 1962–63, and return to college for additional work in economics.
　(d) We recommend that colleges preparing teachers improve the economics courses offered for this purpose, and establish other opportunities for high school teachers to increase their economic understanding.

Materials
(10) We emphasize the need for more effective high school teaching materials and recommend that steps be taken by private publishers, foundations, and others to increase the supply of such materials.

Involvement of others
(11) We recommend that professional economists play a more active part in helping to raise the level of economics in the schools.
(12) We urge widespread public support, both private and governmental, for the improvement of economics in the schools.

Source: Bach *et al.*, 1961, pp. 64–77

TABLE 4.5 *Basic concepts of economic socialization*

Fundamental economic concepts
 (1) Scarcity
 (2) Opportunity cost and trade-offs
 (3) Productivity
 (4) Economic systems
 (5) Economic institutions and incentives
 (6) Exchange, money and independence

Microeconomic concepts
 (7) Markets and prices
 (8) Supply and demand
 (9) Competition and market structure
(10) Income distribution
(11) Market failures
(12) The role of government

Macroeconomic concepts
(13) Gross national product
(14) Aggregate supply
(15) Aggregate demand
(16) Unemployment
(17) Inflation and deflation
(18) Monetary policy
(19) Fiscal policy

International economic concepts
(20) Absolute and comparative advantage and barriers to trade
(21) Balance of payments and exchange rates
(22) International aspects of growth and stability

Measurement concepts and methods
Tables
Charts and graphics
Ratios and percentages
Percentage changes
Index numbers
Real vs. nominal values
Averages and distributions around the average

Broad social goals
Economic freedom
Economic efficiency
Economic equity
Economic security
Full employment
Price stability
Economic growth
Other goals

Source: Saunders *et al.*, 1993, p. 14, pp. 51–54

Opportunity Cost. This is the most valuable opportunity that is lost when a decision is made to do one thing instead of another. This concept is crucial in evaluating alternatives. It is a key component in developing critical thinking and informed decision-making skills in a variety of contexts.

Marginal Analysis. Many decisions do not involve all or nothing choices. It is often possible to substitute a little more of one thing for a little less of something else. Comparing *additional* costs and *additional* benefits of various choices *at the margin* is an important aspect of critical thinking that often helps one make better decisions.

Interdependence. Decisions in one situation often affect decisions in other, sometimes seemingly unrelated, situations. Like marginal analysis, an awareness of possible indirect (interdependent) effects is an important aspect of critical thinking that often helps one make better decisions.

Exchange. Either directly through the often cumbersome process of barter, or indirectly through the use of money, exchange helps increase productivity and expand choices. In turn, increased productivity and expanded choices make decision making and opportunity costs less painful than they would otherwise be.

Productivity. Productivity is the amount of output (goods and services) produced per unit of input (resources) used. An increase in productivity means producing more goods and services with the same amount of resources, producing the same amount of goods and services with fewer resources, or a combination of both. As indicated above, increased productivity expands choices, and expanded choices make decision making and opportunity costs less painful.

Money. Money, either in the form of currency or checking deposits, serves both as a medium of exchange and a unit of account. As a medium of exchange, money facilitates specialization and the division of labour, which are among the main ways of increasing productivity. As a unit of account, money facilitates the comparison of the costs and benefits of alternatives. Such comparisons lie at the heart of critical thinking and effective decision making.

Markets and Prices. Markets are institutional arrangements that enable buyers and sellers to exchange goods and services. Prices are the amounts of money that people pay in exchange for a unit of a particular good or service ($2.00 a pound, $12.00 an hour, $.50 a litre, etc.). The ratios that exist between various prices are called relative prices. Relative price ratios facilitate the comparison and evaluation of alternatives, and thus enhance critical thinking and effective decision making.

(pp.43–44)

In Britain it has even been suggested that primary school children can be taught simple but important economic principles. Ross (1990) has provided the following list of knowledge and understanding objectives (see Table 4.6).

Conclusion

The growing research on children's and adolescents' understanding of money and other economic concepts has been paralleled by an interest in and concern about formal economic education. To have well-informed, economically literate young people must be the ultimate aim of all countries. Research has frequently demonstrated how poorly informed young people are. It may not be until they are in their mid-teens that many young people understand the concept of profit or the principle of exchange. Paradoxically, it is those less protected people from the developing world who are forced into economic activity at an earlier age who seem to be the better informed. Certainly, recent interest in devising an appropriate curriculum for economic education is an important and relevant move in the right direction for parents and their children.

TABLE 4.6 *Types of economic knowledge and understanding*

Limited resource/opportunity cost

KS1 1 Identify and make decisions about resources.

KS2 1 Understand some of the implications of limited resources.

KS2 2 Know that all decisions involve opportunity cost.

Costs and benefits

KS1 2 Understand some of the costs and benefits in situations relevant to themselves.

KS2 3 Be aware of some of the costs and benefits of everyday economic choices: recognize that people can have different and conflicting interests.

Needs and wants

KS1 3 Understand that people have needs.

KS2 4 Appreciate that human needs, unlike wants, are universal, and recognize that for many people, needs are not met.

Consumers and producers

KS1 4 Be aware that they are consumers and that links them to people who produce goods and provide services.

KS2 5 Understand what it means to be a consumer and how consumers and producers relate to each other.

Exchange

KS1 5 Know that buying, selling and giving are ways of exchanging goods and services.

KS2 6 Understand how money is used in the exchange of goods and services and know some of the factors which affect prices.

Work and jobs

KS1 8 Know that there are different kinds of work and that these involve different skills.

KS1 6 Know that people work in different kinds of workplaces and do different jobs.

KS2 7 Understand that workplaces are organized in different ways.

KS2 9 Know about public services, shops, offices and industries in their local community; understand the importance of these to people.

KS2 10 Develop their understanding of the nature of work and its place in people's lives.

Production, distribution and sale

KS1 7 Understand how some things are produced, using different resources.

KS2 8 Have some understanding of how goods are produced, distributed and sold.

(TABLE 4.6 *continued*)

Technological change

KS1 9 Understand how tools and technology contribute to pupils' lives at home and at school.

KS2 11 Develop an awareness of the part played by design and technology in industrial production.

KS2 12 Be aware of some effects of the new technologies and the implications for people and places.

Global and environmental issues

KS2 13 Appreciate some of the environmental and social issues associated with economic and industrial activity.

KS2 14 Recognize similarities and differences between economic and industrial activities in different parts of the world.

Source: Ross, 1990

5

Advertising and Children: Attention, Awareness and Understanding

One main issue in the context of child consumer socialization is the effect of television and other sources of consumer information on the development of young people's consumer behaviour, values and attitudes. Advertising critics have argued that advertising strongly influences young people and results in undesirable socialization in the form of materialistic values and non-rational, impulse-oriented choices. Defenders of advertising practices, however, have argued that parents modify advertising influences, that the main sources of consumer-related ideas and behaviours are parents and peers, and that advertising sets up the agenda for positive parent–child interaction and provides a consumption learning experience for the child (Banks, 1975; Robertson, 1979).

McNeal (1987) has categorized the research into children and television advertising into three areas that involve *processing* of the advertised message, *cognitions* (thoughts) in children, and their consumer *behaviour* as a result of advertising. The processing of the advertised message can be separated into attention to advertising and understanding of television advertisements. The latter is further subdivided into distinguishing programmes from advertisements, discerning the intent of television advertising and lastly, comprehending the content of such advertising.

Attention to advertising will depend on personal factors such as motivation, attitudes towards the commercial, influence of parents and peers, lack of knowledge about advertisements and stimulus factors such as the context of the programmes, whether the advertisements are boring or interesting, the actual content of the advertisement, and the product advertised. McNeal considers three types of consumer behaviour caused by advertising: purchase behaviour itself, which is to be distinguished from purchase request behaviour, and anti-social behaviour, such as parent–child conflict over purchases. The behavioural impact of television advertisements upon children is mediated by a series of important cognitive processes which are activated by exposure to advertisements.

Young (1990) has offered two separate lists of processes and outcomes, which usefully serve to divide up the field of enquiry. Cognitive processes comprise:

(1) Attention to commercials.
(2) Ability to distinguish between commercials and programmes.
(3) The child's understanding of the intent of the commercial.
(4) The child's interpretation of the content of the commercial (including consumption symbolism, gender stereotypes).
(5) The child's memory for the commercial.
(6) Other processes invoked (for example, cognitive defences) by viewing.

(p. 43)

According to Young, the effects of advertising can be divided as follows:

(7) The effect on knowledge, attitudes and values (for example, whether exposure to information in ads for junk foods lowers nutritional awareness, what children feel about advertising). This will have short-term and long-term aspects.
(8) The effect on other people, in particular parents (for example, does the child pester mum for more?).
(9) The effect on choice or consumption behaviour (for example, whether children eat more sweets after watching commercials for that class of product, or whether they consume more of a particular brand by watching a commercial for that brand?)

(1990, pp. 43–44)

Another expert on children and advertising has contrasted two views about the impact of advertising on young consumers (Goldstein, 1994). The standard argument is that television commercials create wants in children, who then pester their parents for the advertised products. The parents, apparently helpless to refuse, succumb to the demands of their children and purchase the advertised product. If they do not give in to their children's demands, so the argument goes, parent–child conflict is the inevitable result. This is schematized in Figure 5.1.

TV COMMERCIAL→WANTS→DEMANDS→CHILD–PARENT→ PURCHASE
CONFLICT   BY PARENTS

FIGURE 5.1 The standard argument. Goldstein, 1994

The standard argument 'explains' that television advertisements are able to create wants because young viewers do not understand advertising and are therefore vulnerable to its appeals. More specifically, the argument is that:

(1) Children do not know the difference between a television programme and an advertisement.
(2) Children do not understand the persuasive intent of advertising.
(3) Those who do not understand persuasive intent are highly vulnerable to commercials.

Goldstein (1994) has argued, however, that there are a number of important elements missing from the argument displayed in Figure 5.1:

- Peer and parental influences, known to play a far more important role in purchasing decisions than advertising.
- Parental responsibility and decision making.
- The highly selective nature of attending to the media and to advertising.
- The multiple meanings and uses of advertising by young people, particularly adolescents (see Figure 5.2).

SELECTIVE

PEER   → WANTS → VIEWING OF → REQUESTS → PARENTAL

INFLUENCE   COMMERCIALS   DECISION

FIGURE 5.2 An alternative approach. Goldstein, 1994

What Goldstein argues is that rather than television forming or shaping consumer wants, the consumer drives of young people (which are acquired from a wide range of social influences) actually determine patterns of television viewing. Goldstein is not the only behavioural scientist to have speculated that television may directly shape the extent to which young people openly express their purchase behaviour and things they have bought (Parsons, *et al.*, 1953; Riesman and Roseborough, 1955). Research that supports this view has indicated that adolescents may aspire to the particular possessions (e.g. clothes) of certain television characters (Vener, 1957). Television may also spark off conversation about buying such items with others. Since nearly all the studies have been correlational, however, it is difficult to determine whether television viewing is a cause or consequence of consumer wants or actual purchasing behaviour.

Churchill and Moschis (1979) reported that television appeared to be an important agent in adolescent consumer socialization, teaching young people 'expressive elements' of consumption. Television also appeared indirectly to affect the acquisition of consumer-related properties by stimulating interactions about consumption with parents and decreasing it with peers. Few doubt the relevance and importance of television advertising, but precisely how it influences young people is much less clearly understood.

There is a substantial body of research which indicates that television plays an important role in the socialization of children, especially as a source of product information (e.g. Caron and Ward, 1975; Reynolds and Wells, 1977; Robertson and Rossiter, 1977). However, the effects of television advertising on children are far from being conclusive. Attention has more often been focused on how (the process by which) television advertising affects children's consumer behaviour and what aspects of consumer behaviour are affected. Some variables also appear to be particularly relevant to the effects of television advertising including viewer demographic characteristics (especially sex, race, age and social class), advertising stimuli, and mediating processes in relation to information acquisition from television advertising (e.g. parent–child interactions). In addition, advertising effects are often difficult to separate from programme-related effects, while effects of cumulative exposure to television commercials over time need to be separated from the impact on consumer behaviour of the growing child's naturally increasing cognitive abilities and maturing view of the world (Rossiter, 1980). Furthermore, there is a need to separate short-term from long-term effects, and advertising effects from the effects of other socialization agents. Advertising effects often disappear when other socialization (interpersonal) processes are taken into account (e.g. Rossiter, 1980), suggesting the value of examining the combined effects of various socialization agents as well (Adler *et al.*, 1980).

Several socialization processes seem to have a significant impact on the development of consumption-related orientations during adolescence. Television appears to be an important source of consumer information. Although a number of studies found strong linkages between television viewing and various aspects of the adolescent's consumer behaviour (e.g. Moschis and Churchill, 1978; Moore and Moschis, 1978, Moschis and Moore 1979a; Ward and Wackman, 1971), the exact process of influence is not well understood. The tendency to use a gross 'amount' of television viewing in the majority of consumer socialization studies has contributed little to the general understanding of the specific learning processes operating. Similarly the distinction between programming and advertising effects of television on consumer socialization have reported positive relationships between measures of television viewing and the learning of various expressive aspects of consumption (e.g. Churchill and Moschis, 1979; Moschis and Moore, 1980b; Ward and Wackman, 1972).

Moschis and Churchill (1978) found that amount of television viewing and consequently the number of television advertisements to which adolescents had been exposed predicted young respondents' social motivations for consumption and materialistic attitudes—suggesting that mere exposure to television may lead to the learning of these 'expressive' aspects of consumption. Though adolescents' frequency of interaction with television appeared to be an important factor in learning certain consumer-related skills, it is questionable as to whether exposure to the medium alone is sufficient to shape young consumers' purchase behaviours. Moschis and Churchill's data showed that learning from television was linked mainly to the uses the adolescent made of television, especially of its advertising content, much of which was found to be of a social rather than a purely consumerist nature.

Although these findings support the contentions of behaviourist psychologists that young people learn the 'expressive' elements of consumption from television, the learning of these skills may not develop through imitation and observation. Rather, social processes (e.g. interaction with peers) seem to condition adolescents' perception and interest in goods and services, which in turn cause them to pay more attention to television programmes and advertisements to learn about the uses of products. Thus, a transactional model of communication effects (see McLeod and Becker, 1974) seems best to describe the learning of consumer skills from television. However, it is possible, for example, that the child's materialistic values affect his or her social uses of television. Moschis and Churchill did not examine the direction of causality between the social uses of mass media and expressive orientation toward consumption. It is most likely that the effect is reciprocal. Essentially one could argue there are five possible relationships between television viewing (TV) and consumption (shopping).

(1) There is no relationship, i.e. watching television is unrelated to shopping behaviour.
(2) Television watching primarily or exclusively leads to particular types of consumption (qualitative and quantitative).
(3) Certain patterns of consumption lead to a particular pattern of television viewing possibly in the process of dissonance reduction.
(4) Reciprocal causation occurs whereby both activities influence the other, i.e. watching particular commercials leads to purchases which in turn influences the choice of particular programmes. Buyers' nostalgia may mean that some people watch advertisement for products they have already bought to justify their purchases.
(5) A moderator variable such as IQ or social class determines both television viewing and consumption which may be related to each other or not. Thus, it could be that middle-class people watch less television and buy less of what is advertised on it, not because of middle-class socialization in both respects.

Children's Attention to Advertisements

When examining the role that advertising plays in shaping the attitudes and behaviours of children as consumers it is important to establish the extent to which youngsters are exposed to advertising and how attentive they are when faced with it. Attention and exposure levels are key variables in any communication context. Attention, for instance, represents a necessary, though not sufficient, condition in information processing. Advertising presents everyone with a remarkable volume and range of information inputs. This array of advertising stimulus materials could prove to be overwhelming for any consumer intent on trying to absorb them all. Attentional processes allow selection to take place, and among young potential consumers these will direct the child towards certain advertisements rather than others.

The degree of attention can influence the child's interpretation of advertising messages and also how much they are remembered. There is evidence too of a relationship between degree of attention to advertising and children's beliefs in the truthfulness of an advertisement (Greenberg et al., 1986). Children who are more attentive to advertising have been found to consider advertisements more truthful. Attention to advertising is also an important factor in connection with the effects advertisements might have on young consumers. Low levels of attention generally lead to low levels of effects (Young, 1990).

Establishing whether or not a child is paying attention to an advertisement requires more than knowing that the child is watching the advertisement. Even when a child is actually watching an advertisement, there can be varying degrees of attention to it. With television, even when a child is not looking at the screen, attention might still be given to the auditory output of advertisements. Although this phenomenon can be investigated experimentally it is rather difficult to determine how much attention any child is paying while watching television most of the time. Any demonstration of attentional processes in a laboratory setting always faces the problem of lacking ecological validity insofar as representing accurately what happens in a natural viewing environment.

Information on children's exposure to TV advertisements

When trying to collect data on children's exposure to TV commercials, most researchers start by trying to find out the amount of TV that is actually watched by children. These results are then compared with the total number of advertisements that are usually broadcast during an hour of television, which enables researchers to reach conclusions about the total number of advertisements a child generally watches. This is, however, a fairly crude index and its results are therefore open to dispute.

According to recent figures, the average American child under 12 watches about 4.2 hours of television per day (Kline, 1991). This figure is by no means exceptionally high, since results from other countries are quite similar (Kline, 1991). Japanese children are reported to watch even more television than their American same-age counterparts (Kojima, 1968). In the UK, children watch around 3 to 4 hours of television per day (Gunter and McAleer, 1990). Research carried out in Flanders indicates that the average Flemish child watches about 2 hours 40 minutes of television per day (Wittebroodt, 1990), whereas in the Netherlands, the amount is reported to be about 1 hour 23 min (Liebert, 1986; Nikken 1991) . Thus, total TV viewing times vary greatly from one country to another, with American and Japanese children reportedly watching three times as much television as those in the Netherlands (Holicki and Sonesson, 1991; Murray and Kippax, 1981; Von Feilitzen, 1991).

This is important to bear in mind since, as a result, children's levels of exposure to TV commercials will differ greatly from country to country. Moreover, it has been found that the total amount of television viewing (which in most cases also has an influence on the total amount of advertising watched) varies significantly according to other factors such as age (the older the child, the more television is watched—until the age of 12) (Nikken, 1991); *social class* (children of lower classes usually watch more television than children from higher classes) (Murray and Kippax, 1981; Young 1990); and other variables, such as the *season* (in winter, levels of television viewing are significantly higher than in the summer) (Wittebroodt, 1990).

After comparing this information about the total amount of television watched by children with information about the number of advertisements present in the various programmes, researchers have tried to measure the amount of advertising to which an average child-viewer is exposed.

Results concerning the total number of television advertisements to which children are exposed have differed greatly. As far as the US is concerned, Riecken and Yavas, 1990 quoted a 1985 figure indicating that 'a child under 12 is exposed to between 2200 and 2500 commercials in a year'. In 1976, however, Galst and White observed that 'the moderate-television-viewing child observes over 5000 commercials for edibles per year'. And in 1980, Adler *et al.* (1980b) estimated that a typical US child viewer was exposed to 20,000 commercials a year. This figure was later obtained in other studies (Christenson, 1982), but in 1991, Kunkel *et al.* concluded that this number of 20,000 advertisements per year was already outdated, since recent evidence had indicated increasing amounts of advertising during breaks in children's programmes.

It should be noted, however, that none of these researchers actually indicated whether they referred to 'children's commercials' or to 'commercials aimed at everyone'. Although there is no agreement as to the exact numbers, these findings nevertheless give the clear impression that children are exposed to thousands of advertisements per year. There are good reasons, however, why these figures should be treated with caution.

(1) Establishing a direct link between television exposure in general and the exposure to television advertisements can be quite hazardous, since a number of technical developments have enabled viewers to watch television without being confronted with any advertisements at all. Not only can children view pay-TV without advertising, the introduction of remote controls allows a great deal of 'zapping'—the changing of channels at the beginning of a commercial break. Moreover, since children are making more use of VCRs, it is possible for them to skip through the advertisements when replaying programmes they have taped ('zipping') (Bovee and Arens, 1989), or to leave out the advertisements when recording the programme (Sepstrup, 1986).

(2) Even if advertisements are being shown intact, we should not forget that much of children's television viewing takes place while other things are going on. Eating meals and snacks is a very common accompaniment to watching television, as are playing with toys and doing homework. Moreover, children also talk to other people when they are watching television, usually about things that are entirely unrelated to television (Dorr, 1986). This indicates that, although children can be 'exposed' to commercials, their attention to them can be at quite a low level.

Children's degrees of attention to advertisements

Attention enables human beings to select which out of a multitude of items of information impinging upon them from the surrounding environment shall be selected for further processing. It is also an aspect of an individual's psycho logical functioning which determines the degree to which an informational item is processed, once selected. The extent to which people pay attention to things in their environment may be influenced by internal factors such as motivation or interest in the content of whatever it is they are paying attention to, and by external factors such as the physical attributes of the stimulus. Thus, children may pay attention to advertisements for products that interest or appeal to them or because these advertisements have special presentational qualities such as fast-moving images, music, sound effects or favourite characters.

Attention to television advertising is difficult to define in operational terms. Observational studies have tended to focus upon the child's visual attention to, or level of 'looking at' or apparent 'eye contact' with the television screen. Attention, however, cannot be fully operationalized in purely visual terms. A person may be looking away from the screen but still paying attention to what-ever is being presented by listening to what is being said.

Using an observational technique which involved the placement of film cameras in a sample of family households, Bechtel *et al.* (1972) monitored chil-dren and teenagers while they watched television in their own homes. They found that children younger than 11 years watched television advertisements only 40 per cent of the time they were broadcast, on average, but older children and teenagers averaged 55 per cent. Winick and Winick (1979) observed more than 300 children at home and reported that they regarded advertisements as rel-atively unimportant with children as young as two years regularly leaving the room when the advertisements came on. Atkin (1978) reported a further study in which mothers observed their own children. They reported that children aged four to nine years paid close attention over half the time whereas only 29 per cent of mothers of children aged 9 to 11 years reported close attention being paid (see Wartella and Hunter, 1983).

Attention to advertising cannot be split simply into 'on' or 'off'. It is not an 'either/or' phenomenon; rather there can be varying degrees of attention. The degree of attention is determined by a range of factors which represent characteristics of the advertising message and of the child audience. *Message* factors comprise *form* and *content* variables. Visual and auditory changes in advertising can affect audience attention, especially among children (Wartella, 1980). Advertisements which contain a large number of visual changes in scene, action and characters, and which have fast-paced production features such as rapid cutting between camera shots, zooming in and out of close-ups and fading the picture up or down to a brighter or darker level of light-ing, can hold the child's visual attention. On an auditory level, lively music, sound effects, unusual voices, children's and women's voices and laughter, are effective for maintaining attention (Greer *et al.*, 1982; Meyer, 1983; Wolf, 1981).

Auditory features and music are some of the formal features of a TV commercial that play an important role in the child's attention to a commercial. Sound effects and music are not only important to keep the child's attention on the commercial, they also play an important triggering function, to bring lost attention back to the TV screen. As has been demonstrated in a number of studies, children quite often turn away from TV or engage in a variety of other activities when watching TV, (Dorr, 1986). Moreover, when two or more commercials are shown one after the other, if the first commercial fails to capture the child's attention, the second commercial will then depend entirely on auditory signals to catch the child's attention again since, quite often, children keep listening to what is going on in the sound track, even when not actually looking at the TV screen. Indeed, children may tend to monitor the sound track at a non-semantic level (i.e. not paying attention to actual words) and listen for particular auditory, non-verbal features which, as they have learnt, signal comprehensible, informative, interesting content. When interest is triggered, children will usually attend visually to the screen, and maintain both visual and auditory attention in order to take in as much as possible of what the commercial is saying for as long as the material is something they can understand (Rolandelli, 1989).

Music plays an important role in this process since it may perform the task of catching and holding attention, thus increasing the likelihood of repeated viewing and listening whenever the advertisement appears, enhancing its potential impact (Calvert and Scott, 1989; Scott 1990). However, most studies reveal that music is by no means an isolated element of a commercial, and only functions in association with other features of an advertisement, such as dialogue, type of voice, and visual elements. As a result of this, the salience and impact of music will vary from advertisement to advertisement, and it is not realistic to expect that the relationship between music and consumer response will be consistent (Young, 1990). For young people it is, of course, probably the type of music played during the advertisement that is of great significance.

Other factors that usually increase a child's attention to a television advertisement include (1) the *overall comprehensibility of its content*, and (2) *frequent changes in character, themes and settings*. Apart from this, a child's attention to an advertisement will also depend on (3) his or her *attitudes towards the advertised product itself* (Verhaeren, 1991). It has also been shown that a content which is (4) *humorous* usually ensures higher levels of attention by children.

As far as the first two factors are concerned, most researchers do point out the problem of finding an ideal balance between elements of novelty, complexity and unpredictability, on the one hand, and familiarity, simplicity and repetitiveness on the other (Rice, *et al.* 1983; Young, 1990). In general, advertisements which are more novel, complex and unpredictable for children will get higher levels of attention than advertisements which are too simple, familiar and expected. The latest type of advertisement will lead to a feeling of *boredom*, and hence very low levels of attention. On the other hand, however, if the content of an advert is too complex, new or unpredictable, this will certainly lead to a greater *incomprehensibility*. If an advertisement is too difficult to grasp, a child's level of attention to it will again be low. Ideally, an advertisement should have content which is 'moderately novel', or of intermediate complexity, but with some familiar and recognizable features as well (Rolandelli, 1989).

A child's attention to an advertisement can also be affected by the presence of humour. Humour has been found to lead to attentional orienting responses from children, thereby increasing the effectiveness of information processing from the commercial message (Stevens, 1988).

Audience factors (meaning demographic and attitudinal characteristics of the people watching) can play a significant part in influencing children's attention to advertising. Thus, an advertisement may attract high levels of attention from some children, but lower attention from others.

One critical audience factor among children is age. As children grow older, their attention becomes less susceptible to special production features within advertisements (Calvert and Scott, 1989; Wartella, 1980). The reason for this seems to be that with greater maturity children search for meaning independent of the perceptual salience of production attributes. More generally, older children grow tired of advertisements more readily (Greer *et al.*, 1982). There is a greater drop in attention to advertisements while watching television among older children than among younger children (see Liebert, 1986).

Gender differences in children's attention to advertising have been reported, although the evidence is not consistent. Greer *et al.* (1982) reported finding that boys were more attentive than girls to television advertising, with boys' attention remaining more stable across segments of advertisements, whilst girls' attention decreased very quickly. Elsewhere, greater attention has been reported to occur among girls than boys (Greenberg *et al.*, 1986). There is no clear-cut conclusion which can therefore be drawn about which gender pays the greatest attention in general to television advertising. Gender undoubtedly does play a part in levels of attention to specific advertisements, however, depending on the nature of the product being promoted.

The role of 'attentional inertia'

'Attentional inertia' refers to a phenomenon that the longer a viewer has continuously maintained attention, the more likely it is that he or she will continue to do so. As attentional inertia increases, the viewer becomes less distractible. Conversely, when a viewer shifts his or her attention away from the screen, it can become more difficult to re-establish attention the longer it has been directed elsewhere (Anderson and Lorch, 1983). Attentional inertia is relatively independent of content. It has been observed to occur in children as young as one year old and is found throughout childhood and occurs in adulthood. This phenomenon is very important in the context of advertising. In a commercial break, the attention that is paid to a particular advertisement will vary according to the degree of attention that has been paid to the preceding advertisements.

Children's Understanding of Television Advertising

Despite concerns about the potential quantity of advertising to which children may be exposed during their young lives, their degree of attention to advertising breaks on television can vary greatly and be influenced by a variety of factors. While children may watch advertising on television, its subsequent impact upon them may depend critically on whether they understand what it means. At a simple level, children's initial understanding takes the form of being able to tell the difference between advertisements and programmes. In addition to this, however, they must be able to recognize the promotional purpose and persuasive intent of advertising.

Distinction between advertisements and programmes

One important issue in the discussion about television advertising's influence on children is children's awareness of television advertising and whether or not children are able to distinguish advertisements from programmes. The importance of this question lies in the fact that a child will only be able to process the information in the advertisement with the appropriate cognitive skills and the necessary 'cognitive defences' if he or she actually recognizes an advertisement as such (Young, 1990). Consequently, the ability to distinguish between advertisements and programmes is seen as an important pre-requisite for the further steps in the child's information-processing.

Many studies have been written on the issue of the child's ability to distinguish between programmes and advertisements, but the research methods that were used differed significantly and led to different conclusions and suggestions, especially concerning the question of the child's age in relationship to his or her awareness of advertisements.

Children's awareness of television advertisements as distinct from programmes has typically been measured in two ways: first, in terms of their verbal responses to open-ended questionnaires, where a positive relationship has been found between age and verbal ability to differentiate between programmes and advertisements (Blatt *et al.*, 1972; Ward *et al.*, 1972; Ward and Wackman, 1972); secondly, in terms of changes in children's visual attention levels between programme sequences and adjacent advertising appeals. Several studies using this technique have revealed a tendency for children to exhibit a drop in attention when an advertisement was shown, compared with their level of attention to preceding programming. Furthermore, attention generally continues to decline during subsequent advertisements within the same series and across the same programme (Ward *et al.*, 1972; Zuckerman, Ziegler and Stevenson, 1978). This attentional decline across the programme and advertising materials, however, tends to be much more pronounced with children aged over eight years than with younger viewers, suggesting that the latter have more difficulty discriminating between the two (Zuckerman, Ziegler and Stevenson, 1978).

On what basis do children distinguish between programmes and advertisements? One of the major problems facing researchers who study children's awareness of television advertising rests with the definition of what this difference really means for young consumers. Children can differentiate between advertisements and programmes by referring to a number of distinguishing features. Television advertisements differ from programmes in terms of a number of perceptually salient features as well as by differences in the nature of their content and purpose.

Levin and Anderson (1976) found that pre-school children's visual attention to the television screen may vary considerably with specific features of the material being presented, such as lively music and active motion. Attention research with television advertisements has shown that changes in attention may be directly attributable to specific audio-visual shifts taking place between advertising and programming sequences and that children as young as three are aware of visual and auditory cues signifying the interruption of a programme by an advertisement (Wartella and Ettema, 1974). This result suggests that the more sudden or dramatic the stimulus change between a programme and advertisements shown in it, the more notice young children will take.

Advertisements clearly differ from television programmes in the following ways:

(1) *Length*—advertisements are much shorter than most television programmes, generally ranging from 10 seconds to 2 minutes in length (Condry, 1989).
(2) *Repetition/frequency*—advertisements appear with a much greater frequency during the broadcast day, and they are repeated much more often than individual programmes are. These repetitions may occur during the same hour, at many different times of the day and week, and on different channels, so that more people are likely to see a specific advertisement than a programme. Moreover, these advertisements are repeated in identical form, as opposed to the dramatic or thematic continuity that can be found in serials and series (Condry, 1989).
(3) *Purpose*—the most important difference between advertisements and other programmes lies in the purpose of advertisements. The basic purpose of advertisements is one of persuasion, often displaying products at their best with model consumers depicted purchasing and gaining satisfaction from

them. This persuasion could be aimed at getting the viewer to adopt new attitudes or engage in new activities, or it may involve reinforcement of already existing attitudes or behaviours. Advertising messages may also entertain and inform the viewer, but the primary psychological mechanism is one of persuasion. Other television programmes, on the other hand, can simply be entertaining or informative (Young, 1990).

Apart from these issues, many other points of difference could be mentioned, such as the presence of a brand name in most advertisements, or differences in formal features of the advertisement, including the presence of jingles, rapid cuts, and differences in sound intensity. Humour, the 'personality' endorsing a product and topicality are other crucially important determinants of attention to and memory for advertisements.

However, these differences between advertisements and programmes are not always so clear, and some counter-examples could be used to make the category boundaries less clear, especially from a child's point of view. Some commentators refer to the fact that some music videos, public service announcements or programme trailers are structured to be very similar to television advertisements, are equally short, and are also frequently repeated (although they do not have the same commercial intent as advertising). Moreover, the use of programme-length advertisements, popular figures or sponsorship are all factors which make the edges of the classes of advertising and programme more fuzzy.

In the majority of cases, however, a very clear distinction can be drawn between commercials and programmes, and this distinction is mainly based on differences in intent, repetition, frequency, length and other features of both form and content.

As far as the awareness of intent is concerned, however, an important question arises from the relationship between children's ability to label a message and their ability to recognize the intent of this message. Researchers have posed the question of which actually comes first: do children recognize an advertisement as 'different' because they notice a difference in intent, or do they notice the persuasive intent of an advertisement after recognizing a commercial as such? Recent findings in the field of child psychology indicate that for messages such as the news and advertisements, identification by name precedes recognition of intent (Blosser and Roberts, 1985). This is also the reason why we followed the approach suggested by most authors who treat the child's ability to distinguish between programme and advertisement before dealing with the issue of the child's understanding of the intent of advertisements.

All this makes clear that even if a child can distinguish between advertisements and programmes, this does not necessarily mean that he or she can also understand the intent of the advertising message. The converse, however, is true: if a child can recognize the intent of a message, this implies that he or she can clearly distinguish between advertisements and programmes.

Age and ability to distinguish advertisements from programmes

At what age can children distinguish advertisements from programmes? Research has provided different answers to this question depending on the methodology used. Children's ability to make distinctions between advertising messages and programmes on television develops with age, varying from one individual to the next and with the type of understanding being considered. From infancy to adolescence, understanding of television advertising follows a three-stage pattern: (1) recognition; (2) growing understanding; (3) scepticism. The young child learns to recognize advertisements, gradually comes to understand their purposes and uses, and with experience grows increasingly sceptical of advertising claims. These processes overlap considerably, in part because no process is ever complete.

Children gradually develop the notion that there are different types of material on television. Pre-school children first base the distinction on salient visual and auditory features that distinguish advertisements from programmes. The most basic of these is that advertisements are short and programmes are long.

The complexity of the format can make a difference to attention levels. This factor also interacts with the age of the child. Thus, advertisements with more scene shifts, special visual and sound effects and changes in tempo attract more attention than less complex messages. These physical attributes of advertising have a more profound effect on the attention levels of younger children, whose attention is more stimulus driven.

Researchers who have based their evidence on non-verbal and observational tests have usually come to the conclusion that children as young as age three or four can distinguish between programmes and advertisements. Studies that have used verbal tests when questioning children, however, usually have found that only children who are nine years of age and older demonstrated their ability to distinguish between programmes and advertisements, with younger children expressing much confusion about the difference.

Five years is most often cited as the age at which the majority of children can reliably distinguish between television programmes and advertisements (Adler et al., 1980; Blosser and Roberts, 1984; Butter et al., 1991; Dorr 1986; Palmer and McDowell, 1979; Young, 1990). 'If they are asked to raise their hands or shout out when a commercial appears during a broadcast, a majority (of five- to seven-year-olds) can do so more often than not' (Dorr 1986). Levin et al. (1982) reported that three- to five-year-olds applied the term 'programme' or 'commercial' correctly about two-thirds of the time when a videotape with both forms was stopped at random points.

In another study, five-year-olds could tell advertisements from programmes with 79 per cent accuracy, while three- and four-year-olds were 65 per cent accurate. Similar figures have been reported for English children (Sweeney, 1988). When children are required to communicate verbally, researchers put the age of awareness of television advertisements at four to seven years.

Research that does not rely on children's verbal abilities finds that children as young as three know the difference between television programmes and advertisements (Butter *et al.*, 1991; Kunkel and Roberts, 1991). Research using non-verbal measures has shown that even very young children exhibit early abilities to distinguish between programmes and advertisements.

Butter *et al.* (1981) attempted to assess the extent to which 80 children aged four and five years were able to distinguish between advertisements and programmes by requiring each child to tell the experimenter 'when a commercial comes on'. The children saw a videotape of a programme with several advertisements inserted at different points. If the child did not answer when an advertisement was being shown, the experimenter asked if this was still part of the programme. Clearly, there is a risk of obtaining false positives with this methodology. Results demonstrated that the majority of four-year-olds were capable of discriminating between advertisements and programmes as were the five-year-olds, who discriminated more successfully.

Levin *et al.* (1982) used the technique of asking early school-age children whether what they had just seen was a 'commercial' or a 'programme' in order to establish when children could differentiate between the two. Segments of programmes and advertisements each lasting 10 seconds were edited on video-tape for this purpose and the child was questioned after each segment. It was found that among children aged between three and five years the percentage of correct identifications was significantly above chance at each age. This result contrasted with earlier findings (e.g. Palmer and McDowell, 1979). Further, the fact that the commercial and programme segments used in this experiment were the same length meant that this particular feature was not available to the children to help their judgments, although the fact that the programme extracts were much shorter than usual programme material may have helped the children more accurately to identify the commercial material.

In a project by Jaglom and Gardner (1981), the two categories of 'television advertising' and 'the rest of television' emerged very early in development, at about three years of age. Unexpectedly they found that 'advertisement' was the earliest category in the children's developing understanding of television content. One of the three children studied intensively by Jaglom and Gardner could identify television advertisements at two years of age!

Using non-verbal measures, Zuckerman and Gianioni (1981) studied 4-, 7- and 10-year-olds. The children were shown photographs of animated characters who appear regularly on children's television programmes and advertisements. Children were asked to identify each character. Two non-verbal tests were performed. Two characters were placed before each child who was asked which one was in a commercial. This procedure was repeated for 10 pairs of different characters, each pair consisting of one programme character and one commercial character. Over half the four-year-olds correctly identified the photograph of the commercial character in practically all pairs. A quarter of the four-year-olds made significantly incorrect responses. They were able to discriminate between the two categories, but failed to apply the correct label to the characters. The 7- and 10-year-olds performed almost perfectly. When children were asked to point to the character in each pair who 'shows you (product name) on television', all age groups performed at near perfect levels.

The symbolic 'meaning' of products grows stronger from ages 9 to 11. Belk *et al.* (1984) studied children's views of 'product symbolism'. Children of 9 to 11 years of age were shown photographs of familiar products, like jeans and bicycles. Each child was asked to say which attributes described the kind of child who owned the product. For example, how wealthy is the child who wears Levi's? The older children had more consistent ideas about the meaning of products. Product symbolism was stronger in girls than boys, and in higher-social-class children than lower-social-class children. Older children, 9 to 18 years of age, show a steady improvement in understanding the ambiguous wording, humour and imagery of advertisements (Brown and Bryant, 1983; Nippold *et al.*, 1988; Weinberger and Spotts, 1989).

Most recent studies on this issue tend to support the view that children as young as three can sometimes distinguish between advertisements and programmes. However, they do emphasize that it is by no means true that *all* children aged three or four can do so: only a small minority of children aged three or four is found to be aware of 'commercials' as something distinct; as the child grows older, the more probable it will be that he or she will distinguish between programmes and advertisements. Research carried out by verbal testing (Blosser and Roberts, 1985) has revealed a steady improvement in the ability of children to identify and label television advertisements as commercial content and programme material as non-commercial content (see Table 5.1).

TABLE 5.1 *Percentage of children correctly labelling TV advertisements*

Message type	0–5 years	5–6 years	6–7 years	7–8 years	8–10 years	10+ years
Child commercial	10%	62%	53%	71%	85%	100%
Adult commercial	10%	58%	63%	79%	92%	100%
News	60%	88%	95%	100%	92%	100%

Source: Blosser and Roberts, 1985

According to these findings, over half the children between five and six years were able to label commercials (both child and adult advertisements), and the proportion increased to 100 per cent by ten years. Moreover, there is also an important difference as to the origin of the child's distinction between programmes and advertisements: this awareness appears to proceed from perceptual discrimination (evidenced as early as age three or four in attentional patterns) through recognition and articulation of perceptual differences by kindergarten and first grades, to a higher level of understanding of continual differences somewhere between kindergarten and second grade (Wartella, 1980). This was an important finding, since it illustrated that identification is not always based on what adults regard as the most important attribute of advertisements: their intent to persuade. Instead, many children distinguish on the basis of concrete characteristics such as length, humour, music, animation and liveliness (Dorr, 1986).

The research findings on this issue can largely be summarized by stating that, although some children are reportedly able to distinguish between programmes and advertisements as early as age three or four, most children below age five do not consistently recognize whether the content they are watching is a programme or an advertisement. Children below this age frequently identify advertisements as part of the show (Kunkel, 1991).

By the time children are six- to eight-years-old they can more often than not differentiate advertisements from programmes. If they are asked to describe differences, the majority can volunteer one or more correct differences. If they are asked to raise their hands or shout out when an advertisement appears during broadcasting, a majority can do so more often than not (Dorr, 1986). And by the time children are 10-years-old, they can all distinguish between advertisements and programmes.

Advertising-related factors

Children's ability to distinguish between programmes and advertisements on television can also be influenced by advertising-related factors. Sometimes these factors can make it easier for the young consumer to distinguish advertisements; on other occasions, such factors cloud the issue. The use of popular television characters or animated cartoon heroes may lead to increasing difficulties for younger children asked to distinguish advertisements from programmes (Verhaeren, 1991; Young, 1990). There is no universal agreement on this issue. However, at least one author has observed that the use of licensed characters (such as Walt Disney characters or the Smurfs) within an advertisement removes some of the formal distinctive features of advertisements and may therefore lead to confusion among younger children as to whether they appear in an advertisement or in a programme (Kunkel, 1988).

Another phenomenon which has been considered within the current context is the existence of a wide variety of advertiser-initiated, product-related shows and sponsorship. Although these commercial and promotional schemes go beyond the usual form of spot advertising, they nevertheless represent a form of marketing designed to raise brand awareness among young consumers. Furthermore, for some observers, this form of commercialism represents an insidious kind of advertising in which the real purpose of ostensibly entertainment-oriented programming is really little more than an extended advertisement for a product (Sepstrup, 1986).

Helping Young Consumers

There are factors which are designed to make it easier for children conceptually to separate advertisements from programmes. Most guidelines concerning the regulation of television advertising require that there should be a separation between programmes and advertisements by using devices known variably as 'separators' or 'bumpers'. Not all researchers, however, accept that these devices are effective.

A number of studies carried out in the late 1970s and early 1980s revealed that most separation devices which were used between programmes and advertisements were quite ineffective (Levin, *et al.*, 1982). They found that the most prevalent technical failing of the existing separators was their lack of sufficient contrast. In most separators, the video was programme-related, and the audio signals did not contrast with what preceded it. Consequently, it was argued that the beginning of the advertisement itself seemed to provide more contrast than the separators and that children have a greater likelihood of recognizing an advertisement if it was *not* introduced (Palmer and McDowell, 1979; Verhaeren, 1991).

However, many recent studies indicate that separators do indeed lead to an increase in children's abilities to distinguish between advertisements and programmes, provided they are clearly different visually and auditorily, and that they use speech which is understood by all children. These studies indicated that a standard separator which featured animated programme characters and a voice-over saying 'programme X will be right back after these messages' did not in any way help children to identify the following advertisements, but that an alternative indication showing a red stop sign and saying 'OK, kids, get ready, here comes a commercial' dramatically increased advertisement recognition by four-, six- and eight-year-old children (Dorr, 1986).

Another method for enhancing children's ability to discriminate between programmes and advertisements has been to cluster advertisements in blocks between each television programme instead of distributing them between and during programmes (Bednall and Hannaford, 1980). This technique of scheduling television advertisements has not, however, been universally accepted and opponents to it have argued that clustering leads to 'clutter' and poor memory for advertisements, which unfairly penalizes advertisers.

In one test of the relative effectiveness of clustering upon children's ability to differentiate programme content from advertising content, Atkin (1975) showed seven advertisements, which were either dispersed throughout a cartoon show or clustered before or following the programme, to groups of 4- to 11-year-olds. Results indicated that overall attention to the advertisements was universally higher in the clustered presentation.

In another study, Duffy and Rossiter (1975) showed 5- to 10-year-olds some 30-second advertisements, either clustered in blocks of six and eight before and after a programme, or distributed in blocks of three, four, four and three before, after and at two logical breaks in the programme. They found that clustering produced smaller changes in attention among 5-year-olds than among 9- and 10-year-olds and apparently did not aid younger children in discriminating between advertising and programme material.

Unfortunately, there are a number of problems with the above studies and the inferences drawn from them. To begin with, children's ability to discriminate between advertisements and programmes was assessed only indirectly on the basis of changes in visual attention. The Duffy and Rossiter study found that the youngest children showed a smaller attention shift in the clustered treatment than in the distributed treatment, which led the authors to infer that clustering did not aid children's discrimination judgments. However, the clustered condition also contained an audio commercial-warning whereas the dispersed version did not, and a further dispersed plus warning condition is needed to separate the independent effects of warning from those of scheduling *per se*.

In a direct examination of the effects of scheduling on memory for television commercials, Bednall and Hannaford (1980) presented groups of 10- and 11-year-olds with one hour of television programming with blocked advertising, distributed advertising, or no advertising. After viewing, recall of commercial material was measured either immediately or three days later. Results showed that block advertising (recalled correctly 36% of the time) was not as well recalled as distributed advertising (recalled correctly 46% of the time). However, no differences between blocked and distributed advertising were found when recall was tested after a delay of three days. Also, whilst recall of distributed advertising changed little with delay, delayed recall for blocked advertising was 15 per cent higher than immediate recall indicating that the clustering had only a short-term inhibitory effect on memory for commercials, which apparently dissipates within a few days. In further tests for recall of programme content, it was found that although this did vary between programme types, with drama better recalled than non-fiction, there was no clear indication that programme recall was affected by the way advertising was scheduled or by its presence or absence.

An inference may be drawn from this that neither blocked nor distributed advertising is any less useful for children or for advertisers. Bednall and Hannaford also claimed that removal of advertising entirely from children's programmes would not improve their recall of those programmes.

Awareness of persuasive intent

The study of children's understanding of the persuasive purpose behind advertising is a key issue in any discussion of advertising regulation. If children are ignorant of persuasive intent, it might be argued that advertising takes advantage of their naivety. As Kunkel and Roberts (1991) state: 'The degree to which children are able to recognize persuasive intent has been a dominant focus of research on children and advertising. Its importance derives from the legal argument that if young children are unaware of persuasive intent, then all commercials aimed at them are, by definition, unfair and/or misleading' (p. 63). In other words, there is an implicit policy-related motive underlying this research.

Most researchers agree that the awareness of the purpose of television advertising is a very important step in the child's acquiring of the necessary skills to become advertising literate (Young, 1990). Recognition of the purpose of an advertisement reportedly influences the assessment of its truth or falsity (Smith and Sweeney, 1984; Young, 1990).

Moreover, it is argued that the child's ability to realize the purpose behind commercials leads to 'cognitive defences' against advertising, which means that the child can mentally generate counter-claims, that it is aware that a special plea is made and that it can adopt a sceptical and distrusting attitude towards the advertiser's claims (Kunkel, 1991).

Other researchers emphasize that understanding intent can be important for the interpretation of the content: 'Because different types of television content are produced for different reasons with correspondingly different standards for accuracy, balance, pleasure, and redeeming social value, attributing motives to those who created the content can have important ramifications for the sense made of it' (Dorr, 1986, pp. 33–34).

Many studies also report that, when children understand that advertisements are intended to persuade them and make them like or buy certain products or services, they often feel quite negatively towards advertisements; they complain when advertisements come on, criticize them, deny their claims, look away or talk, or simply leave the room (Dorr, 1986).

All this indicates that, once children do not only see advertisements as something different from other programmes but also understand their intent, their information processing and interpretation of the commercial content will be much more critical. Consequently, the child's ability to understand the intent of advertising will be a very important requirement in order to obtain cognitive defences against advertisements. However, we should also realize that the child's cognitive defences against advertisements do not necessarily imply that the child will be less influenced by advertising, since cognitive understanding has no necessary relationship to attitudes or behaviour (Ross et al., 1984). Conclusively, we should not forget that knowledge of selling intent alone is not sufficient to import resistance to persuasive appeals (Bruck et al., 1988).

There is a considerable amount of research on the question of children's awareness of the persuasive purpose of advertising. Rarely is an adequate definition of 'awareness' provided. For example, the widely-cited research of Ward, Wackman and Wartella (1977) reports that 96 per cent of 5- and 6-year-olds, 85 per cent of 8- and nine-year-olds, and 62 per cent of 11- and 12-year-olds 'do not fully understand' the purpose of television advertisements. To be considered high in awareness requires the child to verbally express the underlying profit motive of the advertiser. If a child replied that advertisements 'show kids where to buy toys,' this is regarded as 'medium awareness'. If a child said that advertisements are 'short and funny', this is considered 'low awareness'.

According to Robertson and Rossiter (1974), the skills necessary to attribute persuasive intent to an advertisement are: (1) the ability to distinguish programmes from advertising; (2) understanding that there is (a) an external source to the advertisement, and (b) an intended audience for it; (3) awareness of the 'symbolic nature' of advertisements (the idea that advertising settings and devices are not 'real'); and (4) the ability to cite possible discrepancies between advertising claims and product reality. With such a definition, it is not surprising that many young people fail to show 'awareness' of persuasive intent!

Reliance on verbal measures may overestimate the age at which children first grasp commercial intentions. In an exploratory investigation into children's understanding of television advertising, Blatt *et al.* (1972) conducted loosely structured group interviews with children aged 5 to 12 years. During the course of these interviews, the children were asked such questions as 'Do you know what a television commercial is?', 'Who makes television commercials?', and 'Do television commercials always tell the truth?'. A further study among the same age range by Ward *et al.* (1972) used standardized questions. Once again, though, the children were asked: 'What is a television commercial?' Their responses were assigned to three levels of awareness: (1) *Low Awareness*— where children named specific categories of commercial or products in attempting to explain what a commercial is; (2) *Medium-Level Awareness*—where children exhibited some minimal understanding of the notion of advertising; and (3) *High Awareness*—where children showed a clear understanding of the intent of advertising, e.g. to get people to buy a product.

Verbal indicators have suggested that children as young as four or five years old seem to understand the intent of television advertisements when the study requires them to choose certain pictures or to perform appropriate actions (e.g. Gaines and Esserman, 1981). When verbal measures of understanding are used, researchers tend to report older ages (Adler *et al.*, 1980; Paget *et al.*, 1984; Ward, *et al.*, 1977). These considerations and cautions should be kept in mind.

Understanding that advertisements are designed to persuade comes somewhat later than the ability to recognize them. As with other cognitive abilities, awareness of persuasive intent increases gradually with age. In addition to age, another important (age-related) factor is the level of cognitive development achieved by the child. Ward and Wackman (1973) conducted a similar analysis to that of Ward *et al.*(1972) and found that understanding of advertising was not only differentiated by age but also by 'cognitive level'. The latter factor, however, was not independently manipulated, but was based on responses to two questions: 'What is a commercial?' and 'What is the difference between a television commercial and a television programme?'.

Answers were categorized as showing different levels of awareness and differentiation. A low level of awareness to the first question would be noted if the child's reply demonstrated a reliance on perceptual cues as in 'they sell things'.

A medium level of awareness would be recorded if the child had the beginnings of a concept of advertising, such as 'it tells people about things to buy'. A high level of awareness would be indicated if the child could identify commercials in terms of persuasion. 'Cognitive level' was found to be related to the ability of the child to make inferences about the nature of television advertising and to draw distinctions between advertisements and programmes which went beyond the immediate perceptual qualities of each type of content.

Robertson and Rossiter (1974) questioned primary-school-age boys about their understanding of what television advertisements are, what they are designed to achieve, whether they can always be believed and whether they make you want the things you see in them. They found two types of attribution of intent. One, called *assistive*, is where the child sees commercials as informative and the other, called *persuasive*, is where the child sees commercials as trying to make people buy things. Both types of attribution of intent can co-exist in a child, but persuasive intent becomes more frequent as the child gets older. By 10 to 11 years of age, practically all children are able to attribute persuasive intent to commercials.

In a study in which children were asked for their immediate reactions to an advertisement just shown to them on a videotape, which was stopped as soon as the advertisement had finished, Gaines and Esserman (1981) reported that two-thirds of four- to five-year-olds demonstrated an understanding of commercial intent. This result compared favourably even with the performance of 11- and 12-year-olds observed by Ward and his colleagues (1977). The commercial in question was for a breakfast cereal. Over half the four- to five-year-olds exhibited a sceptical response, such as 'might not be as good as they say' or 'can't believe what they say because they want your money'.

Given differences in methodologies, however, it is not possible to equate the findings of Gaines and Esserman with those obtained from the earlier studies of the 1970s using verbal questioning procedures. One conclusion that does emerge from all this work is that different conditions of presentation of advertising can yield different results. Under some circumstances it is possible to elicit an apparently advanced level of understanding even among very young children.

Another methodology has based its measure of children's understanding of television advertising upon a picture selection technique (Donohue *et al.*, 1980). Here, children were first of all shown a television advertisement for a breakfast cereal and then presented with two pictures. One picture showed a mother with a child sitting in her supermarket trolley picking a packet of the same cereal brand from the supermarket shelf. The second picture depicted a child watching a television screen. The children were asked to select the picture which illustrated what the advertisement 'wanted you to do'. Three out of four children chose the supermarket picture, which the researchers interpreted as a demonstration of children's understanding of the intent of television advertisements.

This conclusion has been challenged, however, because the study does not reveal the processes that led very young children to point to the supermarket picture (Young, 1990). It might be natural to expect a child to select the picture containing the advertised product over a picture which makes no reference to that product. Different control pictures in which a different brand was shown being selected, or in which the target brand was depicted in a non-selling environment might have been more revealing.

Stutts *et al.* (1981) asked children two questions derived from a study by Ward *et al.* (1977) on what an advertisement is and why advertisements are shown on television. They found that the majority of seven-year-olds could explain selling intent adequately, but only a small percentage of younger children was able to do so. In a further analysis of the data from this study, age emerged as one of the most significant predictors of children's comprehension of advertising intent (Stephens and Stutts, 1982).

Macklin (1982, 1983) interviewed children aged four and five years and used a variety of measures to assess their understanding of television advertisements. They were asked to respond to the question: 'What is a television commercial?' Then they were shown three advertisements and asked to describe what happened in each one. All four-year-olds showed a low level of awareness, while only a minority of five-year-olds showed a medium level awareness. Recall of advertisements tended to be fragmented and not integrated, and occasionally lapsed into fantasy. However, when a set of non-verbal measures were used with these children their performance improved. The child had to point to different alternatives concerning incidents and information in the advertisements and such recognition measures produced a level of correct performance varying between one-third and two-thirds, depending on the advertisement and the age of the child.

Macklin (1985) replicated and extended the Donohue *et al.* (1980) work by adding to the range of pictures the child had to choose from. Sixty children ranging from three to five years were studied. In one condition, there were three alternatives, the two used by Donohue and a picture of the product being shared between a girl and her friend. In the original study there were only two alternatives, one depicting the product and the other depicting a child watching television. Macklin's results were very different from Donohue's. Eighty per cent of all the children who were given the extended range of pictures failed to select even one correct picture that would indicate an understanding of intent.

There is consistent evidence that younger children who do not understand the persuasive intent of advertisements are more likely to perceive them as truthful messages, whereas older children who can discern persuasive intent tend to express sceptical attitudes towards advertisements. Results of various survey studies indicate that below the age of six, the vast majority of children cannot readily explain the selling purpose of advertising. Between the ages of about five and nine, the majority of children come to recognize and can explain the selling intent of advertising (Meyer *et al.*, 1978; Palmer and MacNeil, 1991; Sheikh *et al.*, 1974).

Macklin (1987) used two non-verbal measures to study 120 pre-school children's responses to television advertisements. She developed a board game to measure understanding of advertisements, and a shopping game to measure persuasive intent. A minority of older pre-schoolers (age 4) was able to indicate an understanding of the function of advertisements. 'This contradicts the accuracy of the prior conclusion by public policy-makers that children under the age of 8 are unable to understand commercial meaning.'

Problems of methodology

When measuring the child's ability to understand the purpose of advertisements, it is important that the methodologies employed by researchers provide valid and accurate indicators of how children respond to television advertising. Much of the early research into children's understanding of the purposes of advertising used fairly crude measures and these methodologies have not gone unchallenged. Some of the methods used to measure the recognition by children of the persuasive intent of advertising have been criticised for giving a misleading impression of how soon children are able properly to understand this aspect of advertising (Adler *et al.*, 1980). It was felt that non-verbal indicators may suggest earlier recognition than does in fact occur. An alternative method was suggested where children are asked about the purpose of advertisements in general in order to establish a concrete context rather than an abstract one.

Young (1990), commenting upon the early American research with children, expresses a legitimate concern about what the data it yielded actually tells us:

> One of the problems with the data obtained from these interviews, and interviews in general, is the difficulty of knowing whether a response or reply that demonstrates say, 'medium awareness' is the *only* response available. Despite the skill of the interviewer in probing to obtain more information, some children are unable or unwilling to express themselves beyond their initial response.
>
> (pp. 79 and 81)

Looking in more detail at the research techniques employed in many of the studies, more specific problems can be identified. First, there is the problem of what is actually meant by the awareness of advertising intent. Throughout the 1970s, many research works were published on the issue of children's understanding of commercial intent, but definitions as to what was exactly meant by this often remained vague. In the 1980s, however, a consensus grew among researchers that this 'ability to understand the intent of TV advertising' actually meant that children should recognize (Kunkel, 1991):

(1) that the source of the advertisement has perspectives and interests other than those of the receiver;
(2) that the source intends to persuade;
(3) that persuasive messages are, by definition, biased;
(4) that biased messages demand interpretation strategies that are different from informational, educational or entertainment messages.

In practice, results concerning the age at which children were found to be aware of advertising intent varied importantly according to what was meant by this awareness. If an awareness of 'selling intent' was taken as the criterion, it was found that most third-grade children were able to understand the purpose of television advertising. If, on the other hand, the criterion was an articulation of the total economic relationship between advertising and programming, even most sixth-grade children were found to be deficient (Wartella, 1980).

Moreover, results concerning the child's age in relation to his or her understanding of commercial intent were also found to differ significantly according to the method which was used for measuring awareness. Researchers who used verbal tests found that young children did not understand the intent of commercial messages (Macklin, 1987), but their research findings may be influenced by young children's inability to understand complicated questions, or their inability to explain verbally what they know mentally.

Some research has not relied upon the children's verbal abilities. Instead children merely have to point at pictures in order to indicate what the character in a commercial wants them to do. These studies reveal that 'although the grasp of concepts improves with age, children as young as three years of age have exhibited some understanding of selling intent' (Donohue, Hencke and Donohue, 1980). Researchers who have used various kinds of non-verbal tests have avoided some of the problems associated with the use of verbal tests with the very young, and have found that even five-year-olds can understand commercial intent (Macklin, 1987).

A number of researchers have tried to establish at what age a child is aware of television advertising intent. The research literature indicates, however, that results can vary significantly according to the research method used to measure children's comprehension of television advertisements. While some researchers have suggested that children as young as age five demonstrate some awareness of the purpose of advertising, many more researchers do not support this view (Young, 1990). Even researchers who claim that children aged five have indicated some awareness of advertising's intent, admit that this tends to happen only for a minority of children (Brucks *et al.*, 1988; Macklin, 1987). From a legislative point of view, it should be assessed at what age a majority of children are aware of advertising intent and in what context.

In general, research findings show that most children understand the selling intent of advertising by the age of eight (Brucks *et al.*, 1988), although some studies which are exclusively based on verbal questions tend to suggest that it is only by the age of nine or ten, the majority of children recognize the intent of commercials (Blosser and Roberts, 1985). Moreover, although a majority of children aged eight do express a certain understanding of commercial intent, such understanding does not fully develop until several years later (Kunkel, 1991).

The issue of cumulative exposure

There is a significant controversy around the influence of 'the total cumulative exposure to commercials' on children's ability to understand commercial intent. Whereas some researchers argue that increasing exposure to television advertisements inevitably leads to an increase in awareness of intent, others report that, paradoxically, higher levels of advertising exposure lead to a lower awareness of the intent of the commercial message (Wittebroodt, 1990). It should also be noted that it can be very difficult to measure this behaviour in a valid way, because of the great number of other factors involved.

Moreover, some researchers note that the variable of cumulative exposure is confounded with age, since the older the child is, the more likely he or she is to have been exposed to a greater number of television advertisements than a younger child. Consequently, it is difficult to establish whether differences in awareness of commercial intent are caused by the fact that the child has been exposed to more advertisements than a younger child, or whether this awareness of intent is a result of psychological maturity (Young, 1990). Studies which have kept one of these variables constant by comparing heavy viewers with light views of the same age, have found evidence in support of the view that an understanding of television advertisements is primarily dependent on cognitive development rather than simple exposure learning (Joossens, 1984).

Does knowledge of the persuasive intention of advertising give children a 'defense' against advertising? Children's ability to recognize persuasive intent in advertisements does not imply immunity to all commercials, any more than it does for adolescents or adults (Huston et al., 1992; Linn et al., 1982; Robertson and Rossiter, 1974). There is little evidence that children who understand the selling intent of advertisements are any less persuaded by them (Condry, 1989).

Young (1990) has summarized both the research on children's awareness of persuasive intent, as well as the political climate surrounding it:

> Given the policy context within which much of the research on television advertising and children was conducted, it is not surprising that the question of whether children understand the purpose of advertising is a central one. If researchers can come up with a firm answer to when children are capable of detecting the persuasive and/or commercial intent behind advertising the policy-makers will be better able to make up their minds on the question of whether or not to ban or restrict advertising to children and, if so, the age below which children should be protected. The boffins and back-room boys did, in fact, come up with answers. The problem was that there were several different answers and they were all supposed to be

correct. There was, in addition, a lack of theoretical precision about what it means to say the child 'understands' the 'purpose' or 'intent' of advertising and this lack of theory in the field led to much muddled thinking.

(p. 68)

Interpretation of the content of an advertisement

Having become aware of the general differences between advertising and pro-gramming, children subsequently develop a deeper understanding of the intent and purpose of television advertising. In relation to this, the age of the child is a significant factor. Many studies have been published about the child's inter-pretation of the content of advertisements. The most important research findings can be grouped under the following headings:

(1) the *truthfulness of the content* of television advertisements;
(2) the *comprehensibility* of television advertisements;
(3) the *influence of famous characters* in television advertisements.

As far as the content of children's advertisements is concerned, in practice, most children's commercials are for toys, breakfast cereals, other foods and snacks, and candies and sweets (Atkin, 1978; Galst and White, 1976; Greenberg *et al.*, 1986). Consequently, most of the research about children's advertisements and their content, actually deals with children's commercials for one of these product categories, even if this is not explicitly mentioned.

Truthfulness of the content
Most researchers who deal with the child's interpretation of the content of advertising have argued that efforts should be made to present both product and its usage in a *truthful way*. It is acknowledged, however, that most advertising codes already put limitations on the discrepancy between the product as pre-sented in advertising, and the product as used in real life (see Young, 1990).

Most studies indicate that children's television advertisements can in fact be misleading because of the various audio-visual techniques and effects that are used. An example of this is the Wonder Bread commercial that showed a child growing when eating the bread. According to some researchers this visual trick could easily be misinterpreted by children who are unfamiliar with what can be done with special effects (Condry, 1989).

Elsewhere it has been noted that advertisements for toys can be misleading because they use special photographic effects to make the toy appear longer or faster than it actually is. One study which examined children's toy advertise-ments for racing cars found that advertisements which included real racing footage influenced two aspects of children's understanding of the advertise-ments: it led them to perceive the product in an exaggerated way, and it made them less likely to understand that the advertisement was staged and synthetic (Ross, 1984). This study also added that because of this presentation of real-life racing pictures, the viewer proportionately had less time to see the product in action and to make objective judgements about it.

Other studies that examined the truthfulness and accuracy of toy advertisements also found that toys can appear to offer much more than is actually possible, through editing and other technological devices. The majority of commentators therefore suggest that, since younger children have a limited capability for evaluating the credibility of what they watch, advertisers have a special responsibility to protect children from their own susceptibilities (Bovee and Arens, 1989). Only minority support has emerged for the view that no true restrictions should be imposed as far as the reliability of children's commercials is concerned. Indeed, children soon learn to discount the claims by advertisers that toys possess extra-ordinary capabilities, particularly when real life experience with it has taught them differently (Donohue and Meyer, 1984).

Comprehensibility
Research has indicated that not all children of all age groups are able to understand all children's advertisements. The child's comprehension of an advertisement has been found to vary importantly according to a number of factors, including child-related and commercial-related influences. As far as child-related influences are concerned, the most important factor influencing the child's comprehension of an advertisement is reportedly the child's age (Dorr, 1986; Ross et al., 1984; Werner, 1989). Advertisements which are perfectly comprehensible to most 10-year-olds may cause comprehension problems for younger children, due to a difference in their level of cognitive development. Apart from the child's age, other child-related factors include the child's parents, and peer group.

Most researchers, however, have focused on the characteristics of the advertisement itself when studying 'comprehensibility'. Certain advertisements may pose comprehension problems because they include more 'information' than a child can process at one time. It is worth remembering, however, that advertisements are usually repeated so that children are exposed more than once to the same advertising message. Re-viewing the same advertisement a number of times may therefore help children in their comprehension of the content of the advertisement.

One issue studied in relationship to the child's comprehension of television advertisements is whether or not a child understands disclaimers which frequently appear in various toys and food advertisements. A disclaimer is a disclosure made with purpose of clarifying potentially misleading, ambiguous or deceptive statements made within an advertisement.

Stutts and Hunnicutt (1987) studied 106 children ages three to five to determine whether they could understand the nature and intent of disclaimers. Children's verbal responses to disclaimers were directly related to the age of the child: five-year-olds gave more correct verbal answers than four-year-olds, who in turn gave more correct responses than three-year-olds. Regardless of age, most respondents gave incorrect verbal responses to disclaimers concerning omitted factors, accessories, or the terms of sale. The ability to understand disclaimers increases with age and verbal skills.

A number of researchers have reported that these disclaimer messages were quite ineffective and by no means influenced children's knowledge, attitudes or values about the products which were advertised. However, most researchers now agree that disclaimer messages could play an important role provided they are understood by children (Faber *et al.*, 1984; Liebert *et al.*, 1977). Research findings have illustrated that it is not the disclaimer message in the advertisement that is largely ineffective, but that the language and the wording which are used in such messages may be too difficult for children.

Toy advertisements which use a standard disclaimer such as 'some assembly required' do not invariably lead to a better understanding among children that the toy in question has to be put together than do toy advertisements without such a disclaimer. However, it seems that if the disclaimer is reworded to the child's own level of comprehension, it is understood by nearly all children, even as young as ages four and five. Thus, advertisements that state 'you have to put it together', or 'it must be put together before you can play with it' have been found to be quite effective at telling the child what is required with a toy.

Influence of famous characters

Research studies have been conducted on the role and influence of 'famous characters' in children's advertising. It was mentioned earlier that programme personalities and cartoon characters may contribute to children's confusion between programmes and advertisements, and that this confusion effect can be heightened when the characters involved appear in advertisements that are shown within and adjacent to their own programmes.

Apart from this, some researchers also argue that a celebrity whose area of fame and presumed expertise is superficially related to the product advertised (e.g. a pilot in an advertisement for an electronic football game) may be incorrectly perceived as having special expertise about the product (Ross *et al.*, 1984). The use of celebrity endorsement in advertisements for toy cars has been found to influence children's cognitive and affective responses to the advertisements. Whereas some research suggests that this influence is greater among younger children since they lack the necessary cognitive skills to develop 'defences' against this, other studies report that the influence of celebrity endorsement on product preferences was equally strong for older as for younger children, and that there was no evidence of a developmental shift towards increased resistance to endorsement (Ross *et al.*, 1984; Wittebroodt, 1990).

Children's memory for advertising

Many studies that examine the possible effects of television advertising on children also deal with the child's memory for advertisements. The reason for this is that it is the memory for information extracted and stored during watching and listening that will be used afterwards, in the formation of knowledge, attitudes or values about the products or services that were advertised, or when activities such as purchase or purchase request behaviour occur. Consequently, it is expected that advertisements which are remembered and memorized by the child will have a greater influence than those that are not remembered.

It seems that whilst there is generally no intent among young viewers to seek information from television advertisements to use in a purchase decision (Ward et al., 1977), except perhaps at Christmas-time when they may be looking for gift ideas (Caron and Ward, 1975; Robertson and Rossiter, 1974), children may nevertheless use information which they have already learned from advertisements to guide product requests of parents at a later date (Robertson and Rossiter, 1977).

Advertising may influence a child to buy a particular product by raising its salience above other brands of the same product class and one way in which it may do this is by suggesting that a certain brand has more of a particularly attractive or highly valued attribute than other brands of the same type (Wright and Barbour, 1975). Research has indicated that children, even the very young, may remember advertisements in terms of their component attributes (Wartella et al., 1979). It was shown here that, in researching this question, it is important to employ more than *recall* measures to assess memory, however. On recall, eight-year-olds showed considerably better overall memory for the product appeals contained in advertisements than three- to four-year-olds. But when *recognition* was used, this difference was substantially reduced and the percentage of younger viewers remembering the commercial product elements improved considerably.

Research suggests, for instance, that when children have to choose a brand from a wide range of largely similar products, one of the factors that will influence their choice will be the most salient advertisement for an available brand retrieved from memory, rather than the most recent television advertisement or other promotion seen or heard (Young, 1990). Of course, salience could depend upon recency of exposure suggesting that these variables are inextricably linked.

The child's 'memory' for advertisements, however, is a very complicated issue. Brands do not simply exist in isolation in children's minds, but they are clustered in groups of products having similar characteristics. Consequently, it is suggested that the child's viewing of a chocolate commercial of a certain brand not only increases the response salience to that brand, but at the same time also increases response salience to other associated brands, products and sub-classes of products (Young, 1990). In this sense, any advertisement for a particular brand may encourage purchase behaviour across that product category.

However, television advertising is but one factor out of the large number that influence the child in the consumer context. Thus, while television commercials which are memorable for children may have a certain influence on them, the significance and strength of this influence can depend upon a variety of mediating variables which persist within the child's social environment. High levels of advertising recall offer no guarantee that the desired product purchase effects will follow (Kinsey, 1987).

Children's memory for advertisements has been researched since the early 1950s. A number of studies have tried to assess children's memory for individual toy, cereal, or snack advertisements. Some of these studies have been conducted by the advertising companies themselves in order to measure the reported effectiveness of certain advertising campaigns. Their results have usually not been made publicly available. Apart from this kind of research, other studies have been conducted by social scientists, communication specialists and child psychologists in order to collect more general data on the child's memory for commercial information.

Studies that try to examine the child's memory for advertisements are usually faced with the problem of whether to use *recall* or *recognition* tests (Bryant and Anderson, 1983). The results yielded by studies vary significantly according to the method which was used, with studies based on recognition generally reporting higher levels of memory than studies using recall tests. Some studies report that the validity of the method actually depends on the child's purchasing or choice situation. If the child usually chooses products by selecting a certain brand out of a large number of brands present on shelves (as when shopping in a supermarket), the recognition method is reportedly the most valid. If, however, the child has to ask for the brand he or she wants (as in the case of buying sweets from a corner shop, where the child has to make a request to the shopkeeper), the most valid method turned out to be based on recall (Young, 1990).

Influencing factors

Research on the child's memory for advertisements found that child-related and advertising-related factors may influence the degree of recall or recognition of a certain advertisement.

Child-related factors. Many researchers have reported that children's recognition and recall of the advertising messages increased as children grow older, and that major increases in memory seemed to occur between kindergarten and third grade (Wartella, 1980). Moreover, most studies report that, as children grow older, their recall for advertisements becomes more complete, coherent and unified. Whereas younger children usually recalled a single element of an advertisement, older children were found to recall more product and commercial plot-line information. Older children also recalled more information about the advertisement and more different kinds of information, such as information about the storyline, brand name and product attributes (Ward *et al.*, 1977). Results, however, have been found to vary according to the research methods that were used: if multiple-choice tests were used, young children scored significantly better on recognition of product information than when open-ended questions were used.

When examining the causes of these age-related differences in memory for commercial information, stage of cognitive development has emerged as significant. Young children do not always generate the necessary internal models ('schemas') which are important for the structure of content, and for the selection, encoding and recall of information. However, it has also been found that young children who do not know much about the structure of advertisements could increase their recall of commercial content after learning about the types of information advertisements usually contain (Dorr, 1986).

Advertising-related factors. Many advertising-related factors have been found to influence the child's degree of recognition or recall of an advertisement, including the *content* of the advertisement and the *production features* of the advertisement. Some studies provide evidence which indicates that children's recognition and recall scores are significantly higher for those advertisements in which they are interested than for advertisements with a content that does not appeal to them. Research showed that even kindergartners answered three out of four recognition measures accurately in a multiple-choice recognition test. This level of performance was particularly likely where information was presented about a relatively simple game product which they appeared interested in (Wartella, 1980).

The child's memory for advertisements has also been found to vary according to some production characteristics of the advertisement, including both visual and auditory features (Rolandelli, 1989). It has been shown that some visual representations in advertisements (making use of action, famous cartoon characters, animals, heroes, etc.) lead to increased attention, recall, and recognition among children, sometimes even regardless of the product which is advertised. Similarly, auditory signals such as music and certain slogans were found to increase children's memory for advertisements. However, although music plays an important role as to memory, it is often emphasized that music only interacts with the other elements of the advertisements, and that, therefore, it is not realistic to expect that the relationship between music and recall will be consistent (Scott, 1990).

As far as slogans are concerned, evidence suggests that even young children learn particular brand name slogans, and that memory for slogans is well established by the time children reach grade school (Wartella, 1980).

Scheduling aspects of television advertising, such as whether advertisements are presented in clustered or dispersed format and their frequency of repetition, can make a difference to children's memory for advertising on television. The evidence concerning the influence of these factors has not always been clear-cut. Although experimental results indicated that clustered advertising was not recalled as well as distributed advertising if recall occurred immediately after presentation, most studies report that no differences in recall are found after exposure to clustered versus distributed advertising (Young, 1990). Research findings suggest that repetition of certain elements within one advertisement (e.g. the brand name), and repetition of the entire advertisement usually increase the child's memory for it (Atkin and Heald, 1977).

Attitudes towards TV advertisements

'The advertising industry suffers from a credibility gap among children', according to Riecken and Yavas (1990, p. 145). By age eight, few children believe that television advertisements tell the truth. By age 10, three-quarters of children are sceptical of advertising claims, and hardly any 12-year-olds still believe advertisements tell the truth (Gaines and Esserman, 1981; Gunter and McAleer, 1990; Ward et al., 1977).

Despite their scepticism, young people often have highly favourable attitudes towards specific advertisements (Riecken and Yavas, 1990). There is evidence that repeated exposure to any stimulus, including a television advertisement, enhances its appeal, a process known as the *mere exposure effect* (Zajonc, 1968). Attitudes toward advertisements tend to become more favourable with repetition.

Collins (1990) found that 65 percent of 9- and 10-year-olds in Belfast, Northern Ireland, believe advertisers tell the truth only some of the time or never. Despite their negative global evaluations of advertisements, the children in the study said they enjoy them, especially advertisements featuring humour. Action was the second most preferred advertisement feature, with music third. Content and information ranked fourth and fifth.

Children particularly enjoy humour in advertising. This is further illustrated in a French study by Arnal et al. (1984–85). One hundred adolescents viewed 30 selected advertisements and indicated their perceptions of the humorousness of the ads and their reactions toward them. Perception of an advertisement as humorous was strongly related to the attraction that it had for the student.

Condry (1989) suggests that viewers may have negative attitudes towards advertisements if they interrupt the programme in progress, as they do in the US. Many viewers, Condry writes, see the advertisements as annoying and intrusive, though he cites no evidence to support this. The implication of such speculation is that if a particular advertisement persistently disrupts programme enjoyment, it may cause dislike of the brand being advertised.

Hite and Eck (1987) sent questionnaires to a national sample of 690 consumers and a national sample of 310 companies. There were significant differences in attitudes towards advertising. Consumers had more negative attitudes regarding advertising directed at children, and towards advertising in general, than did business respondents. The consumer respondents reported significantly greater agreement with statements that advertising to children stifles creativity, promotes materialism, and encourages poor nutritional habits. The respondents from manufacturing firms and from larger firms had a significantly more positive image of advertising to children and of advertising in general. They felt advertising is beneficial because it provides useful information on new products and that the advertising industry is decreasing the number of unfair and deceptive children's advertisements through self-regulation.

Summary and Conclusion

This chapter has examined research concerned with children's attention to, memory for and comprehension of advertising, with special reference to advertising on television. Before commercials can exert any influence over a child's consumer-related attitudes or behaviours, the child must first have processed the message contained in the advertisement to a sufficient degree. This information processing occurs in a number of stages. An advertisement must attract the young viewer's attention, and hold his or her attention long enough for the central message to get through. Attention on its own is not enough. A child must be able to differentiate the advertisement from surrounding material and comprehend what its message means. Finally, the message must be remembered after the advertisement has finished.

The following summary attempts to encapsulate the character of the principal stages of a child's processing of television advertising:

(1) *The child's attention to advertisements*
Here, the evidence is that 'attention' is a necessary but not sufficient requirement for having an effect, and that children's degrees of attention to advertisements depend on various characteristics of the message, the child and the viewing environment. Younger children especially like advertisements better than older children, while the latter were often found to exhibit a loss of attention when advertisements came on.

(2) *The child's ability to distinguish between advertisements and programmes*
A majority of six- to eight-year-old children have been found to distinguish advertisements from programmes, and by age 10 nearly all children can do so. Thus a child's awareness of advertisements as something distinctive can be enhanced by using separators between programmes and advertisements, provided these separators are clearly different from the programmes they precede or antecede. The use of popular cartoon characters in contrast has been found to lead to confusion, especially among younger children.

(3) *The child's ability to understand the purpose of the advertising*
In general, it has been found that most children of age eight have a moderate understanding of advertising intent. Younger children as well can under-

stand the intent of advertisements, but this will largely depend on influences exercised by their parents, peers, school and by their cumulative exposure to advertisements. Understanding commercial intent does seem to be important for developing 'cognitive defences' against advertisements, due to an increase in the child's scepticism towards the commercial message.

(4) *The child's interpretation of the content of the advertisement*

As far as truthfulness is concerned, some advertisements for toys and foods have been reportedly misleading for younger children, since the special visual and auditory techniques used require certain cognitive skills for evaluating the reliability of the message. Moreover, special efforts should be made to ensure that the commercial information is presented in a form which is comprehensible to younger children as well. Disclaimer messages can be effective, provided they are understood by children.

(5) *The child's memory for the advertisement*

The child's memory for a certain commercial is influenced by child-related factors (such as age, cognitive development), advertising-related factors (content, usual features, slogans, music, etc.), and external factors (such as the viewing environment).

6

Advertising and Children: Influences and Effects

Effects of Advertising

Despite many years of research by advertisers and social scientists, there is still no widely accepted model of the way advertising influences young consumers. Researchers have not yet succeeded in reaching a consensus on the effects of television advertising on children. Some believe that the effects of advertising can be quite strong, whereas others acknowledge only weak effects. Other researchers have recognized that the effects of television advertising can be complex, operating on certain levels, though not on others.

It is important to distinguish between different kinds of effects in establishing the power of advertising's influence. Advertising may operate to increase the young consumer's product awareness, attitudes towards a product, inclination to purchase, or purchase-request (of parents) behaviour. Thus, it is important to realize that the effect of an advertisement can be measured not only in terms of its impact upon purchase behaviour. Advertising can influence children's consumer-related knowledge, attitudes, values and most importantly their purchase. The latter effects may be quite distinct from purchase behaviour influences, and may occur in the absence of any behavioural impact of advertising. Effects can also be either intended or unintended.

When examining the relationship between television advertising and children's consumer-related perceptions, values and behaviour, some important problems have to be faced. First, it is very dangerous to conclude anything definitive about television advertising and children on the basis of some of the findings about the effect of television in general. The reason for this is that advertising is very clearly different from other programme categories and can simply not be treated in the same way. Consequently, conclusions about the effects of television content in general are by no means automatically valid for the effects of television advertisements.

Research suggests, for instance, that the same act on television (e.g. someone punching someone else in the face) will evoke different reactions when it occurs in a comedy than when it occurs in more serious programming. The reason for this is that the effects of negative emotions such as anger, fear, dread or disgust

137

will be diminished if contextual cues suggest that the context is unrealistic or not meant to be taken seriously. Moreover, negative actions that would be taken seriously and evoke negative reactions in everyday life, such as insults, aggression and accidents, are more likely to evoke humour when placed in a context that suggests the content is unrealistic or is not meant to be taken seriously (Dorr *et al.*, 1983).

Consequently, the same act will lead to different reactions when it occurs in more serious programming than when it occurs in a comedy, a cartoon or a televised commercial. This once again shows the ultimate importance of the child's ability to distinguish between the aims of commercials and programmes. All this indicates that it is quite dangerous to extend findings or theoretical models about the effects of television in general to the effects of television advertising.

Some authors have therefore tried to develop various specific theories about the precise nature of advertising effects on children (Adler *et al.*, 1980b). Most of them summarize their theoretical findings in various schemes, thus trying to represent the way in which television advertisements affect children (Kapferer, 1985). However, most of these theoretical models have only a small relevance for the practical question of what the effects of commercials on children are, however great their theoretical and scientific value may be. They usually provide an insight into the construction of the effect-process, but they do not reveal what these effects are, nor how strong they are.

Effects on knowledge, attitudes and values

Television advertising can have effects upon children, potentially, at a number of psychological levels. It may influence what children know about products and consumerism, their attitudes towards products and brands, or their consumer values. Advertising may also affect purchase behaviour. Before turning to the evidence concerning the latter subject, how does advertising impact upon children's consumer knowledge, attitudes and values?

Researchers who have studied this topic have produced varying and equivocal answers. Different investigations have revealed evidence of both strong and weak effects of television advertising. In some instances, there is a belief that advertising affects, in a direct sense, children's attitudes towards products: the more children see, the more positive their attitudes are likely to become. Elsewhere, a view has emerged that advertising's influences may operate more subtly upon wider consumer values.

Even if advertising produces favourable attitudes towards products, it does not automatically follow that this will lead to purchase behaviour on the part of children, or even to a predisposition to request purchases of parents. The relationships between attitudes and behaviour are complex and not consistent (Ajzen and Fishbein, 1980). The nature of the research has varied and produced varying results. A great deal of the research on advertising effects on children has used survey interviews and correlational analysis. Such methodology cannot prove cause–effect relationships, but merely demonstrates degrees of association between reported advertising exposure levels and reported product attitudes, purchase or purchase-request levels. Many correlational surveys indicate fairly weak relationships between reported advertising exposure and consumer-related attitudes (Goldberg, 1990).

The actual measures of advertising exposure also vary in their degree of specificity. Some survey researchers rely on broad-brush measures of reported commercial television viewing. Such 'mere exposure' of children to television has been found to exhibit degrees of positive association with children's level of familiarity of advertisements and perceived product attractiveness (Atkin, 1980).

A different, and empirically more sound, approach to the study of advertising effects is to manipulate children's exposure to specific advertising material under controlled circumstances. This has been done either in laboratory settings or in rather more naturalistic viewing environments. Gorn and Goldberg (1982) showed children aged between five and eight years a 30-minute video-taped cartoon containing advertisements for snack foods. Some children were shown advertisements for orange juice and various fruits each day for two weeks, while another group viewed advertisements for sugary food and drinks products. Each day, after viewing, the children were given a selection of fruits or confectionery as well as a sugared drink or natural orange juice. All this took place at a summer camp. The children's snack food and drinks choices tended to reflect the types of product advertising to which they had been exposed.

Elsewhere, however, advertising effects have largely failed to emerge, or if they do, to persist for only brief periods of time. For example, a German study (Haedrich et al., 1984) measured attitudinal and behavioural effects of television advertising on 306 children, 10 to 12 years old. After presentation of test products in television advertisements, no change in attitude could be detected, although a significant behavioural effect was found, 'but this was only for a brief period of time. After two to three hours, no further influence of the test products was observed on behaviour.' Despite these meagre findings, the authors still insisted that: 'Children can obviously be influenced in their behaviour by television. The fact that no attitudinal change was observed can be attributed to two factors: either it has to do with the test products as such . . . or the design of the test was not sensitive enough to measure attitude.'

Television advertisements for medicine have been found to play only a limited role in the formation of children's beliefs and attitudes toward medicines. The charge that OTC (over-the-counter, i.e. non-prescription) drug advertisements encourage excessive reliance on pills and create a pill-reliant syndrome (as suggested by Winick et al., 1973) is questionable (Milavsky, Pekowsky and Stipp, 1975).

In two experiments, eight- and nine-year-olds were relatively uninfluenced by a series of television advertisements. Butter et al. (1991) investigated the influence of advertisements for OTC medications upon children's choices. In the first experiment, 115 children aged eight and nine years were exposed to advertisements for six different OTC medicines or advertisements for other products. They were then asked to recommend either a medicine or non-medicine remedy for a child and an adult with various illnesses or problems. The OTC medicine advertisements appeared to influence their recommendations only with respect to use of sleeping pills, but not for the other five products. In another experiment, 234 children in the same age range were exposed either to fever and cold medicine advertisements intended for a child audience, or to non-drug advertisements. Only the fever medicine advertisements appeared to influence the children. In both experiments, the effects of advertisements were specific to particular products.

Rossano and Butter (1987) conducted two experiments of television drug advertisements and children's attitudes concerning medication. The studies examined whether direct exposure to television drug advertisements would affect the attitudes of 8- to 12-year-old children. Attitudes toward drug use were assessed by means of questionnaires. No influence of advertisements was detected in either experiment.

Do attitudes towards advertisements in general predict attitudes toward specific commercials or products? Riecken and Yavas (1990) reasoned that if children's attitudes toward different advertisements vary, this argues against the notion that children are indiscriminate in accepting and reacting to advertisements. The researchers believed that such differential responses argue against a uniform ban on children's advertising. More than 150 children aged 8 to 12 participated in a before–after experiment. Children's attitudes toward television advertisements were assessed using a measure developed by Rossiter (1980). The child indicates how much he or she agrees with statements such as 'Television commercials tell the truth', 'Television commercials try to make people buy things they don't really need', and 'I like most television commercials'. Three product categories were studied: cereals, OTC drugs, and toys, as well as specific products within each category.

Surprisingly, Riecken and Yavas found that children held negative opinions about advertisements and in a majority of cases questioned whether or not they were telling the truth. Furthermore, children did not always believe that advertised products represented the best buys. Advertisements were regarded as giving an excessively rosy impression about products, which ought not to be taken at face value.

Children's overall attitudes toward advertisements in general, and toward OTC drug, cereal and toy commercials were different. Attitudes toward toy advertisements were less negative than toward other product advertisements. 'Based on the overall results, covering eight brands across three product categories, the conclusion is that the attitudes children hold toward television commercials for a particular product category are not indicative of how they will evaluate brands within that category . . . The children expressed generally negative views of advertisements; they may, however, deem brands advertised in a positive, negative, or uncertain manner ... Children's reactions to specific product advertisements are not shaped by their pre-existing attitudes towards commercials in general ... Children's attitudes toward specific product advertisements do not have any bearing on brand attitudes' (Riecken and Yavas, p. 144).

Behavioural effects of food advertising

A number of researchers have investigated the impact of televised advertisements on children's food consumption. There has been a degree of concern over the impact of advertising for certain kinds of food products upon the health of children. In particular, concern has centred on advertising for sweets and snack foods, excessive consumption of which has been linked to weight problems, heart disease and dental cavities. Critics of television advertising for these products have pointed to the frequency with which such advertising occurs, especially at times when large numbers of children are known to be watching television (e.g. Dibbs, 1993).

The issue has been studied using survey and experimental methodologies. The surveys frequently employ insufficiently robust measures of advertising exposure and food consumption, however, while the experimental studies often lack ecological validity. Despite their ability to exert close control over exposure and consumption variables, experiments conducted under contrived circumstances may reveal little about how children actually behave in everyday life. It is worth taking a closer look at some of the evidence nevertheless in order to get an impression of the how this subject has been studied.

Gorn and Goldberg were interested in the behavioural effects of television advertising on children. They conducted a series of studies during the late 1970s and early 1980s to investigate this issue. The paradigm they typically adopted involved showing children a television programme with advertisements edited in. The children were then given an opportunity to choose from a range of alternative brands, the one they would most like to consume. The advertised brand was of course among the choices offered.

Goldberg et al. (1987) used this paradigm of choosing from a mixed set of alternative brands with five- and six-year-old children and found that short-term snack and breakfast food preferences tended to reflect their exposure experience. Children were more likely to select highly sugared foods if they had previously viewed television commercials for such products and they were more likely to choose nutritious snack and breakfast foods if they had just seen pro-nutrition public service announcements. There must be doubts about the ecological validity of such studies in that they do not reflect real life experience, but they nevertheless demonstrate the kind of impact certain experimental stimuli can have on children.

Gorn and Goldberg (1980) were interested in the effects of repeating the same commercial to children and recorded several videotapes, some of which repeated the same commercial (a new brand of ice cream) at intervals in a half-hour cartoon programme. The study was conducted with children aged 8 and 10 years. The child's brand choice was assessed from a range of ice creams including the advertised brand, and actual consumption behaviour was measured by allowing the child to eat the chosen brand and, afterwards, weighing what was left. Exposure to a television advertisement for the brand influenced choice of that brand in the expected direction and there was also evidence that exposure to more than one advertisement for that brand increased the probability that the brand would be chosen from the array of different brands of ice cream at the end. There was no effect on actual consumption behaviour, though.

Gorn and Goldberg (1982) reported another study conducted in field conditions (summer camp) with children aged five to eight years. Their exposure to television advertisements was manipulated during brief permitted spells of television viewing at camp. Brands of drink or snack foods that were advertised to the children proved to be the ones they most often chose and consumed from a range made available to them a short time after viewing.

Galst (1980) presented 65 children between three and seven years of age with videotapes of cartoon programmes. These were recorded with different combinations of food commercials and/or pro-nutritional public service announcements edited in. Each child selected a drink and a food from a range of snacks after viewing. The difference with this study was that children viewed and chose each day for four weeks. In addition, one condition was the presence or absence of comments from an adult after the advertisement, these comments being designed to promote a pro-nutritional message. Although there was a tendency for children to select sugared snacks in any case, Galst found that the most effective combination for reducing the children's selection of snacks with added sugar was the presentation of commercials for food products without added sugar together with pro-nutritional PSAs with accompanying evaluative comments by an adult co-viewer. Mere exposure to any television presentation, however, did not influence the children to select sugared snacks with greater frequency. This study is important because of the medium-term time scale used. Whereas some of the short-term 'view and choose' studies seem to demonstrate a choice that is a direct function of what the child has previously seen advertised, this medium-term piece of research would suggest that reducing sugared-snack consumption requires a high level of counter-propaganda from more than one source.

In an attempt to evaluate the relative effectiveness of different kinds of appeals in advertisements, Cantor (1981) placed either a humorous or a serious television advertisement for oranges just before a commercial for either a sweet dessert or a toy. These were embedded in a videotape of a children's programme and shown to 37 children aged from three to nine years, at a child-care centre. The behavioural measure was an index of the frequency of choosing a fruit or sweet at lunch over a week. The results were not completely conclusive but suggested that a serious advertisement for good nutrition would be more effective than a humorous one, at least in the absence of an immediately subsequent counter-advertisement (the advert for the sweet dessert).

Stoneman and Brody (1982) introduced another variable into the experimental literature looking at the effects of television advertising on food-choice behaviour. They ingeniously simulated peer pressure on behaviour by getting children (peers) to indicate to other children (experimental subjects) which one out of an array of foods they (peers) preferred. The peer would stand in front of a group of experimental subjects and point to the food he or she liked on a projected slide of a selection of foods. Unknown to the experimental subjects, their peers had been told to choose a category of food (salty snacks) by the experimenter. Using a similar experimental paradigm to other researchers in this area, that is, a variety of treatment conditions followed by a food choice task, they found that the effect of peer group influence and television advertising influence was additive, that one reinforced the other.

Dawson *et al.* (1985) were interested in the role of television advertisements in influencing the ability of the child to delay gratification. Delaying gratification is waiting before acting to obtain a desired goal rather than immediately going through a 'want–act–get' sequence. Television advertisements for sugared foods provide an immediate temptation to the child. How will this affect the young consumer? In this study, six-year-olds were shown a television advertisement for a breakfast cereal. A game was devised which involved the child waiting for a while and getting a non-preferred reward. This game was designed to simulate delay of gratification and the measure would be the length of time the child could wait for the desired reward. It was found that in the presence of a television advertisement the child would wait longer. Children with the food in front of them and no television to distract them waited a relatively shorter time. The researchers concluded that many television advertisements provide distraction and that the child can generate 'fun thoughts' that help their delaying. In other words, the television advertisement, although it presents a brand in an attractive and tempting light, can function by delaying gratification in that the entertainment provided by the advertisement can block and distract thoughts about eating.

Factors influencing advertising effects

When trying to assess the precise nature of the effect of television advertising on children's knowledge, attitudes and values, it is important to realize that, first, the actual effects of TV advertisements on children will largely vary according to a number of mediating factors that operate in direct relationship to the advertisements (such as level of exposure, repetition, and child's age) and that, secondly, apart from advertising there are many other factors that affect and shape a child's knowledge, attitudes and values, which are entirely unrelated to advertising. Consequently, we are faced with the problem that it is practically impossible to disentangle the impact of advertising from that of other relevant factors.

As far as the actual effects of a television advertisement on children are concerned, the most important factor is undoubtedly the nature of the advertisement itself, and the way in which children process the information in this advertisement.

Many researchers, however, do emphasize that a number of mediating factors are operative in the process of influencing. Most studies refer to three such factors: the role of advertising exposure levels; dispositional factors associated with the child's age; and the role of the parents, especially their social class and educational background (Robertson and Rossiter, 1977).

Advertising exposure levels and effects

Are the degrees of exposure to advertisements in general or the repetition of a single advertisement in specific important in the effects an advertisement has on children? Research on this matter does not reach a consensus. Some studies suggest that the repetition of an advertisement has no effect at all (Gorn *et al.*, 1977). Other research works indicate that repetition usually has a negative influence on an advertisement's effect, since increasing exposure may produce a negative attitude and hence decrease results (Kinsey, 1987). We should, however, draw attention to an earlier conclusion that for younger children (approximately until age seven), repetition by no means led to a negative attitude, but was a source of pleasure through recognition. This again indicates that the child's age should certainly be taken into account when assessing the effects exercised by television advertising.

Most researchers, however, do find a positive relationship between the amount of exposure to advertisements and the degree of effect exercised by them (Joossens, 1984; Kinsey, 1987). One of the reasons for this is that high levels of exposure and repetition lead to an increase in the child's memory for advertisements, which can be important when assessing long-term effects. It should be said, however, that a high level of memory by no means automatically implies a high effect: it has been reported that children can literally repeat a certain advertisement by heart without their knowledge, values or attitudes being affected by it.

Moreover, most researchers also indicate that, even though there seems to be a relationship between the exposure to advertising and the degree to which children's knowledge and attitudes are influenced, it is by no means sure that television advertising alone is responsible for these effects (Young, 1990). One reason for the differences in attitudes, knowledge and values found with children that were exposed to a greater amount of advertisements could be a result of differences in social class (Goldberg, 1990; Kapferer, 1985).

The child's age

If the effects of television advertising on the child's knowledge, attitudes and values are studied, it is often suggested that younger children are more susceptible to the effects of television advertising than older children. Various explanations are provided to prove this thesis. Older children have greater cognitive skills, which result in a growing understanding of the advertiser's commercial intent and of the content of the commercial. Consequently, older children will more often use an entire apparatus of cognitive defence against the commercial, often resulting in negative attitudes such as cynicism and distrust towards the advertisement. Research therefore indicates that, in the USA at least, older children have less favourable attitudes towards television commercials than younger children (Young, 1990). Since attitudes such as distrust and cynicism are considered to be effective neutralizers of the commercials' effects on knowledge, attitudes and values, most researchers do suggest that television advertising effects on younger children are more important than on older children.

Parent's educational background/social class
An important role in the effects of television advertisements on a child's knowledge, attitudes and values is played by his or her parents, who are partly influenced by their educational background and the social class to which they belong. This influence by parents is exercised both in an indirect and in a direct way. Indirectly, parents mediate the effects of television advertising by influencing the overall viewing environment in which the interaction between the child and television advertisements takes place. Most research studies, for instance, link parents from lower social classes to higher amounts of television exposure and higher exposure to advertisements for their children (Goldberg, 1990).

Parents, however, also exercise a direct influence on the effect of television advertisements for children by directly providing comment on television advertisements. Parental intervention is sometimes considered to be the most effective tool in the management of television's influence on children and young people (Donohue and Meyer, 1984). The reason for this is that children and television advertising usually function in a social and familial context. This context, provided mainly by the child's parents, influences what messages children take away from television, how they use the medium, and how literate they are as television viewers. Much of the time and in many ways, parents (and others) can influence the messages children take away from television (Dorr, 1986).

In practice, this means that the effects that television advertisements for children's products (such as toys, sweets, breakfast cereals, etc.) have on children's knowledge, attitudes and values (e.g. about nutritional standards) can be largely influenced by the parent's verbal comments on these advertisements. Moreover, this parental mediation will also play an important part in the way advertisements influence children's purchase behaviour or purchase-request behaviour (See chapter 2).

Many studies suggest that it is the parent's moral judgement, their explanations about and their comments on the issues presented in television advertisements which play a mediating role in the effects of advertisements on children's long term values (Robertson, 1979). These parental comments can either be direct or indirect (Messaris and Sarett, 1982). Research also suggests that these parental comments are positively related to the parents' educational backgrounds: the higher their education, the more often parents will be found to mediate the effects of televised advertisements by commenting on it.

Parental interaction with children about television advertising and its effects can take place either when children are or are not watching advertisements. Some researchers hereby draw attention to the fact that, especially for young children, parental mediation will have optimal results when parental comments are given during the actual watching of the advertisements (Dorr, Kovaric and Doubleday, 1989). The reason for this is that in this situation, parents can be certain what the child is watching, help them to understand the medium and its content, encourage them to accept only those messages which the parents endorse, intervene immediately should there be desirable or undesirable content, and gain first-hand knowledge of children's reactions to the medium and its content (Dorr et al., 1989).

However, although most researchers agree that parents can play an important role as responsible mediators of children's interactions with television, the literature provides little empirical support for this image of parents. Even though some surveys found relatively high levels of co-viewing, for instance, most surveys that tried to measure the amount of co-viewing between parents and children found that the actual amount of parent–child co-viewing is less than estimated by the published literature, and is, in fact, quite low.

Carlens (1990) reported a survey which found that parent–child co-viewing was usually more frequent with older than with younger children, since the older children's tastes will be more similar to those of their parents. This also suggests that, when co-viewing, parents do not usually do this out of concern or in order to mediate television influences. One should not conclude that levels of co-viewing are automatically related to parental interaction. This is also illustrated when children and parents from lower social classes are examined: levels of co-viewing between parents and children are reportedly higher than in other classes, with levels of parental interaction being reportedly lower (Desmond et al., 1990).

All these research findings illustrate that parents can play an important role in mediating the effects of television advertisements on children's knowledge, attitudes and values, but that, at present, it is doubtful whether the majority of parents do realize this responsibility and effectively make use of it. It is also suggested that although the importance of the parental role in this matter is vital, advertisers should not deny all responsibility but contribute to this parent–child relationship in a constructive manner (Bovee and Arens, 1989).

Purchase behaviour of children

If the effect of television advertising is seen as a series of processes that can be arranged in a certain order, then the end of the line is *doing* something. Very often, researchers are therefore interested in the question of whether or not advertising causes children to actually 'buy more sugared sweets, spend too much money, or buy toys they don't really need' (Young, 1990). Some commentators notice that 'this is the kind of common-sense question asked of researchers and they will get short shrift if they answer that they don't really know or that it all depends on what you mean by . . . ' (Young, 1990, p. 147).

Of more concern, however, are research findings concerning the influence of television advertisements on children's consumption and purchase behaviour. Children themselves, of course, usually have only a very limited amount of money at their disposal, which they can use for purchasing snacks or inexpensive toys. Most purchases for children are made by the parents, though this is changing as children acquire more personal disposable income.

It is difficult to suggest anything conclusive about the actual influence of advertisements on children's own purchase behaviour. It was noted earlier how most researchers encountered important difficulties when trying to assess the effect of commercials on children's knowledge and attitudes. Measuring the impact of advertisements on children's purchase behaviour seems even more difficult, since there can easily be a huge gap between attitude and behaviour. Moreover, the indeterminacy of decision making and the many other influences exercised by the social world all pose difficult problems. Finally, many detailed advertising studies about the effectiveness of certain advertising campaigns directed at children are never made public, which keeps away some very interesting data from most scholars. As a result of all this, the problems which arise when assessing the effect on children's purchase behaviour seem nearly insurmountable.

However, this issue is too important to be evaded. Many research studies have therefore tried to provide an answer to the question of the effects of TV advertising on children's purchase behaviour. Most of the studies on this topic actually belong to one of the two largely different research categories: 'experimental research' or 'survey research'. The research method used can be an important indicator as to the results presented by the studies. Studies that can be described as 'experimental' usually support the view that the effects of commercials on children are considerable, whereas survey research studies have more usually reported that these effects operate ultimately at a low level.

Experimental research

Faced with the enormous problems of the complexity and amount of other intervening factors, many researchers chose, for various kinds of experimental situations, to study the effects of television advertising on children's purchase behaviour. In most experiments, children were shown several advertisements, usually for different sorts of toys or snacks. After being exposed to these advertisements, children were invited to select a snack or toy out of a range of various presents. On the basis of these choices, research findings were formulated.

The most important drawbacks of this kind of research are that: (1) it does not actually examine children's *purchase* behaviour, but only deals with the child's choice out of a number of prizes which are offered as a free gift; (2) the effects that are measured are short-term effects, since the "choosing phase" usually took place immediately after exposure; (3) it does not explore any of the processes that mediate between watching and doing; and (4) it does not simulate the social activities of watching advertisements and consuming. Thus, this kind of research has only a limited external validity. Consequently, it is sometimes criticized as being 'naive' for not simulating what goes on in the real world (Young, 1990).

The strength of this kind of research, however, is that it has the ability to assess causality unequivocally (Goldberg, 1990). That is, unlike correlational studies, causal factors can be established. Consequently, although it is unlikely that the experimental procedure used in this approach has much external validity, these studies are important since they can tell us something about the relative effectiveness of various stimulus presentations.

The results found by experimental research generally supported the view that children's television advertising has a considerable influence on children's choice behaviour. Some researchers reported that children were more likely to select highly sugared foods if they had previously seen TV commercials for this, but were likely to choose a nutritious snack instead if they had just seen pro-nutrition Public Service Announcements (PSAs) (Goldberg *et al.*, 1987). Similar experiments have been done with toy commercials of various brands, and results were similar (Ross *et al.*, 1984), with some researchers even commenting that 'toy commercials can be more persuasive than the child's mother' (Prasad *et al.*, 1978).

In summary, most of the experimental studies do provide evidence that exposure to television commercials for particular products (especially sugared snacks and toys) have an immediate short-term influence on the child's choice behaviour. Given the limited external validity of this kind of research, this does not tell us very much about how children make up their minds to pick and choose in a supermarket or shop as a consequence of having seen advertisements on television.

However, some studies in this field yield certain findings which could tell us something about the 'real' world as well, especially as far as age differences are concerned. In one research study, it was found that children aged nine based their choice of a 'prize' they could take home on an evaluation of the advertised product rather than on a comparison of the various alternatives (Roedder *et al.*, 1983). Children aged 13, on the other hand, were found to weigh up all the alternatives before deciding which prize to choose. The researchers noticed however that when the range of alternatives was reduced, younger children too were less influenced by recent advertising when selecting a prize and relied on their original preference instead (i.e. the preference they had before exposure to advertisements). From this it was concluded that young children's abilities of comparison and evaluation can be overtaxed when the range of alternatives is increased or when the various alternatives are equally valued (Roedder *et al.*, 1983).

These findings may be relevant for the child's real-life experiences on the matter, since the wide range of equally valued alternatives might correspond to a cluttered market place where there are many quite similar products (e.g. all the different kinds of largely similar toy guns, race cars or computer games available at stores or supermarkets). Consequently, under these circumstances, the most likely determinant of choice may be an 'advertisement', which is presumably the most salient advertisement for an available brand retrieved from memory, rather than the most recent television advertisement or promotion seen or heard.

Survey research

In contrast to the experimental research, many researchers used a survey research to study the effects of advertising on children's purchase behaviour (Goldberg, 1990). Most research studies that follow this approach emphasize that television advertising is only one of a large amount of simultaneously interacting influences on children's purchase behaviour. Consequently, they usually conclude that television commercials have but a fairly minor role in influencing children's purchase behaviour.

What is positive about this method of research is that the external validity usually tends to be high, particularly given the broad range of potential influences considered. That is these studies look at everyday behaviour, not behaviour under laboratory conditions. The weakness of this survey research method, however, lies in the difficulty of attributing causality, because assessing the direction of causality on the basis of correlational evidence is often difficult (e.g. does viewing more television advertisements for toys lead to wanting more toys or vice versa?).

Survey research studies usually claim that consumer choices actually result from a complex mix of various factors, including the consumer's cognitive skills, information on show at the time, social pressure and experience (Ross *et al.*, 1984). They stress that, quite often, effects from television advertisements on children's purchase behaviour will be mediated by communication within the family (including parent–child communication) or within larger social groups (e.g. child's peer group) (Moore, 1990), and by many other factors, such as the actual size and appearance of the package of the product (Young, 1990).

A product that is unnacceptable to parents may not be taken up by the child, and there have been many examples of products (such as new sweets or chocolate bars) which failed to find a respectable child market despite being heavily advertised to children (Smith and Sweeney, 1984). What the child thinks about a product in his or her own right is also a significant factor. The product itself will have to provide the necessary reasons for the child to buy it again. Otherwise, if the product in one way or another does not fully meet the child's expectations, it will not be bought a second time, regardless of the total amount of advertisements trying to persuade the child to do so (Schneider, 1987). This seems to be one of the reasons why, in the US, even a candy bar with Reggie Jackson's name on it at the peak of his baseball career did not make it across the candy counters, or why Procter and Gamble, despite a huge advertising campaign, did not succeed in launching Pringles, a new potato chip of which children were to be the major consumers (Schneider, 1987). Since there are so many other factors, a conclusion which is often drawn from this is that advertising does not dominate children's choices (Wolfe, 1990).

Conflicting conclusions can be derived from the above findings which suggest, on the one hand, that advertising does not significantly influence children's product choices, and, on the other hand, that children's product preferences can be moulded by advertising. However, when looking into the matter more carefully, it seems that these two conclusions are not so irreconcilable as might first be thought since both are based on similar facts. The problem is that although they are both correct, they each represent only part of the truth.

The finding that advertising 'clearly does not dominate children's choices' corresponds with a large number of empirical data which have been collected through survey research and which indicate that advertising in general, and television advertising in particular, is but one of a large variety of influences that play a role in the child's decision-making process. The other factors include what the child experiences in the shop itself, the comments made by peers and parents about the product in question, and many other sources (including catalogues).

A large number of studies have tried to assess the role of the various influencing factors. Although the exact percentages differ slightly from study to study, the overall importance of the various sources of effect are quite the same in all the studies examined.

A survey by De Bens and Vandenbruane (1992) also reported that TV advertising was one of the children's criteria for choosing toys, but that other factors were reportedly more influential. This was especially the case as far as brochures, the child's friends, and the child's direct experience with the toy in the shop were concerned.

These researchers found that television advertising is only one out of a number of influencing factors, and, as such, it can hardly be accused of 'dominating children's choices'. On the other hand, this evidence also shows that, indeed, advertising is an important influence in the child's decision-making process, but that it is by no means the only one. Consequently, the statement that 'children clearly form preferences for playthings dependent on toy advertising' also presents part of the truth. The statement is incomplete, however, in that it does not mention that there are other influencing factors as well.

The above findings again clearly illustrate the sometimes biased presentation of certain findings. Both presentations actually started from the same observations, each formulating conclusions in such a way as to illustrate some biased preconceptions. The result of such an approach is that when examining the research material available one too often gets the impression that nothing conclusive can ever be achieved because of the contradictory findings. If, however, the research data themselves are examined, one finds that many research conclusions which at first seemed quite contradictory turn out to be quite reconcilable.

When this is applied to the issue of television advertisements and their effects on children's purchase behaviour, we can reconcile the findings suggested by the experimental research with those offered by the survey research, concluding that: (1) television advertisements play an important role in the child's purchase behaviour, but (2) there are many other factors which have an equally or even more important influence in this matter.

research prov. by

Balance f.

C

Quasi-experimental research

In order to avoid some of the drawbacks of the two previous research methods, a number of researches have tried to follow a 'quasi-experimental' approach. This method actually combines the two other approaches by inducing the experimentalist to consider the broader network of variables operating in the environment, and by inducing the survey researcher to recognize the shortcomings of the correlational method as a basis for establishing causal relationship. In particular, the quasi-experimental research method allows for the determination of causal relationship (as in the laboratory experiment), but in a broader real-world context (as in survey research) (Goldberg, 1990).

An interesting quasi-experimental research study was conducted by Goldberg (1990), who examined a group of French-speaking and a group of English-speaking children in Montreal. He described how, as a result of a Quebec law eliminating advertising to children on Quebec stations, the only source of television commercials for toys and children's cereals became American border TV stations. The fact that English-speaking children in Montreal watched more children's TV on these American stations than did French-speaking children provided an ideal situation for a comparative analysis between the two groups. Goldberg reported that English-speaking children were able to recognize significantly more toys available in the marketplace and that they had more children's cereals in their homes than did French-speaking children.

These differences, however, cannot be attributed to the influence of television advertisements alone. Goldberg's data showed that there were already important differences between the toy awareness of English- and French-speaking children regardless of the hours of American children's television viewed. Similarly, there were also differences between the two groups of children concerning the amount of children's cereals that were purchased, even if the number of hours of American television which were watched remained the same. Other factors, such as cultural environment, may have also contributed to the observed differences between the two groups.

On analysing the results within the same language groups, it was found that increasing exposure to American children's television (and, consequently, increasing exposure to children's commercials) was indeed associated with increasing levels of toy awareness and amount of cereals purchased. Higher scores were gained by the English-speaking children, who watched more American television than their French counterparts.

Goldberg (1990) concluded from all this that 'the Quebec law served to reduce children's exposure to commercials for sugared products and hence appears to have reduced consumptions of those cereals' (p. 453), and that 'there is no reason to believe that comparable legislation in the US would not have comparable results'. As far as toys are concerned, he concludes that 'the expectation was that reduced exposure to commercials would leave children unaware of the toys and thus less able to pressure their parents to buy them', and that 'the law seems to have been effective in this context' (p. 453).

However, it should be pointed out that:

(1) Although it has been firmly established that higher exposure to American TV (advertisements) is associated with higher numbers of cereals purchased, it is by no means sure that TV is the cause.

It could be that children who view more television advertisements buy more cereals, but, vice versa, it can well be that children who buy more cereals also will watch more television.

Moreover, an important explanation for the differences between English- and French-speaking children can be that they simply have different eating traditions. Whereas English-speaking Canadian children eat more cereals (as American or English children do), French-speaking Canadian children reportedly prefer other breakfast foods (such as bread or croissants, as French children tend to do).

(2) It is quite surprising to find that a greater awareness of toys is directly associated with a greater pressure on the child's parents to buy these toys. Although awareness of a toy will certainly be a prerequisite for purchase-request behaviour, one can hardly argue that the mere awareness of a product (regardless of the attitudes towards it!) directly leads to a purchase request for that product. On the contrary, from the perspective of consumer socialization, a greater awareness of the various toys available on the market may be interpreted as a positive fact, since this will enable the child to compare the advantages and disadvantages of various products and, consequently, make a better choice when being confronted with the enormous amount of toys that are present in shops and supermarkets.

We have tried to illustrate by this Goldberg study that even 'quasi-experimental' studies by no means provide the 'ideal' research method for analysing the complex issue of the impact of television advertising on children's purchase behaviour.

Summary and Conclusions

The effects of television advertising on children are neither uniform nor do they occur at a single psychological level. In examining the research evidence, this chapter has found that television advertising can influence children's knowledge, attitudes and values. It can also impinge upon consumer-related behaviours, whether these take the form of a child's own purchases or of a child pestering others (most notably parents) to make purchases on his or her behalf.

In connection with effects on knowledge, attitudes and values, a difficult problem facing researchers is to disentangle the impact of television advertising from that of other relevant factors. A number of interesting and fairly consistent findings have nevertheless emerged. Television advertisements have more effects on younger than on older children. Television advertisements can have an effect on the child's consumer socialization, nutritional awareness, degrees of materialism and other matters.

Turning to the effects of television advertisements on children's purchase and consumption behaviour, principal findings include:

- Children's advertising indeed has an effect on the child's purchase and consumption behaviour, but this effect is by no means the only effect since many other factors intervene (e.g. parents, peers, social situations).
- The influence of television advertisements on children's consumption behaviour is not greater than that of other factors.

In respect of the influence of television advertisements on children's purchase-request behaviour, evidence has emerged that:

- Television advertising increases children's purchase-request behaviour.
- The amount of children's purchase requests also differs importantly according to other variables, including age, socioeconomic level, parental education, cultural background, product category and peer integration.
- Consequently, television advertising is not the only influencing factor in children's purchase-request behaviour, nor is it the most important one.
- Parental denial of children's purchase requests can in some cases lead to increased tensions and parent–child conflict.

The above findings illustrate that television advertisements indeed have effects on children, but that there are many other factors (such as parents, or real-life experiences) that have an even stronger effect on children, and that play an important mediating role between TV advertising and children's purchase and consumption behaviour.

As a result of this, the precise influence of an advertisement on a child will vary from child to child, and from advertisement to advertisement. It has been shown, however, that *younger children* and *children from lower social classes* are more susceptible to the influence of television advertisements than other children.

Various suggestions have been made in order to protect children against certain influences of television advertising. Our research findings yielded no evidence to support the suggestion of a *ban* on television advertising for children, which is the 'protection' offered in some countries. The influence exerted upon children by television advertising is by no means greater than the influence by other factors; consequently, there is no scientific reason why there should be a complete ban on one factor influencing children's consumption behaviour, while other factors continue to influence the child—sometimes in an even stronger way. Moreover, a ban on television advertising for children could have negative effects since this deprives children of an important consumer-learning facility, and could also lead to an increase in other forms of advertising influence, including sponsorship and product placement.

Most researchers therefore suggest that 'education' is better than censorship. Children should be helped and guided in their interaction with television advertisements. *Parental guidance* and *public education* should play an important role in preparing children to cope with the kind of society in which they will have to live. In practice, children could be taught about television advertising, its intent and function, and this by parents, teachers and all kinds of consumer training programmes. Advertisers should also contribute to this by ensuring special care and attention as far as certain products aimed at young children are concerned.

In conclusion, most researchers also suggest that while children are still in the process of learning, society should provide the necessary laws to protect them. Whether these laws and restrictions should be imposed by governments or be adopted as self-regulating codes by advertising agencies themselves is a matter which is open to public debate.

7

Reaching Child Consumers

The preceding chapters have established that there is a young consumers' market comprising teenage and pre-teenage children. This market segment is a heterogeneous one in terms of demographic and psychological character, and in respect of purchase patterns. Children can, as consumers, also be distinguished in terms of the developmental stage they have reached. Young consumers are responsive to advertising, but the nature of this behaviour also changes as children mature.

As a potential market, children pose a challenge to marketers because they represent a market which is far from static. Traditionally, much advertising aimed at children has attempted to get them to influence the purchase of their parents. Increasingly these days marketers are devoting their attention directly to children themselves as consumers. Reflecting this shift of emphasis, even department stores and supermarkets are placing products that appeal to children at lower shelf levels for the convenience of these shorter consumers.

Manufacturers have been quick to recognize the potential of the child market and have provided it with a wide array of products ranging from fashions to sweets. These same manufacturers have heavily promoted these products directly to children via television programmes for children, comic books, product packages and other media. Producers of children's products have even entered the school environment in order to promote the goods. They give teachers such items as pencils and books which are then passed on to the children. In some cases manufacturers are even furnishing books containing advertisements of their products.

Marketing to children is not without its problems, however. To some parents the idea of selling to children conjures up visions of exploitation of the innocent. In the next chapter, we consider issues relating to the protection of young consumers.

Reaching young consumers effectively requires accurate knowledge about where they obtain their information about consumer matters. As earlier chapters have shown, children and teenagers utilize a variety of information sources to guide their product and brand choices. Members of their own family and friends and peer groups are among the most significant influences. Knowing that this is the case might suggest that by influencing these opinion-formers, young consumers can be reached indirectly. In addition to these interpersonal sources of information and advice, however, young consumers turn to various mass media for consumer-related information. Advertising on television and radio, at the cinema, in newspapers, magazines, and on posters and billboards all play a part. Depictions of role models in non-advertising media contexts (in television programmes or magazine articles) can also have an influence. Where media influences are concerned, it is important for retailers to know which media are predominantly used by different sections of the young consumer market. It may also be the case that some media are more significant than others in relation to particular types of products. This understanding of the young persons' market comes through research. Research findings can then be used to guide effective promotional or marketing campaigns, product placement and packaging.

Indications from research have suggested that some retailers are more young-person oriented than others. McNeal (1992) described a survey of retailers in the United States which was designed to find out how child-oriented they were in their retailing practices. Rather than sending out a questionnaire he sent a letter to the Chief Executive or Chief Operating Officers of 176 American retailers. The letter posed a number of open-ended questions about retailing arrangements for children. Ten broad categories of retailer were surveyed: department stores, variety stores, convenience stores and discounters, restaurants, drugstores, apparel stores, hotels/motels, and other (specialty) stores. Although there was a low response rate of only 35 per cent, this survey nevertheless provides some interesting evidence about retailers' attitudes towards this target group.

The survey found that 68 per cent of respondent stores were child-oriented in 1991 compared with 37 per cent in an earlier survey reported in 1984. A company was judged to be child-oriented if it stated it had one or more policies or practices targeted to children as potential customers. The improved attitude towards children was not restricted to particular retail categories. Nine out of the ten categories of retailer surveyed exhibited a higher rate of child-orientation in 1991 than in 1984.

There were a number of specific aspects of retailing which addressed the needs of children. First, the presence of shopping or buying facilitators had become more widespread. This means that more retailers acknowledged children as special customers who require special assistance. This might take the form of eye-level displays and fixtures, smaller (child-sized shopping carts, children's menus, and bicycle racks). Second, more retailers were targeting some kind of promotion aimed specifically at children, in the form of in-store promotions or media advertising. Third, there had been an increase in store personnel training for purposes of assisting children. Fourth, a growth in ethical practices was observed which were designed with children in mind. These included keeping dangerous products and sexually oriented magazines out of children's reach.

McNeal (1992) concluded that retailing practices for children have improved in the USA. Children are increasingly included in retailers' marketing strategies. Some retailers treat children as a market in their own right, with their own purchasing power and own product tastes. Others regard them as a secondary influence upon the primary purchasers—namely parents. Yet other retailers see children as an adult market of the future.

Despite these promising signs, it was clear from even McNeal's limited survey that not all retailers regard children as a significant market in any of these respects. McNeal found that drugstores did not perceive children to be a segment of any importance to them either as a current primary or secondary consumer market or a market of the future. Retailers have not made a complete set of positive steps. While promotions aimed at young consumers have increased, there has been no equivalent increase in the amount of in-store staff training, nor in the level of consumer education or critical practices designed to protect children.

Reaching young consumers—teens and pre-teens—effectively means knowing about the way this market segment thinks and feels. It comprises an understanding of how best to communicate to young people when producing advertising and promotional campaigns for them, and how best to obtain information from them about what they need and desire. Although marketers and retailers often believe they know their target markets, where children and teenagers are concerned this is frequently not the case.

Researching Young Consumers

One of the problems facing marketers is that the children's market is far from homogeneous. It is segregated by age, gender and other demographic factors which, unfortunately, create a vicious circle. Children are becoming adept at 'reading' marketing and advertising campaign objectives. A cardinal sin appears to be to position a product towards anyone younger than the oldest of the target market. Products will frequently spiral downwards in terms of age appeal after holding cachet for the older children. The young children see older ones using the product and want to be there too. But when older children see younger ones with what used to be 'their' product, its appeal plummets. Often, a break will be needed before the cycle can be restarted.

There are certain rules within children's research that are worth bearing in mind. They need to be interviewed in specific age groups preferably among children from the same age year, otherwise older children will tend to dominate younger children when placed in the same interview groups. Some specialists in children's market research recommend that boys and girls should be interviewed separately. Each gender may have distinctive views about consumer and related issues and may respond differently in group situations. Girls will tend to work more co-operatively in discussing a topic, while boys tend to be more competitive and want their own opinions to be heard. Changes in self-perceptions among the genders is another reason for keeping them separate. Changes in self-perceptions among the genders can also create problems for mixed-gender focus groups, although do not necessarily count as a legitimate reason for keeping boys and girls separate.

Research techniques have to be tailored to the age groups being interviewed. The younger the children, the less able they are to rely on verbal skills to explain what they mean and certain projective tools do become valuable. However, there us a fine line to be drawn here. Children already 'inhabit' a rich fantasy world and their imaginations can extend the original idea in unforeseen directions. Role playing has to be used with caution, therefore, since you could end up with a room full of hyperactive children.

Consumer researchers (e.g. Ward and Wackman, 1973; Ward, Wackman and Wartella, 1977; Wartella and Ettema, 1974) have demonstrated that cognitive development and related information processing skills are important considerations in designing marketing strategies to define which children are a target market. Children use more and different kinds of information in purchase decision making as they grow older (Ward *et al.*, 1977).

It is usually valuable and sensible to include parents in most research evaluations of children's products. They remain the primary purse-holders. Although children are given far greater say in the family, the adult has final veto on unsuitable or expensive products. When both children and parents are interviewed, there can be a problem determining where the weight of response lies, although it can be instructive to listen to the children. In family interviews, parents will often give the 'correct' response such as 'we don't let them eat sweets' only to be immediately corrected by the child.

The child consumer is not just a pint-sized version of an adult. The methods used to conduct research among youngsters are becoming ever more subtly designed to enable a better understanding of how child consumers think, feel and act.

Focus groups

The focus group is a popular marketing research technique with all age groups. It is certainly widely used to study young consumers. The technique can be an effective way of finding out what children want from different products and services. Handled with care by skilled moderators, focus groups can yield valuable information from young consumers about the factors which influence their consumption habits and preferences, and provide a better understanding of the language they use to discuss these matters.

Focus groups tend to involve open-ended discussion about products, although researchers may also try to steer them through a planned series of questions designed to get the children to think about and comment upon specific product attributes and issues. Often the children will be presented with the item(s) under discussion and are allowed to touch it and, if appropriate, to play with it while offering their observations.

Children can be valuable focus group participants if moderators tune in properly and researchers modify their speech to talk with youngsters on their own terms. Unlike adults, young consumers provide information through more than just conversation, and focus group moderators who vary their style from conference table conversation can reap increased and better information. Often, valuable information for marketers resides not simply in what children say about consumer matters, but in how they say it. Some researchers have found that getting children involved in behavioural simulations or exercises can add considerably to a straightforward group-discussion approach. Role playing and simulated shopping can provide valuable insights into important aspects of children's consumer-related behaviours which they cannot always readily articulate (Dailey, 1985–86).

The drawbacks of focus groups with children include the effort often needed to put them together, since parental permission has to be sought for children's participation. Keeping groups of young children under control and preventing their attention from straying too far off the point require real skill. Some children may dominate the discussion, while others may be too shy to speak. The confidence of all the children must be won if focus groups are to work effectively. Despite these problems, focus groups are generally regarded as a worthwhile exercise and can generate many ideas and opinions, as well as demonstrating the language of the young consumer.

One factor which can affect the success of focus groups is the power of peer pressure. Peer pressure is recognized as playing an increasingly important role in shaping children's consumer values and preferences. Child focus-group participants may discuss consumer issues in a way which mimics an acceptable 'party-line', but which does not necessarily represent their own views. Marketing researchers have used techniques designed to diminish the influence of peer pressure including giving young participants some degree of anonymity when they are invited to express their opinions. One way to avoid peer pressure completely is to conduct individual interviews. Interviewing children on their own has been found to create conditions under which they are more open and willing to talk about their tastes and preferences without worrying about how much other children may frown upon them.

Another technique is known as 'secret balloting' and here children are invited to write down their product preferences or wider consumer attitudes which are examined later and cannot be traced to any one respondent.

Despite concerns about peer pressure, focus groups can engender verbal interactions between children that can prove extremely valuable. It is important, however, not to mix together widely disparate age groups within the same focus group. It is generally regarded as advisable to keep focus group numbers within a two-year age span, and to separate boys from girls. Mixing together different age groups can backfire because younger children may often be intimidated by older children.

Keeping girls and boys apart is often recommended, even when testing reactions to products designed for both sexes. Girls develop psychologically at a faster rate than boys in a number of important respects and thus even when drawn from the same age group, the two sexes will behave differently in focus groups. One sex may become a significant distraction to the other when answering questions about consumerism. Clearer opinions will generally emerge if the sexes are kept apart.

In evaluating the usefulness and effectiveness of group discussions with children McDonald (1982) distinguished three different approaches: *Creative Drama Approach*, *Adult-Oriented Approach* and *Structural Approach*. The Creative Drama Approach has as its foundation methods used in schools to stimulate involvement in classroom activities. Games and play are combined with drawing and acting out. Research projects are addressed as if they were classroom activities moderated by a teacher. Children are treated as children, and are expected to engage in child-like activities. A high degree of creativity on the part of the children is expected. While the games are designed to stimulate open-ended responding, children tend to be led through a predetermined topic agenda. This approach is used by advertising agencies as a tool for getting children to evaluate new product concepts or ideas for advertising campaigns. Drawing techniques are sometimes combined with role playing.

The Adult-Oriented Approach involves group discussions conducted by moderators with much experience conducting adult consumer groups, but little understanding of children. This approach expects children to behave like adults. Generally no use is made of games or play activities to encourage group participation.

The Structural Approach, developed by McDonald (1982), takes into account the cognitive developmental stages through which children pass as they mature. The information-processing skills associated with these stages are important guiding considerations in conducting and analysing group sessions. Questioning is therefore designed to be appropriate to childhood abilities. Special supportive materials designed to help the children with the research task are used. These materials add structure to the group situation by providing the children with visual aids, thus making an idea or concept more understandable and easier to conceptualize.

Picture drawing

The use of pictures to obtain information from children has been a part of psychological research practice for many years. These techniques are also being used increasingly by marketing researchers. They are helpful on those occasions when children either cannot or will not articulate what is on their minds. Children retain a great deal of what they learn as images. It therefore makes sense to refer directly to pictures when questioning young consumers about products. Verbal questions often fail to work in this context because young children may not yet be able adequately to describe pictures in words.

Children are generally very eager to help the researcher by drawing a picture of something. Unless specifically asked to do otherwise, children will generally draw pictures of things they value, or find interesting, or are thinking about at the time. The drawings can be done in pencil or pen, with crayons or colour markers. The sessions can be conducted on a one-on-one (especially where several pictures are required from each child) or group basis. If done on a group basis however the researcher must make sure that copying does not take place. The children are given specific instructions and are then allowed anything from 15 minutes to one hour to complete the task.

Getting the instructions right is important. The frame of reference given to children can be broad or relatively narrow. Piloting can help to fathom out which type of instruction works well. Often it is best to allow children considerable latitude in expressing their views of the world. Different statements about what to draw can elicit varying imagery. McNeal (1992) describes the results of one study in which several distinct statements of what to draw were applied. 'For instance, "Draw what you would like to buy when you go shopping" typically elicited drawings of two or three products special to the children. "Draw what comes to your mind when you think about going to the store" usually produced a picture of a toy store, convenience store or departmental store. These trial-and-error efforts did demonstrate how much was already stored in the minds of children about consuming and how easy it was to elicit parts of it by choosing specific cue words' (p. 217).

The 'data' produced by picture-drawing techniques can be analysed using a variety of clinical, content analysis and statistical approaches. A clinical approach would focus on what objects the picture emphasizes, how big they are, their shape and colour. Over-emphasis of certain items can indicate that children attach a great deal of importance to them. Content analysis objectively categorizes objects in drawings and provides a frequency count of how often particular features appear. The frequency of appearance of items can again signal how important they are to the child. Once all the content of the drawings have been listed, a variety of other operations can be carried out with the data. Complex statistical analyses which are capable of analysing large numbers of different variables together can be used to lend further shape to the information supplied by drawings. Such techniques can even be applied to classify the children into different consumer types.

Depth interviewing

Focus groups together with supplementary techniques (such as picture drawing) and observational techniques (to be examined later) represent popularly used methods for finding out about children as consumers. Relatively little evidence has emerged about how effectively more conventional interview procedures can be used with young consumers, during which questions of depth may be posed to children individually. Interview techniques have been used indirectly to find out about children's consumption attitudes and habits. Typically, interviews are carried out with mothers rather than with the children themselves. This technique can prove to be adequate when investigating certain kinds of product, especially those where the mother has a major influence on the purchase (usually nonfood items) (Berey and Pollay, 1970). It is not always the case, however, that mothers can supply information which accurately reflects children's own opinions, tastes and preferences.

Marketing researchers have explored techniques which can elicit consumer-related information from children, as young as five or six years. Interviews are conducted with individual children accompanied by their mothers. Such interviews, which can be used to obtain opinions about products as well as to evaluate advertisements, generally begin with questions being posed to the mothers. Having been given an opportunity to air their views, however, mothers are then primed at key points to invite their children to offer their views. The aim is that, once the child has been drawn into the interview in this way, they then answer practically all the remaining questions. This technique has been found to prove effective in securing the confidence of young children and getting them to volunteer more about their personal consumer tastes and preferences than they might otherwise disclose (Neelankavil *et al.*, 1985).

Observational techniques

Watching and listening to children avoids the problem of dealing directly with them and their relative immaturity. It also avoids the reporting of children's behaviour by their parents, who are not always aware of some of their behaviour and may not be objective about some topics.

Observation can take place in central or field locations. For instance, children might be invited in to play with new toys or games at a venue where researchers can observe their behaviour unobtrusively from behind a two-way mirror. Under these circumstances, children are able to play with the items under study in any way they please. Their remarks to each other about toys or games can be recorded as well as their physical behaviour. If they are playing with or testing out a new game with fixed rules, the researchers can observe how long it takes the children to understand how the game is played and whether its level of difficulty is too great for certain age groups (or too easy).

Observational techniques in the field can be applied to study how children behave when out shopping either with their parents, with their friends or on their own. Once again, the length of time children spend in a store or particular section of it, their attention to layout and packaging details, and what they buy themselves or pester their parents to buy for them can be examined without research intervention, which might alter the behaviour young consumers display.

In one such study, observations were made of parents and children shopping together to find out if in-store behaviour varies with the age of the child. Its aim was to identify a range of factors which were shown to be linked to the way parents and their children interact in the shopping environment. The observations were supplemented by anecdotal comments obtained from 200 sets of parents and children who were shopping in supermarkets and toy stores (Rust, 1993). Young children (under 10) were much more likely than older children to point at products or other things in the store and to exhibit some sort of physical involvement with products, displays or packaging while in the store. Parents' interactions with older children took on a different form and indicated a degree of teamwork in choosing what to buy. There were other signs that shopping with older children had involved planning prior to the trip.

Observational techniques do not always produce quality data. For example, observations usually cannot be obtained in the home setting, where many products are actually used. However, there is no way to adequately simulate the home setting and its atmosphere in a laboratory. This means that when observations are made in artificial settings the results are always somewhat distorted, despite employing an otherwise objective research method. There is also a question to be dealt with in the case of the observational technique, namely its invasion of privacy, because the subjects normally do not know they are being studied.

Laboratory experiments

Performing laboratory experiments on young consumers provides accounts of their behaviour under varying conditions. Because the conditions are created by the experimenter, however, there is almost always reduced realism, particularly as compared to the standard observational method (which is often used in tandem with the experimental method). In laboratory experiments, researchers can exercise control over various facets of the consumer experience by manipulating product attributes, advertising attributes or features of the retailing environment.

Experimenting is a necessary research procedure for testing new products for children. Laboratory research can allow for the creation of various conditions under which a product's use can be examined. Through experimentation, variations can be made in the product itself, the way it is used, or in aspects of the environment in which it is sold. The experimental method may also be used for testing new premiums, packages and advertising campaigns. It is nearly always the case that new marketing communications need to be compared with old ones, alternative ones or those of competitors. This approach is also useful in the store environment for measuring children's responses to displays, fixtures, fittings and in-store communications.

The inherent disadvantage of the experimental method is that the research conditions are created, rather than real, and therefore may not be representative enough of actual conditions. Testing a new product's play value against one or more competing products, for example, may not produce accurate enough results because the test does not take place in the children's natural environment, where play may have a different meaning. There is also the possibility of an experimenter effect (the characteristics of the experimenter influencing behaviour) as well as evaluation apprehension (feeling anxious about being observed and thus behaving uncharacteristically).

Role playing

This technique is a special variation of the experimental method and usually involves the observation technique as well. It requires children to pretend to be someone else while playing or shopping, with the researcher observing their behaviour. For instance, rather than question a boy about how his mother reacts when he asks her to buy something when they are shopping together, he may be invited to pretend to be his mother and to demonstrate her typical reaction in that context, by acting it out.

This technique can indicate the child's perspective on different states of affairs. Its down side is that role playing is nevertheless tinged with a degree of artificiality. As a technique it needs to be handled with care to ensure that children do not use it as an opportunity to be silly or perform socially undesirable behaviour. It can, however, yield useful insights into children's views of consumerism which they would not be able to articulate as well via some other line of questioning.

Problems with researching children

Children are not easy to study in the consumer context. McNeal (1992) made the following observations:

(1) We still do not have a good understanding of how children think and why they behave as they do in the consumer role. Therefore, there is a need for much more basic marketing research among them, and just as important, there is a need for these results to be shared in some non-competitive way.
(2) Our research findings about children's consumer behaviour are almost always suspect, so we need to fix our research procedures and reproduce these findings under a new set of theoretical guidelines.
(3) Errors made in marketing to children have more downside risk than those made in marketing to others, so it therefore deserves more research underpinnings.
(4) There are people who, because of their special training, experience, and perhaps a sixth sense about kids, have a better than average grasp of kids' thinking and behaviour, and this type of person should be responsible for much of the marketing research among children.

(p. 220)

Large numbers of failures in the children's market point to a failure to understand young consumers. But there have also been large numbers of successes which are testimony to an understanding of them. Research has an important job in providing essential information to guide decision makers in charge of designing, packaging, advertising and selling products for children. Research should play a pivotal role in marketing strategy targeted to children, perhaps even more so than it would in the case of adult markets.

As one leading researcher advises though, it is important to recognize that no matter how much research is carried out among child consumers, marketers can never be absolutely sure they know what makes young consumers tick. Even with continual refinements to research techniques, it is important always to remember that research findings may have limitations and should be used sensibly as part of the information mix in determining a marketing strategy. Research techniques may not always be sufficiently sensitive to measure the full range and complexity of young consumers' opinions, perceptions and behaviour. Nevertheless, there is an important degree of understanding to be gained about children as consumers from conducting carefully planned research. Such is the rate of development of the children's market and the sophistication of young consumers that research techniques will need to evolve if marketers are to keep on top of this growing market sector.

Advertising to Young Consumers

Advertising to children is far from simple. As preceding chapters have indicated, children's reactions to advertising can be complex and change significantly as children pass through different stages of cognitive and conditional development. Understanding of commercial messages begins at a low level among very young children, in their infancy, but eventually develops to reveal a pattern of discrimination and scepticism.

McNeal's advertising model

McNeal (1992) presents an interesting model which provides a schematic picture of how an advertising campaign can influence children's attitudes and behaviour. The attitudes that are affected are linked to the product, the brand, its producer, seller and the promotional message itself. Behaviour that is influenced takes three forms:

(1) behaviour toward the product—looking for it, at it, comparing it with others; (2) behaviour toward the parents—influence attempts on parents by children in order to get them to buy the product advertised or to provide necessary funds; and (3) peer influence.

(p. 146)

The influence on parents results in behaviour by them such as purchases, provision of funds to the children, negotiations with the children and refusals. The parents, in turn, form attitudes based on these possible behaviours—toward the product, the brand, the producer, the seller, the advertisement and advertising in general.

The resulting attitudes of the children and the attitudes of the parents interact to produce a liking or dislike of products, brands, sellers, advertising, which will determine later behaviour toward these objects by children and/or parents. The likes and dislikes that result are often referred to as *preferences* and *loyalty* (for brands, stores, and product types). The likes, importantly, also become part of the children's parents' evoked set—the two or three brands that come to mind when the purchase of a product is contemplated.

The model suggests possible outcomes of advertising that are favourable to marketers who focus on children as any one or more of three markets. As a *primary* market, advertising may produce a purchase and favourable attitudes. As an *influence* market, advertising may cause the child to inform and persuade the parent, who in turn may buy may the product and/or form favourable attitudes toward it. As a future market, advertising produces liking and other favourable attitudes that can trigger behaviour toward a product at a later time.

The model of advertising to children has been roughly divided into three stages:

(1) Advertising influences children to buy products and/or to get parents to make purchases.
(2) Parents consider the product at the recommendation of the child.
(3) The attitudes of the child and parents that have been induced by advertising and purchase behaviour determine their future behaviour toward advertised products.

McNeal (1992) indicates that there are limitations to the model. It shows advertising effects in isolation, without the use of other communications effects and without the influence of other products and retailers. There are so many marketers advertising to children in order to get them to purchase, influence their parents and form favourable attitudes toward the marketed product that children cannot and will not process all the messages. Other communications tools are obviously necessary. Sales promotion efforts such as coupons, contests and premiums can often stimulate action faster and more effectively than advertising or advertising alone. Public relations programmes may work better with children. Properly designed packaging can have enormous impact on children and their parent once they enter the purchase environment.

McNeal (1992) recommends the three 'P-tests' to marketers in order to make their advertising effective. These are *pre-test*, *parent test* and *pilot test*. The *pre-test* is an examination of advertisements by a person who is professionally trained and experienced in understanding children. This might be a child or educational psychologist, a marketing communications expert or an education expert. Such a person would bring their experience to bear in judging whether a particular promotional message or campaign contained the right ingredients to get through to young consumers. A *parent test* utilizes a panel of parents who would be recruited to offer an opinion about advertising aimed at children. They can give a view about how parents would perceive an advertisement as well as about how children might respond to it. Finally, a *pilot test* is a small-scale study of the effectiveness of an advertisement among an appropriate group of children. Such a test can be done internally by the marketing organization or be contracted out to an external specialist agency. The aim of the pilot is to place the advertisement in a critically evaluative situation where any problems are identified early on before the campaign gets fully in motion. The combined purpose of these 'P-tests' is to make advertising aimed at children as effective as possible.

Programme-length commercials

A more subtle technique of reaching young consumers than standard spot advertising on television has been the idea of the programme-length commercial. This approach recognizes the need for a more complete marketing mix in shaping the behaviours of an increasingly media-wise and sophisticated population of child and teenage consumers.

The phenomena in toy marketing of creating associations between merchandise and popular television themes, or characters, has been around for many years. Examples can be found as early as the 1950s, when television series on the American networks such as 'Davy Crockett', 'Wyatt Earp', and 'Dragnet' had licensing agreements with toy manufacturers who wished to capitalize on the popularity of these television series. More recently, Davy Crockett caps and Mickey Mouse watches have been replaced in childrens' affections by He-Man dolls, Transformers robots, and G.I. Joe army equipment. The experience has generally been that products associated with successful television shows enjoy remarkable sales (see Kunkel, 1988).

One of the concerns of regulators and critics of television advertising has been, not simply the pervasiveness of these television-merchandise relationships, but the way they come about. A distinction has been drawn between the traditional programme-related agreements, whereby toys or other merchandise are produced as a result of the success of the programme, and those instances where the programme follows from and is created out of pre-existing merchandise. The concern here is that the programme is little more than a longer than usual advertisement for the merchandise rather than an original television entertainment creation. The issue of protection of children from advertising is a topic we return to in the next chapter.

Even more effective as a marketing device is the combining of programmes featuring characters who are also available as toys, and spot advertising embedded in, or shown adjacent to, such programmes. While there are restrictions on the forms such advertising can take, this double-whammy approach can significantly and quickly raise a manufacturer's profile among the target consumer market.

Promotion and publicity aimed at children

Promotion and public relations aimed at children rapidly gained importance during the second half of the 1980s and have today become at least equal in importance to advertising. In the USA, annual spending on promotion and public relations exceeds that on advertising, where marketing to children is concerned (McNeal, 1992). McNeal noted that the increased expenditure on promotion and publicity aimed at children has not derived from a reallocation of advertising expenditure. It represents new and additional expenditure which underlines the growing significance of the young consumers' market.

The term 'promotion' embraces a wide range of marketing activities that include coupons, contexts, sweepstakes, premiums, samples and telephone services. Promotions can enhance brand identity and improve brand image among children and teenagers. They can also build brand loyalty so that children at the point of purchase consistently want to buy the promoted brand over a non-promoted one.

Child-targeted public relations is becoming an increasingly integral part of marketing to young consumers. The three main tools used by public relations when targeting children are *publicity*, *event marketing* and *school relations*. Publicity involves the placement of stories in news media such as children's magazines and newspapers or items about a product or the product's manufacturer. This technique can attract consumer attention to the product, render consumers better informed about it and boost its credibility. One of the major problems faced by child-targeted publicity is the shortage of appropriate media outlets through which to reach children. Much of the load falls on magazines, given the limited child-oriented television and radio airtime.

Event marketing involves associating the name of a product or service with an event which is known to be very popular with children and preferably is one in which children themselves participate. Sponsorship of such events can be an effective route for boosting a brand's profile among young consumers, especially if the event runs for some time and allows for repeated exposure of the brand name.

School relations can provide valuable opportunities to present marketing messages to school officials, teachers, children and their parents. They also provide an additional public service of contributing financially to local and national educational programmes. Large numbers of children can be reached this way and a positive public image can be established if a product's promotion generates much needed funds to meet the costs of educational or teaching resources. According to McNeal (1992) ' . . . kid-targeted promotion could do more than just clinch the sale. Promotion also could be used for developing brand and seller identity among children and for building preferences and loyalty toward firm and its products' (p. 177).

Promotional messages aimed at young consumers must be carefully designed because this market segment is becoming increasingly sophisticated and sceptical about advertising. Even a quarter of a century ago, there was clear evidence that young people did not accept advertising at face value. An American survey of teenagers and young adults found that 24 per cent of respondents said that advertisements directed at them were not believable; 19 per cent found much advertising uninformative; 28 per cent thought that advertising was silly; and only 7 per cent regarded adverts as sincere. Nevertheless, 87 per cent of young consumers (aged 14 to 25 years) said they would rather buy advertised than non-advertised products.

Effectively reaching young consumers with advertising messages requires knowing how they respond to different types of product and product promotions. It is important to understand the character of the children's market and to design communications to which they will be responsive. Marketing professionals and media researchers have identified a number of important factors and rules of thumb which should be taken into account when marketing to young consumers. There appear to be four important points to bear in mind:

(1) Never talk down to youngsters.
(2) Be totally straightforward and sincere.
(3) Give young people credit for being motivated by rational values.
(4) Be as personal as possible.

Elsewhere, research into children's responses to marketing communications has identified a number of additional attributes which can make advertising messages stand out more for children:

(1) Know your niche.
(2) Position your product.
(3) Talk the talk.
(4) Pictures sell.
(5) Put it to music.
(6) Move it along.
(7) Don't preach.
(8) Make it fun.
(9) Groups are dynamic.
(10) Be new, but familiar.

The first point, *know the niche*, recognizes that children are not a homogeneous market. Young consumers can be differentiated by age, stage of cognitive development needs, desires, interests and personality. Marketers and advertisers need to establish which segment(s) they are aiming for. Promotional messages must clearly position the product with the target group in mind. The product or service has to have a point of view and a unique selling proposition which will appeal to young consumers at whom it is directed.

Using the most appropriate communication techniques is vitally important. Advertising messages must use the right language. Language is integral to group belonging and binding. Visuals can enhance the marketing message, but must display images which have known significance for the target market. Music also is an integral part of youngsters' lifestyles, but care is needed to select appropriately fashionable music and music icons.

Promotional messages must have pace to appeal to young consumers who are accustomed to processing information through first-morning audio-visual channels. Production values must be kept at a high level, but the creative challenge is to achieve a blend of all the appropriate visual, musical and linguistic elements in a stimulating package.

A further key aspect relating to style of presentation with any promotional campaign is not to preach to children. Young consumers can be very aware. They want products and services that are going to do something for them, make them look or feel better, have more fun and be better accepted within their peer group.

Making promotional and marketing communications fun can also enhance their impact because children enjoy humour, with visual humour being especially effective with younger children and verbal humour being more effectively deployed among older children.

It has been observed previously that peer groups can have a dynamic influence upon young consumers' product tastes and preferences. The peer group generates and constrains perceptions of what is most acceptable or fashionable. Advertising messages must not ignore these definitions and boundaries.

Novelty value is important. Fashions can change rapidly among children, so it is important that marketers and advertisers are aware of what is new to children as well as what is familiar. Familiarity can work well in certain circumstances where it represents 'tried-and-tested', though it is important not to parade the 'familiar' as 'new'.

Conclusion

Reaching child and teenage consumers can be a highly skilled exercise. Young consumers can often be more difficult to reach than their parents. They are more constrained than are most adults in terms of their purchasing behaviour as well as being more fickle and capricious in their purchases.

Understanding young consumers' psychology is therefore essential to marketers who wish to reach them. This understanding can be attained through a variety of techniques, though these techniques may not always be the same as those which would be used to examine the adult market. This fact underlines the need for expert help and guidance in researching as well as reaching young consumers.

Marketers need to know where young consumers get their information about consumer matters. They also need to know how youngsters respond to different consumer information sources. The mass media may be important sources of consumer information, but their significance may vary depending upon the type of product or service being considered. Young consumers may turn to television for information about one product, but to comic books or magazines for information about others. In other instances, point-of-purchase information may be the key to successful marketing and sales.

Within the retail setting, it is important for marketers to know how youngsters shop. The way products are packaged and displayed may make a crucial difference between completion of a sale and rejection of a product by the young consumer. These represent topics which need to be investigated through appropriate research techniques. Catering for the needs and desires of children and teenagers means understanding what these needs and desires are.

The same techniques as those used for adults may not, however, work with youngsters. Single sex and same-age groups of children may work better in qualitative research than mixing them up demographically. This is a much more important point to note than would be the case with adults. With some children, especially younger ones, the use of techniques which utilize children's capacity for fantasizing about things may yield insights which their verbal utterances might not reveal. Indeed, standard interview techniques may not work at all well with young children, who may be both intimidated by the interview situation and unable to articulate their feelings about products.

Allowing young children an opportunity to react to actual products or retail environments, to play act or role play, and to engage in games or pretend activities which stimulate shopping or product usage, may be far more revealing simply because this places the research on their wavelength.

With older children and teenagers, face-to-face interviews can be used with greater effectiveness, but even here it is probably advantageous to combine this data collection technique with other techniques such as role playing or observation of behaviour in natural or quasi-natural conditions.

Research evidence should be carefully and thoughtfully utilized to guide campaigns that are designed to expose young consumers to products and encourage direct or indirect purchase behaviour.

In understanding how to shape young consumers' product preferences, it is important to acknowledge the role played by parents, who often control the purse strings. Some advertising might therefore be better aimed at parents rather than at children, since it is parents who ultimately control the means to purchase. Children may pester their parents to purchase something for them, but parents must be convinced that this product is one worth buying. To have greater confidence that an advertisement is going to work, it should be pre-tested with both children and parents before it is placed within various media.

Advertising is not the only way of reaching young consumers with product-related messages. Other forms of promotional activities can prove to be effective under certain circumstances. Public relations activities aimed at children have been gaining in importance over the past 20 years. This approach might involve event sponsorship, school visits, and other forms of publicity. Events which are known to be popular with young people may provide ideal opportunities. Through association, positive feelings about the event may be equated with the sponsor's brand names. Whichever technique for reaching children and teenagers is used, marketers should always remember the importance of knowing their market. One particularly important feature of the young consumers' market is that its tastes and interests can change very quickly. It is therefore essential to remain constantly vigilant so that any such changes and their marketing implications can be detected almost as soon as they occur.

8

Protecting Child Consumers

So far this book has established that children as consumers represent a substantial and often influential segment of the population. The size and spending power of this market segment mean that it represents an important target for advertisers and marketers. Reaching this target market is seldom simple or straightforward because children can be complex and sophisticated consumers. They are heterogeneous in both character and modes of responding to the consumer environment. Communicating effectively to children as young consumers means understanding the psychology of this market segment.

The children's market has distinct psychological characteristics. Children vary in terms of their self-confidence, consumer competence and experience, susceptibility to peer group pressures, and ability to understand and absorb promotional messages. Critics of advertising aimed at children argue that youngsters are more susceptible to the persuasive appeals of commercial messages because their psychological immaturity renders them vulnerable. Further arguments against advertising to children claim that it can create artificial needs among young people, which parents may be reluctant to gratify, thus producing unnecessary intra-family tensions and conflict. Advertisers, it is claimed, take advantage of children's natural credulity and lack of experience.

The research literature reviewed in earlier chapters would suggest that while children pass through a stage of vulnerability, they generally emerge from it as informed and knowledgeable consumers able to make their own minds up about what they wish to buy. As they grow older, children develop the abilities needed to challenge the claims of advertisers.

Arguments for Restraint of Advertising

Criticism of advertising or promotional activities designed to influence young consumers stems from a number of worries people have about the abilities of children and teenagers to make effective judgements about claims that are made about products. The lack of intellectual and emotional maturity of children is believed to place them at a significant disadvantage with adults in being able to fend off the persuasive messages of marketers and advertisers, and resist the temptations to purchase or to pester others, to purchase on their behalf.

Since children do not always have much disposable money of their own, they are dependent upon their parents for many of the items they wish to own. One concern is that advertising contributes to intra-family conflicts by encouraging children constantly to pester their parents to buy them things. Parents may not always listen or give in to children's purchase requests with the result that the child becomes resentful. Arguments between parents and their offspring about product purchases would probably occur even if there was no advertising. The question is whether such arguments occur more often because of advertising.

Marketers and advertisers have become increasingly subtle and sophisticated in the techniques they employ to raise product or brand profiles. One area of controversy has centred on the so-called programme-length commercial. This form of television production reflects a growing trend in multi-faceted marketing whereby consumers are exposed to messages about products through a variety of channels on television, radio, print media, in retail outlets and almost anywhere else it might be possible to reach consumers.

With spot advertising, commercial messages are clearly demarcated. Consumers generally know that when they are watching an advertisement they are being exposed to a message which has a selling intent. Even children come to recognize this factor as a primary distinguishing attribute of advertisements. However, when the programme itself becomes a sales vehicle by featuring characters based upon pre-existing merchandise, such as toys, the sales message becomes integrated within an entertainment form and its presence may be less clearly detected by audiences, especially by young audiences.

Regulators have been inconsistent in the way this sort of marketing phenomenon has been dealt with. While such advertising forms as 'host-selling', whereby characters from a programme also appear in commercials within that programme, have been outlawed, manufacturers whose products feature as programme characters can nevertheless place commercials within such programmes for other products they make. The breaking down of the dividing line between what is clearly defined and generally recognized as a sales message and advertising which is disguised as entertainment, with no ostensible sales purpose, can, it is argued by some critics, place consumers at a disadvantage, because such subtle marketing techniques may undermine the abilities of experienced as well as inexperienced consumers to know with what type of content they are dealing.

Questions such as whether advertising needs to be regulated, to what extent it should be regulated, and whether regulation in respect of certain forms of marketing needs to cut deeper than others, require careful reflection. The protection of innocents needs to be weighed against the significance of advertising to national economies and the right of manufacturers and their advertisers to speak freely about their products within democratic societies.

It cannot be fairly argued, however, that all advertising aimed at children is beyond criticism. Advertisers are not given a free range to do or say anything they choose. Most countries draw up and implement regulations which attempt to control advertising and offer protection to consumers. Key questions here are whether regulations are effective as far as children are concerned and to what extent they are necessary.

Protectionism and Regulation

Many people are in favour of various forms of consumer protectionism. Most countries have laws intended to protect adults *and* children from exploitation. *Censorship* and *protectionism* have essentially different aims. Censorship is most frequently applied to sociopolitical and 'artistic' materials, such as political writings and pornography. Protectionism, on the other hand, is most commonly aimed at commercial exploitation of both children and adults.

Naturally the issues of censorship and protectionism stimulate considerable discussion. At one extreme one finds *libertarians*, who are usually uncomfortable with any form of censorship. Many are in favour of sexual freedom, artistic licence, political freedom and the operation of the free market. On the other hand, *protectionists* argue that laws need to be passed to protect adults, and particularly children, from various forms of exploitation.

Naturally children and adolescents are seen to be particularly vulnerable to various forms of exploitation. Libertarians argue that it is the duty of parents and teachers to protect, and more importantly, to educate young people into the motives of advertisers, polemicists and manufacturers. Protectionists, on the other hand, argue it is duty of the state, and/or specific regulatory bodies, to pass laws that protect people from exploitation of various kinds. There are, of course, also those who are less consistently libertarian or protectionist. For instance, there are some who are 'artistic libertarians' while being at the same time 'commercial protectionists' (Furnham, 1993). The issue for consumer protectionism revolves around two issues: the role of protectionism in the wider society on the one hand and children's/adolescents' understanding of and experience in the economic world.

The children's market has grown enormously over the past 20 years and whereas 40 years ago children were piggy-bank savers, pocket-money spenders and *future* consumers, they are now recognized to be significant spenders and consumers in their own right. Though constrained in terms of mobility and disposable cash, in western societies children soon learn to become sophisticated and knowledgeable consumers (Furnham and Stacey, 1992).

Children become consumers through a process involving a *socializing agent* (parent, teacher, peer), a *method of teaching* and a *medium for teaching*. Parents are the major consumer socializing agents. It is parents who introduce their children to the supermarket, corner or high-street shop, the store assistants, the

Censorship cw.
Protectionism.

shelves of products and the niceties of the rituals of shopping and buying. It is parents who initiate young children into the use of money by asking them to give money to the shop assistant, put coins in the vending machine or count money from the purse/wallet. It is usually parents who encourage and allow their child to make his or her first trip alone to the shop.

Children closely observe their parents' shopping behaviour: choosing between what appear to be two similar heads of lettuce or bunches of celery, squeezing fruit or bread to test freshness, scrutinizing meat or fish from various angles. They might equally be puzzled by their parents looking at packages for E numbers, checking the country of origin on labels or trying to determine the calorific content of the total contents of a package. They are also observant of the parent who throws pre-prepared meals, alcohol, cigarettes and sweets into a shopping trolley seemingly oblivious to price, packaging, alternatives or health concerns. Children learn consumer behaviour by observational learning.

During what may be called the child's 'consumer training period' (lasting from four years old to adolescence) parents may permit and model various degrees of participation in the consumer role: advice as to what to buy for a meal, choosing between two brands of a favoured product or independently seeking out food stuff from another part of the supermarket. While in the shop parents can and do use it as a laboratory—showing the child subtle differences between similar-looking products or explaining expiry dates. In the home, parents talk about products, often giving elaborate and complicated evaluative judgements and reasons for the purchase. Children may also hear their parents passing judgements on magazine, radio and television advertisements. Questions arise naturally as to the different role of the mother versus the father or indeed the role of other relatives, such as grandparents or older siblings. So far, relatively little research has been done in this area.

Of course not all parents are equally conscientious in training their children in the various activities and nuances of consumer behaviour. However, parental influence in consumer socialization is mediated by parental concern and involvement. To quote researchers in this field:

> Today there is no fast line that separates the consumption patterns of the adult world from those of child except the consumption objects themselves.
>
> (Riesman et al., 1953)

> Parents are teaching their children a great deal of consumer behaviour: in fact, we might worry that parents who are ineffective consumers also are teaching their children ineffective consumer behaviour.
>
> (McNeal, 1987)

Children learn from and copy their peers but such influence appears to decline as they get older. Schools also attempt both implicitly and explicitly to educate their pupils.

Business organizations also attempt to act as powerful consumer socializing agents. This influence may operate through advertising, particularly on television, though this is strictly controlled by laws governing 'adult' products as well. Shops themselves may try to influence parents and their children since they know that loyalty to a service supplier (like a bank) can last a lifetime. Thus shops may do any of the following to activate long-lasting loyalty:

(1) Provide rest or play facilities for children and their parents.
(2) Be attentive to eye-level displays for children or even specific store- or age-specific credit cards.
(3) Provide consumer education to elementary school classes such as field trips to part of the store/factory.
(4) Undertake in-store promotional efforts such as window displays particularly for children.
(5) Train shop assistants to be particularly responsive or helpful to children.
(6) Co-operate with parents' ethical dilemmas such as removing certain products or ensuring the law is observed (selling cigarettes and alcohol to minors).

Naturally shops and stores want business and many have realized that they can appeal to children most effectively via their parents. If parents are only concerned with appeasing demanding children, and uninterested (or even disinterested) in the children's consumer education, stores may then be more likely to try to appeal to the children directly. If, on the other hand, the store notices parents' concerns and interests, they may be more likely to attempt to appeal to them.

The focal point of most concern for regulation and protection however is not parents or teachers, but rather the product itself. Because a product may be so intermingled with many other aspects of consumption (pre-, actual- and post-purchase) it may be difficult to delineate the product's unique and special role in the consumer socialization of children.

For McNeal (1987):

> Parents are practically partners with the retailers in the consumer training of children in the sense that parents provide children with much of their income (one-half or more) and then encourage the children to make independent purchase efforts at stores. Further, parents give retail stores legitimacy by visiting them often, themselves, and also by taking the children with them . . . over a period of time children make more independent purchases in a greater variety of stores when with parents than without them. Thus, the retail store, in general, is parent-blessed. This seems much less true of the advertising that concerns parents so much. Also, parents can buffer much of the influence of advertising to their children that occurs in the home, but it seems much more difficult to buffer the influence of retailers when the children are engaged in an independent purchase act with them. Thus, what children learn in their interactions with retailers is probably determined more by the retailers than by the parents, but it has at least tacit approval of the parents.
>
> (p. 59)

Children clearly need education and protection, but the question remains who should do it: the state, the parent, or both? Parents are probably the most efficient and effective of educators. It is they who implicitly or explicitly inculcate values, beliefs and behaviour patterns into their children. However, many parents feel that they need 'state' support in the difficult task of child-rearing. McNeal (1987) has suggested five types of question about parents, children and money:

(1) Are parents aware that giving their children money to spend gives the children market power? While the money that one child receives is minor, the combined amount for all children causes children to have buying power and to be recognized as a market by some producers and retailers.

(2) Why do parents really need to give their children money, particularly during preschool years? The parents meet the children's needs already and do it better than the children can.

(3) Are parents cognizant of retailers' feelings about children being given money to spend and being encouraged to spend it? Regardless of what motives the parents have for giving their children money, by virtue of giving it to them they set in motion certain activities at the retail level, such as stocking and displaying goods. Yet parents may not know the viewpoint of retailers.

(4) Are parents giving their children money, encouraging them to spend it, but relying principally on business and elementary school to teach the children appropriate consumer behaviour? There is not much evidence that parents deliberately teach their children consumer behaviour, yet they encourage them to be consumers. Because knowing how to be a consumer is not a genetic matter, someone must teach them both prior to and during consumer activities.

(5) If parents insist on their children being consumers by giving them money and encouraging them to spend it, are they also giving approval to marketers to court their children as potential customers? We hear a lot of condemnation of marketers, particularly advertisers, for pursuing children as consumers, but from a theory of business standpoint, it would be more surprising if they did not.

(p. 39)

Parents and businesses make various assumptions about children as consumers, some of which are correct, others less so:

- *Children are gullible.* By and large this is true, but then so too are many adults. The important question is what they are gullible about, and whether protectionism prevents and encourages gullibility.
- *Children possess limited understanding of business operations.* This is also partly true. Children do not know how businesses price their products and services, the reason for taxation or the purposes of advertising, selling, displaying and promotional packaging. On some of these issues, parents may be equally ignorant.
- *Children have limited dexterity.* This is definitely true. Because children have greater difficulty twisting and turning compared to adults they can easily be prevented from 'getting into' products.
- *Children have limited mastery of language.* This is true. Children cannot always understand commercials, warnings on products and so on, which can be as frustrating to business as to protectionists.

- *Children have critical and caring parents.* This is only sometimes true. Certainly if children want a product which their parents prefer them not to have, parental denial can cause conflict, argument and temper tantrums. Rather than deal with the conflict and educate the child some parents prefer quite simply to legislate against it, so preventing the conflict in the first place.

Certainly many children of 10 years old and more can be as gullible or as sophisticated as their parents with respect to consumer affairs. The significant difference is that they do not have the disposable cash of their parents.

There are, however, limited data on children's actual consumer-related behaviour.

- *Frequency and purpose of children's shop visits.* Studies have shown that five-year-olds can give extensive descriptions of their parents' (mostly mother's) buying activities on a typical shopping trip, and about half give explanations for their decisions. Most children appear to have been to a shop alone by the age of 7 or 8 years, and by the age of 10 many may make two or three visits a week, but tend to be restricted both in the shops they go to and the purchases they make. About half of all children as young as five years old make unassisted purchase while with parents, and all of them by the age of seven. It is parents who sanction and encourage children's shop visits.

  (McNeal, 1987; 1992)

- *Children's store knowledge and preferences.* Because most children enjoy shopping they quickly learn a lot about them in terms of their purposes, styles of operation, product offerings, choices and prices. Like their parents, children show strong preferences for stores and as they get older prefer speciality to convenience stores. Again, like adults, children prefer and value contact with helpful and informed assistants in a shop.

  (McNeal, 1987; 1992)

Children are clearly much more educated and sophisticated than the consumer protectionist lobby would have us believe. It makes their task of infantilism all the more difficult and necessary. The innocent, gullible, consumer-behaviour-naive child hardly exists, except, of course, in totalitarian society.

Consumer education and protection for children

Consumer education has been taken seriously in America since the 1920s and by the second world war the focus on consumer education had shifted from a 'cynical anti-business philosophy' to that of a 'rational approach to life' (Roger and Nolf, 1980). President Kennedy set up a committee on consumer interests which emphasized consumer education. The following quotes come from page 111 of the President's Committee on Consumer Interests (1970):

Every effort should be made to help our *young* citizens become alert, responsive, and responsible consumers.

Consumer Education is not merely a rhetorical exercise in buymanship. It is a continuing, *lifetime* learning experience.

Consumer Education provides our *youth* with a useful frame of reference not only for the future but also for the sometimes difficult and perplexing *present*.

The idea of consumer education is rarely disputed, though some might prefer less money being spent on education and more on legal prohibitions. However, it raises three important questions: *Who* should do it?; *When* should it be commenced?; *What* should the content of the education be?

Who should be the educator?

Essentially there are three groups, each or all of whom may play an important part in the business of consumer education. Obviously parents and families explicitly or implicity do this sort of teaching. Whatever they explicitly teach, however, children will model their actual behaviour. As all parents have found to their cost, 'Do as I say not as I do' rarely, if ever, works. Secondly, *schools* could acts as educators. Although it may be done informally in some schools or explicitly in others it rarely features on the curriculum. Certainly, few doubt that it is important preparation for adulthood; but some object that it is not an important preparation for childhood (Walstad and Watts, 1985). However, there are serious difficulties with using schools as major agents in consumer education:

- Disagreements about the subject matter (*what* as well as *how* it should be taught).
- An image problem, because it is seen as having insufficient intellectual content or rigour.
- Anti-business attitudes of some teachers who see an 'us vs. them' between manufacturers/retailers on the one hand and consumers on the other.
- Prioritizing consumer education in a crowded syllabus.

Because actual consumer-related education is sparse, patchy and varied in nearly all countries it becomes very difficult to assess its effectiveness. It could be integrated with the teaching of maths or economics but there are no teachers trained specifically to do this.

A third group of potential educators are *businesses* and *manufacturers* themselves. For some there is no way of separating promotional intent from educational benefits. Hence industry-led consumer education is seen as an oxymoron on a par with military intelligence. McNeal (1987) has argued:

Business has a legitimate contribution to make children's consumer education. Business knows more about its products and services than anyone, and it has at its disposal some of the most powerful educational tools ever invented—its communication mix of advertising, selling, packaging, sales promotion and publicity. Logically, its teaching assignments would be the nature, use and benefits of its products and services. These are the very topics that teachers and parents often know so little about, yet feel competent to explain to children. The synergism is apparent. What products and services should businesses educate children about? Certainly, it should include all of those items targeted to children. These would include cereals, snacks, candies, soft drinks, frozen desserts, toys, games and crafts. Part of this consumer education drive should be aimed at parents when it would be more appropriate, such as, for example, with nutrition information about snack foods or uses and care of some toys.

Most product and service education for children logically would be the responsibility of their producers. Retailers probably should be involved at least in the education about services because they ordinarily provide them. Retailers also could assume the responsibility for educating children about gift decisions and gift purchases when these items are for adults and not ordinarily targeted to children. The stores that seek this business from children should be responsible for the related customer education.

Retailers, like parents, should help children understand some of the concepts taught in the classroom, such as counting money, calculating sales taxes, and comparing products. Retailers could also post information where appropriate for parents and children. For example, fast food restaurants could post nutritional information about its main products, such as sandwiches, chicken, fish and beverages. Retailers should offer their store environments as laboratories to parents and teachers for demonstrating consumer education concepts taught in the class room. Parents already use the stores for this purpose in an informal manner, and retailers often invite elementary classes to take field trips to their stores. These activities only need more structure.

(pp. 168–169)

When should consumer education be taught?

This is not so much a policy question as a research one. It has exercised educational and psychological researchers since the turn of the century. The question is really at what age do children show sufficient intellectual development to group the concepts being taught. For some researchers the idea about economics and consumerism can be taught in the kindergarten, while for others it needs to wait for high school (Furnham, 1993). On the one hand the issue is a psychological question about cognitive development and the age at which young people can assimilate this type of knowledge. On the other hand, the question is really one of social policy concerning when the necessary funding is best provided for that education.

What type of education?

Most of the research evidence would support the view that education is better than censorship or proscription where children are concerned. Such is the complexity, variety and prevalence of media these days that children need to be taught the critical skills to reach their own judgments about advertising.

Parental guidance and public education both have an important role to play in preparing children to cope with the kind of society in which they will have to live. Through talking to their children about advertisements, the cost of products and what represents good or bad value for money, parents can have a significant influence on children's consumer awareness and ability to critically appraise advertising. Television literacy projects based in schools have also been found to produce greater consumer literacy among children (Christenson, 1982; Dorr, Graves and Phelps, 1980).

Methods of protectionism

Once manufacturers recognize that children are a potential market and begin advertising directly to them, various questions arise both for the manufacturer and for parents. Manufacturers will want to know about the child's ability to understand advertising messages, how best to display goods (e.g. the appropriate height and price) to appeal to young shoppers. If a product appeals to the child, parents may get pressurized to buy it and may in some instances find themselves objecting on the basis of cost, ethico-political grounds or simply because they do not want their children to have them.

There thus arise various protectionist polices which take usually, one of three forms.

(1) *Organization in pressure groups.* 'Concerned citizens', as they like to think of themselves, form organizations to 'cope with' some of the issues resulting from the interaction between marketers and children. Because this is such an appealing political platform for those with anti-business attitudes, sceptics may observe that these concerned parental protectionist groups are homogeneously left-wing.

(2) *Regulation and legislation.* It is frequently the aim of protectionists to use legal sanction with so-called protectionist and safety policies to ban certain products, severely limit advertising, etc. Depending on the political persuasion of the local or national government this could be an easy or difficult task.

(3) *Education.* It is possible to encourage or indeed legislate for consumer education to make children (and their parents) more knowledgeable discriminating consumers.

The first issue of the 1991 volume of the *Journal of Social Issues* was concerned almost exclusively with the human sciences research perspective on consumer protection issues. Here it was noted that Kennedy's speech on consumer rights in 1962—the right to be informed, the right to choose, the right to safety and the right to be heard—was the major stimulant to this research. Thus it is possible to conceive of 'rights' being violated in the following examples:

- A four-year-old hurt by a defective toy may be a violation of the right to safety.
- A food-processing company that chooses not to print 'sell-by' dates may be conceived as violating the right of consumers to such information.
- A manufacturer who for one reason or another has a near monopoly can be accused of denying the consumer the right to choose.
- If a new car spends considerable time being repaired and no replacement is given, this might violate the consumer's right to recourse and redress.

Not all accept these 'rights' as valid and it is not clear if they have protection in law. However, the concept of rights was a major boost to protectionist interests. According to Friedman (1991) the consumer movement in America can be split into two groups: the first one consisting of *reformists* who are primarily concerned with consumer problems that result from the inefficient operation of markets and work within the system in legislate regulatory and judicial areas. The other group comprises the radicals who seek to institutionalize consumer representation in government through the creation of new agencies; to police consumer purchasing power through use of consumer co-operators, boycotts and the like and to increase corporate (and individual) accountability through federal chartering of corporations, placing the public on various management boards, and passing laws making manufacturers criminally responsible for the misbehaviour of their companies.

Brobeck (1990) distinguished between liberal and conservative reformists. Conservative reformists stress improvements in efficiency of markets through increased information. They are most comfortable advocating improved consumer education, expanded product testing and evaluation of consumer services and require disclosures. Liberal reformists, on the other hand, are more concerned about exploitation and discrimination, especially against the poor, that 'invariably' are found in capitalist economies. Accordingly, they emphasize government interventions to prevent and redress fraud and to ameliorate structural discrimination in free markets. Specifically, they address the pricing of insurance, banking, telephone and energy services where the poor are often forced to pay higher prices (or costs) than are other consumers. Their solutions involve government subsidies or government interventions where there is minimal disruption of markets.

According to Mayer (1991), it is in progressive eras that consumer problems are turned into consumer issues. Furthermore, he argued that nearly all issues or campaigns follow a pattern: some 'disasters' with people poisoned, insured or disabled by a product; research to elucidate the problem and its cause; a groundswell of orchestrated public protest; the emergence of, at first poor, legislation. He distinguishes between three quite different agendas: that of the *media*, manifest in articles and features; that of the *public*, as demonstrated in surveys and concerned with such things as taxes, prices and government-regulated rates, goods/services availability, consumer representation and environmental quality; and a *policy* agenda, concerned with the drafting and introduction of legislation.

Pope (1991) concentrated on advertising as a consumer issue which, particularly in America, has seen various historical phases. He notes:

> The 'new consumerism' that began in the 1960s owed little directly to the changing character of marketing. Rather, it was the product of a broader challenge to established authority, a partial delegitimation of dominant institutions. Reawakened environmentalism, a multifaceted women's movement, challenges to business and government secrecy, and the skill of consumer activists in using modern methods of propaganda and publicity all played their roles. Yet although its origins lay elsewhere, the modern consumer movement has had to contend with the new advertising and market climate.
>
> (p. 51)

Since the 1960s television advertising to children has provoked a fierce debate about fairness: Are young children fair targets for advertising? Is it fair to allow unlimited advertising during children's programming? Does fairness require special action to limit certain types of advertising strategies directed at children? In 1974, the Federal Communications Commission (FCC) required that television stations place limits on children's advertising of 9.15 minutes per hour on weekends and 12 minutes per hour on weekdays,

But as Kunkel and Roberts (1991) argued:

> But if children's television advertising present problems of fairness, why would 12 minutes of commercials be acceptable whereas 14 minutes would not? And how could 12 minutes of ads be considered reasonable on weekdays, but not on weekends, when only 9.5 minutes per hour were allowed? According to the commission, the limits imposed struck a balance between the needs of children, who were judged uniquely susceptible to commercial influence, and the needs of broadcasters, who were dependent upon advertising revenue to maintain their children's program offerings. The FCC was concerned that more stringent limits on advertising could result in the demise of children's programming by removing the basis for its profitability.
>
> (p. 61)

This compromise satisfies nobody. It is clearly not based on any principle save perhaps expediency.

In 1977, again in America, the National Science Foundation commissioned a review of the 100 or so published studies on children and advertising and concluded that young children (below five years) experience difficulty distinguishing perceptually between programmes and advertisements. A substantial proportion of children, particularly those below the age of eight years express little or no comprehension of the persuasive intent of advertisements. Younger children who are unaware of the persuasive intent of television advertising tend to express greater belief in advertisements and a higher frequency of purchased requests (Kunkel and Roberts, 1991).

In the late 1970s the American Federal Trade Commission (FTC) decided to ban all advertising directed at children too young to understand a message's persuasive intent but this caused an immense backlash and claims were made naming the first amendment. In the end FTC lost and had their powers reduced. Kunkel and Roberts (1991) note:

> The FTC case also demonstrates that research evidence generally does not play a central role in determining policy outcomes. The conclusions that young children lack the abilities necessary to evaluate and defend against advertising was never successfully challenged. The evidence could hardly have been any stronger. Yet it was not the findings, but their meaning when viewed from a societal value perspective, that became the key issue of contention.
>
> While child advocates may be chagrined, there is an inescapable conclusion associated with the FTC proceeding. When forced to choose at an extreme level, society (at least in the form of its representative government) valued the protection of private enterprise, commercial speech, and some degree of the concept of caveat emptor more than it valued the protection of children in their interaction with these institutions. When the scientific 'facts' did not

appear consistent with the most valued outcome, the political means were pursued to obtain the desired end. The research evidence was ultimately made irrelevant in order to accommodate the predominant values.

(p. 67)

Hermann (1991) has attempted to categorize various types of consumer movement organizations and produced the typology shown in Table 8.1.

TABLE 8.1 *A typology of consumer organization*

Beneficiary Constituency	*Conscience Constituency*
Volunteer leadership	
Organizations seeking benefits for their members (others may benefit incidentally)	Organizations seeking benefits for all consumers
Examples: food-price protest, rent strikes	Examples: state and local consumer groups (information, education, redress assistance, lobbying)
Precipitating factors: sudden price increases or shortage of food or other basic needs.	Precipitating factors: product safety concerns (e.g. adulteration, contamination); fraud; misleading ads; redress problems
Facilitating factors: availability of short-term local leadership; media coverage and/or communications among potential supporters; recruitment of existing organizations (unions, housewife groups, etc.)	Facilitating factors: local leaders with organizational expertise; media coverage, public support, contributions, volunteer work
Professional leadership	
Organizations that provide advice or assistance to individuals	Organizations that seek change in the social, political and economic structure, benefiting all consumers
Example: Consumers Union (U.S.)	Examples: Nader organizations; 'umbrella organizations' (federations of consumer groups)
Precipitating factors: increasing product complexity; health/safety concerns	Precipitating factors: rise of concerns about corporate and government performance affecting consumers; inadequate voice for consumers in corporate and government decisions
Facilitating factors: careerist professional staff; adequate support base; recruitment of technical expertise	Facilitating factors: charismatic leadership; professional cadre; reform-oriented contributors

Source: Hermann, 1991

Furthermore, he considers the factors that affect the success of the consumer movement. These include the development of popular, saleable ideas and solutions; obtaining media access and maintaining organizational credibility. He believes that consumer organizations of the future are likely to be built around a professional specialist staff capable of dealing with relatively complex issues and providing relatively sophisticated services.

In the same spirit, Friedman (1991) tried to specify the dimensions of consumer boycotts, where much seems to depend on the target of the boycott, the time and place, and the boycott sponsors. Some boycotts are merely expressive tokens; others very radical and instrumental aims at immediate consequences. Friedman's consumer boycott strategies model is presented in Table 8.2. This model divides up consumer boycotts according to two dimensions: media-oriented boycotts versus marketplace-oriented boycotts, and surrogate boycotts versus non-surrogate boycots. Friedman noted that the type of boycott which had received most academic attention in economic literature, namely the marketplace-oriented, non-surrogate boycott, may be the least frequently occurring in reality. Media-oriented boycotts, whether of the surrogate or non-surrogate type, are more likely to occur in actuality. The reason for this has mainly to do with the allocation of resources to a boycott. A media-oriented boycott is less costly to resource. A marketplace boycott can require considerable organization and economic support (involving picketing, demonstrations and leafleting over the course of an orchestrated campaign), if it is to be successful; this level of support is seldom forthcoming.

TABLE 8.2 *Strategies envisioned by boycott leaders for various types of instrumental boycotts*

	Target	
Boycott	*Non-surrogate*	*Surrogate*
Media-oriented boycott	Adverse effects on target firm's image lead to desired change in target firm's behaviour	Adverse effects of target firm's image lead to pressure applied by target firm on offending party, leading to desired change in behaviour of offending party
Marketplace-oriented boycott	Adverse effects of target firm's image and sales lead to desired change in target firm's behaviour	Adverse effects on target firm's image lead to pressure applied by target firm on offending party, leading to desired change in behaviour of offending party

Source: Friedman, 1991

It seems that to be successful, media-orchestrated boycotts need to follow certain simple rules:

- Announcements and pleas should be made by well-known organizations and individuals.
- Announcements should identify a few well-known organizations as the target.
- Complaints and objections against these organizations should appear legitimate and relatively uncomplicated.
- If possible, passion and drama should accompany all announcements.

Factors that seem to predict the success of marketplace-oriented boycotts include:

- Boycotted products/services should be easy for consumers to identify.
- Boycotts should target just a few brand names, ideally one primary target.
- Boycotts should be planned at a time when there are few, if any, competing boycotts.
- It is crucial that there are acceptable and readily available targets for the boycotted products and services.
- Ideally boycott targets need to be selected so as to ensure that consumer violations of the boycotts are publicly visible.

Friedman (1991) has, interestingly, pointed out that a boycott is a new form of social action—a *boycott*! The lobbyists and protectionists are becoming increasingly sophisticated. Indeed there are now boycott consultants who advise nascent pressure groups how to proceed. Some, curiously and paradoxically, recommend approved, politically correct products. The purpose of this reverse discrimination to encourage consumers to buy products and services provided by organizations that are somehow favoured (for ethical, political or other reasons). To this extent one might even see the boycott as an extremely clever bit of marketing!

Conclusion

This chapter focused on the issue of the protection of young consumers. Protectionism and regulation, which is found in all countries to some degree, apply to the advertising, distribution, manufacture and sales of all sorts of goods.

Some argue that there are three basic reasons why children need protection: first, because of the gullibility, naivety, and therefore persuasability of children; second, because of the subtlety, sophistication and avarice of various companies; and third because artificially stimulating children's needs causes needless parent–child conflict.

Others argue that children are far from naive and that protectionists have 'infantilized' the young consumer for their own political ends. Furthermore, they believe it is the parents' duty to socialize their child into the consumer world and that certain parents should not expect legal sanctions to do what they should be doing.

Most agree that children (and adults for that matter) require education and some form of consumer protectionism but the question remains as to who should do this. The idea of consumer education is far less politically charged than the idea of protectionism, but important questions still need answering: *who* should educate *whom*, about *what* and *when*.

Over the past 20 years protectionists and lobbyists have become increasingly sophisticated, organizing boycotts, campaigns and demonstrations. Some have been very successful, others less so.

As the turn of millennium approaches it is apparent that increased consumer needs will cause government and other bodies to consider more carefully how to educate, facilitate and protect their citizens. The growth of modern, capitalist economies as well as the rapid growth of the electronic communication revolution mean that the world's growing number of young people will be eager to acquire the many products and services they see advertised. Parents, educators and legislators, as well as marketers and manufacturers, have different goals when it comes to the young consumer. It seems unlikely that this situation will change.

References

Abramovitch, R., Freedman, J. and Pliner, P. (1991). Children and money: Getting an allowance, credit versus cash and knowledge of pricing. *Journal of Economic Psychology*, **12**, 27–45.

Adelson, J. and O'Neil, R. (1966). Growth of political ideas in adolescence: The sense of community. *Journal of Personality and Social Psychology*, **4**, 295–306.

Adler, R.P., Lesser, G.S., Meringoff, L.K., Robertson, T.S., Rossiter, J.R. and Ward, S. (1980). *The Effects of Television Advertising on Children. Review and Recommendations*. Lexington, MA: Lexington Books.

Ajzen, I. and Fishbein, M. (1980). *Understanding Attitudes and Predicting Behaviour*. Englewood Cliffs, NJ: Prentice-Hall.

Anderson, D. R. and Lorch, E.P. (1983). Looking at television: Action or reaction? In J. Bryant and D.R. Anderson (Eds.), *Children's Understanding of Television: Research on Attention and Comprehension*. New York: Academic Press.

Angrist, S.S., Mickelson, R. and Penna, A.N. (1977). Sex difference in sex-role perceptions and family orientation of high school students. *Journal of Youth and Adolescence*, **6**, 179–186.

Armentrout, J. and Burger, E. (1972). Factor analysis of college student's recall of parental child-rearing behaviours. *Journal of Genetic Psychology*, **121**, 155–161.

Arnal, M-J., Chossiere, J., Lebreuilly, J. and Saurat, F. (1984-85). Sensibilité de lycéens à l'humour de la publicité televisée. *Bulletin de Psychologie*, **56**, 1345–1357.

Assael, H. (1981). *Consumer Behaviour and Marketing Action*. Boston, MA: Kent Publishing.

Atkin, C.K. (1975). Effects of television advertising on children: Second year experimental evidence. Report 2. Ann Arbor, Michigan: Michigan State University.

Atkin, C.K. (1978). Observation of parent–child interaction in supermarket decision making. *Journal of Marketing*, **42**, 41–45.

Atkin, C.K. (1980). Effects of television advertising on children. In E.L. Palmer and A. Dorr (Eds), *Children and the Faces of Television. Teaching, Violence, Selling*. New York: Academic Press, 287–306.

Atkin, C.K. (1982). Television advertising and socialization to consumer roles.

In D. Pearl, L. Bouhilet and J. Lazar (Eds), *Television and Behaviour: Ten Years of Scientific Progress and Implications for the 80s.* Vol. 2. Rockville, MD: NIMH.

Atkin, C.K. and Heald, G. (1977). The content of children's toy and food commercials. *Journal of Communication*, **27**, 107–114.

Atkin, C.K., Reeves, B. and Gibson, W. (1979). Effects of televised food advertising on children. Paper presented to the Association for Education in Journalism, Houston, Texas.

Atkin, C. and Rheingold, C. (1972). *The Impact of Television Advertising on Children.* Paper presented at the meeting of the Association for Education in Journalism, August, 1972.

Avery, R.K. (1979). Adolescents' use of the mass media. *American Behavioural Scientist*, **23**, 53–70.

Bach, G., Bellack, A., Chandler, L., Frankel, M., Gordon, R., Lewis, B., Samuelson, P. and Bond, F. (1961). *Economic Education in the School.* New York: Committee on Economic Development.

Bahn, K.D. (1986). How and when do brand perceptions and preferences first form? A cognitive developmental investigation. *Journal of Consumer Research*, **13**, 382–393.

Bandura, A. (1973). *Aggression: A Social Learning Analysis.* Englewood Cliffs, NJ: Prentice-Hall.

Banks, S. (1975). Public policy on ads to children. *Journal of Advertising Research*, **15**, 7–12.

Baumrind, D. (1968). Authoritarian vs. authoritative parental control. *Adolescence*, **3**, 255–272.

Baumrind, D. (1971). Current patterns of parental authority. *Developmental Psychology Monograph*, **4**, 1–103.

Baumrind, D. (1978). Parental disciplinary patterns and social competence in children. *Youth and Society*, **9**, 239–276.

Baumrind, D. (1980). New directions in socialization research. *American Psychologist*, **35**, 639–652.

Bayer, A. (1975). Sexist students in American Colleges: A descriptive note. *Journal of Marriage and Family*, **37**, 391–397.

Bechtel, R.B., Achelpohl, C. and Akers, R. (1972). Correlates between observed behaviour and questionnaire responses on television viewing. In E.A. Rubinstein, G.A. Comstock and J.P. Murray (Eds), *Television and Social Behaviour*, Vol.4. Washington, D.C.: U.S. Government Printing Office.

Becker, W.C. (1964). Consequences of different kinds of parental discipline. In M.L. Hoffman and L.W. Hoffman (Eds.), *Review of Child Development Research*, Vol.1. New York: Russell Sage, pp. 169–204.

Bednall, D. and Hannaford, M. (1980). *Television and Children: Recall of Television Advertising and Programmes by Children.* Melbourne: Australian Broadcasting Tribunal Research Report.

Belch, G.E., Belch, M.A. and Ceresino, G. (1985). Parental and teenage child influences in family decision making. *Journal of Business Research*, **13**, 163–176.

Belk, R., Mayer, R. and Driscoll, A. (1984). Children's recognition of consumption symbolism in children's products. *Journal of Consumer Research*, **10**, 386–397.

Bennett, W. (1991). Young shoppers hold sway over parents' choices. *The Independent*, 25 October.

Berey, L.A. and Pollay, R.W. (1970). The influencing role of the child in family decision making. In St. H. Britt (Ed.), *Psychological Experiments in Consumer Behaviour*. New York: Wiley, pp. 141–145.

Berti, A. and Bombi, A. (1979). Where does money come from? *Archivio di Psicologia*, **40**, 53–77.

Berti, A. and Bombi, A. (1981). The development of the concept of money and its value: A longitudinal study. *Child Development*, **52**, 1179–1182.

Berti, A. and Bombi, A. (1988). *The Child's Construction of Economics*. Cambridge: Cambridge University Press.

Berti, A., Bombi, A. and de Beni, R. (1986). Acquiring economic notions: Profit. *International Journal of Behavioural Development*, **9**, 15–29.

Berti, A., Bombi, A. and Lis, A. (1982). The child's conceptions about means of production and their owners. *European Journal of Social Psychology*, **12**, 221–239.

Birds Eye Walls (1990). Pocket Money Monitor. Produced by HCPR Ltd for Birds Eye Walls, Walton-on-Thames, Surrey, UK.

Blatt, J., Spencer, L. and Ward, S. (1972). A cognitive developmental study of children's reactions to television advertising. In E.A. Rubinstein, G.A. Comstock and J.P. Murray (Eds.), *Television and Social Behaviour. Vol.4. Television in Day-to-Day Life: Patterns of Use*. Washington, DC: US Government Printing Office, pp. 452–467.

Blosser, B.J. and Roberts, D.F. (1984). Age differences in children's perceptions of message intent; responses to TV news, commercials, educational spots and public service announcements. *Communication Research*, **12**, 455–484.

Blosser, B. J. and Roberts, D. F. (1985). Age differences in children's perception of message intent: response to TV news, commercials, educational spots, and public service announcements. *Communications Research*, **12**, 455–484.

Bocker, F. (1986). Children's influence on their mothers' preferences: A new approach. *International Journal of Research in Marketing*, **3**, 39–52.

Bonnett, C. and Furnham, A. (1991) Who wants to be an entrepreneur? A study of adolescents' interests in a Young Enterprise scheme. *Journal of Economic Psychology*, **12**, 465–478.

Bovee, C.L. and Arens, W.F. (1989). *Contemporary Advertising*, Third edition. Homewood, Ill: Richard D. Irwin.

Brittain, C.V. (1963). Adolescent choices and parent–peer cross pressures. *American Sociological Review*, **28**, 385–391.

Brobeck, S. (1990). The consumer movement in the 1990s. *Proceedings of the 36th Annual Conference of the American Council on Consumer Interests.* Columbia: ACCI.

Bronson, W.C. (1972). The role of enduring orientations to the environment of personality development. *Genetic Psychology Monographs*, **86**, 3–80.

Brown, D. and Bryant, J. (1983). Humour in the mass media. In P.E. McGhee and J.H. Goldstein (Eds), *Handbook on Humour Research: Vol.2. Applied Studies.* New York: Springer-Verlag.

Bruck, M., Armstrong, G.M. and Goldberg, M.E. (1988). Children's use of cognitive defenses against television advertising: A cognitive response approach. *Journal of Consumer Research*, **14**, 471–482.

Bryant, J. and Anderson, D.R. (Eds), (1983). *Children's Understanding of Television. Research on Attention and Competition.* New York: Academic Press.

Burgard, P., Cheyne, W. and Jahoda, G. (1989). Children's representations of economic inequality: A replication. *British Journal of Developmental Psychology*, **7**, 275–287.

Burgess, E.W. and Locke, H.J. (1960). *The Family: From Institution to Companionship.* (2nd edition) New York: American Book Co.

Burr, P.L. and Burr, R.M. (1976). Television advertising to children: What parents are saying about government control. *Journal of Advertising*, **5**, 37–41.

Burris, V. (1983). Stages in the Development of Economic Concepts. *Human Relations*, **36**, 791–812.

Butter, E.J., Weikel, K.B., Otto, V. and Wright, K.P. (1991). TV advertising of OTC medicines and its effects on child viewers. *Psychology and Marketing*, **8**, 117–128.

Calvert, S. L. and Scott, M.C. (1989). Sound effects for children's temporal integration of fast-paced television content. *Journal of Broadcasting and Electronic Media*, **33**, 233–246.

Campbell, E.Q. (1969). Adolescent socialization. In D.A. Goslin (Ed.), *Handbook of Socialization Theory and Research.* Chicago: Rand McNally.

Cantor, J. (1981). Modifying children's eating habits through television ads: Effects of humorous appeals in a field setting. *Journal of Broadcasting*, **25**, 37–47.

Carlens, D. (1990). *Kinderen, Televisie en de Vlaamse media-markt. Een terreinverkennend onderzoek naar het kijkgedrag van 9- tot 12-jarigen en hun houding t.o.v. BRT en VTM: een klassikale schriftelijke enquete.* Brussels: Licentiaatsverhandeling V.U.B.

Carlson, L. and Grossbart, S. (1988). Parental style and consumer socialization. *Journal of Consumer Research*, **15**, 77–94.

Caron, A. and Ward, S. (1975). Gift decisions by kids and parents. *Journal of Advertising Research*, **15**, 4, 15–20.

Cateora, P.R. (1963). *An Analysis of the Teenage Market*. Austin, TX: Bureau of Business Research.

Chaffee, S., Mcleod, J.M. and Atkin, C.K. (1971). Parental influences on adolescent media use. *American Behavioural Scientist*, **14**, 323–340.

Childers, T. and Rao, A. (1992). The influence of familial and peer based reference groups on consumer decisions. *Journal of Consumer Research*, **19**, 198–213.

Chizmar, J. and Halinski, R. (1983). Performance in the Basic Economic Test (BET) and 'Trade-offs'. *The Journal of Economic Education*, **14**, 18–29.

Christenson, P.G. (1982). Children's perception of TV commercials and products. *Communication Research*, **9**, 491–524.

Churchill, G.A. and Moschis, G.P. (1979). Television and interpersonal influences on adolescent consumer learning. *Journal of Consumer Research*, **6**, 23–35.

Clancy-Hepburn, K., Hickey, A.A. and Neville, G. (1974). Children's behaviour responses to TV food advertisements. *Journal of Nutrition Education*, **6**, 93–96.

Coleman, J.S. (1961). *The Adolescent Society*. New York: Free Press of Glenco.

Collins, J. (1990). Television and primary school children in Northern Ireland: The Impact of Advertising. *Journal of Educational Television*, **16**, 31–39.

Condry, J. (1989). *The Psychology of Television*. Hillsdale, NJ: Lawrence Erlbaum Associates.

Connell, R. (1991). *The Child's Construction of Politics*. Carlton: Melbourne University Press.

Cram, F. and Ng, S. (1989). Children's endorsement of ownership attributes. *Journal of Economic Psychology*, **10**, 63–75.

Crosby, L.A. and Grossbart, S.L. (1984). Parental style segments and concern about children's food advertising. In J. H. Leigh and C.R. Marton (Eds), *Current Issues and Research in Advertising, 1984*. Ann Arbor: Graduate School of Business Administration, University of Michigan.

Cummings, S. and Taebel, D. (1978). The economic socialization of children: A neo-Marxist analysis. *Social Problems*, **26**, 198–210.

Dailey, B.D. (1985-86). Communicating to the youth market: The child's perspective. *Journal of Advertising Research*, **22**, RC-7–RC-8.

Danziger, K. (1958). Children's earliest conceptions of economic relationships. *The Journal of Social Psychology*, **47**, 231–240.

Davidson, D. and Kilgore, J. (1971). A model for evaluating the effectiveness of economic education in primary grades. *The Journal of Economic Education*, **3**, 17–25.

Davis, H.L. (1970). Dimensions of martial roles in consumer decision making. *Journal of Marketing Research*, **7**, 168–177.

Davis, H.L. (1976). Decision making within the household. *Journal of Consumer Research*, **2**, 241–260.

Davis, J. (1990). *Youth and the Condition of Britain: Images of Adolescent Conflict*. London: Athlone Press.

Davis, K. and Taylor, T. (1979). *Kids and Cash: Solving a Parent's Dilemma*. La Jolla: Oak Tree.

Dawson, B., Jeffrey, D.B., Peterson, P.E., Sommers, J. and Wilson, G. (1985). Television commercials as a symbolic representation of reward in the delay of gratification paradigm. *Cognitive Therapy and Research*, **9**, 217–24.

De Bens, E. and Vandenbruane, P. (1992). *TV Advertising and Children, Part IV, Effects of TV Advertising on Children*. University of Ghent, Belgium: Centre for Media, Opinion and Advertising Research.

Dennis, J. and McCrone, D. (1970). The adult development of political party identification in Western democracies. *Comparative Political Studies*, 243–263.

Department for Education and Employment (1996) *Youth Cohort Study: Trends in the Activities and Experiences of 16-18 Year Olds: England and Wales 1985-1994*. Issue 7, June. London: HMSO.

Desmond, R.J., Singer, J.L. and Singer, D.G. (1990). Family mediation: parental communication patterns and the influences of television on children. In J. Bryant (Ed.), *Television and the American Family*. Hillsdale, NJ: Lawrence Erlbaum Associates, pp. 293–309.

Dibbs, S. (1993). *Children: Advertisers' Dream, Nutrition Nightmare?* London: National Food Alliance.

Dittmar, H. (1992). *The Social Psychology of Material Possessions*. Hemel Hempstead: Wheatsheaf.

Donohue, T.R., Hencke, L.L. and Donohue, W.A. (1980). Nonverbal assessment of children's understanding of television commercial intent and program market segmentation. *Journal of Advertising Research*, **20**.

Donohue, T. R. and Meyer, T.P. (1984). Children's understanding of television commercials: The acquisition of competence. In R.N. Bostrum (Ed.), *Competence in Communication*. Beverly Hills, CA: Sage.

Dorr, A. (1986). *Television and Children: A Special Medium for a Special Audience*. Beverly Hills, CA: Sage.

Dorr, A., Graves, S. B. and Phelps, E. (1980). Television literacy for young children. *Journal of Communication*, **30**, 71–83.

Dorr, A., Doubleday, C. and Kovaric, P. (1983). Emotions depicted on and stimulated by television programmes. In M. Meyer (Ed.), *Children and the Formal Features of Television*. Munich: K.G. Saur.

Dorr, A., Kovaric, P. and Doubleday, C. (1989). Parent–child co-viewing of television. *Journal of Broadcasting and Electronic Media*, **33**, 35–51.

Duffy, J. and Rossiter, J.R. (1975). *The Hartford Experiment: Children's reactions to TV commercials in blocks at the beginning and the end of the programme*. Paper presented at the 1975 Conference on Culture and Communication, Philadelphia: Temple University.

Dunlop, R. and Eckstein, J. (Eds), (1995) *Cultural Trends 1994: 23. Film, Cinema and Video; The Benefits of Public Art.* London: Policy Studies Institute.

Emler, N. and Dickinson, J. (1985). Children's representations of economic inequalities: The effects of social class. *British Journal of Developmental Psychology*, **3**, 191–198.

Emmerich, W. (1973). Socialization and sex-role development. In V.L. Bengtson and D.K. Black (Eds), *Life Span Developmental Psychology: Personality and Socialisation.* New York: Academic Press.

Enis, B.M., Spencer, D.R. and Webb, D.R. (1980). Television advertising and children: Regulatory vs. competitive perspectives. *Journal of Advertising*, **9**, 19–26.

Ermisch, J. (1990) *Fewer Babies, Longer Lives.* York, UK: Joseph Rowntree Foundation.

Faber, R.J., Meyer, T.P. and Miller, M.M. (1984). The effectiveness of health disclosures within children's television commercials. *Journal of Broadcasting*, Fall, **4**, 463–476.

Feshbach, S., Feshbach, N.D. and Cohen, S.E. (1984). Enhancing children's discrimination in response to television advertising: The effects of psychoeducational training in two elementary school-age groups. *Developmental Review*, **2**, 385–403.

Fierman, J. (1980). Reaching teens: Less emphasis on the product. *Advertising Age*, April 28, 5–24.

Filiatrault, P. and Ritchie, B. (1980). Joint purchasing decisions: A comparison of influence of structure in family and couple decision-making units. *Journal of Consumer Research*, **7**, 131–140.

Friedman, M. (1991). Consumer boycotts: A conceptual framework and research agenda. *Journal of Social Issues*, **47**, 149–168.

Fox, K. (1978). What children bring to school: The beginnings of economic education. *Social Education*, **10**, 478–481.

Foxman, E.R., Tansuhai, P.S. and Ekstrom, K.M. (1989). Adolescents' influence in family purchase decisions: A socialisation perspective. *Journal of Business Research.* March, 159–172.

Fry, J.N., Shaw, D.C., Lanzenauer, H von. and Dipchaud, C.R. (1973). Customer loyalty to banks: A longitudinal study. *Journal of Business*, **46**, 517–525.

Furby, L. (1978). Possessions in humans: An exploratory study of its meaning and innovation. *Social Behaviour and Personality*, **6**, 49–65.

Furby, L. (1980a). Collective possession and ownership: A study of its judged feasibility and desirability. *Social Behaviour and Personality*, **8**, 165–184.

Furby, L. (1980b). The origins and early development of possessive behaviour. *Political Psychology*, **2**, 30–42.

Furby, L. (1991). Understanding the psychology of possessions and ownership. *Journal of Social Behaviour and Personality*, **6**, 457–467.

Furnham, A. (1982). The perception of poverty among adolescents. *Journal of Adolescence*, **5**, 135–147.

Furnham, A. (1987). The determinants and structure of adolescents' beliefs about the economy. *Journal of Adolescence*, **10**, 353–371.

Furnham, A. (1990). *The Protestant Work Ethic*. London: Routledge.

Furnham, A. (1993). *Reaching for the Counter: The New Child Consumers: Regulation or Education?* London: Social Affairs Unit.

Furnham, A. and Argyle, M. (1997) *The Psychology of Money*. London: Routledge.

Furnham, A. and Cleare, A. (1988). School children's conceptions of economics: Prices, wages, investments and strikes. *Journal of Economic Psychology*, **9**, 467–479.

Furnham, A. and Gunter, B. (1983). Political knowledge and awareness in adolescence. *Journal of Adolescence*, **6**, 673–685.

Furnham, A. and Gunter, B. (1987). Young people's political knowledge. *Educational Studies*, **13**, 91–104.

Furnham, A. and Gunter, B. (1989). *The Anatomy of Adolescence*. London: Routledge.

Furnham, A. and Jones, S. (1987). Children's views regarding possessions and their theft. *Journal of Moral Education*, **16**, 18–30.

Furnham, A. and Stacey, B. (1992). *Young People's Understanding of Society*. London: Routledge.

Furnham, A. and Thomas, P. (1984). Adults' perception of the economic socialization of children. *Journal of Adolescence*, **7**, 217–231.

Furnham, A. and Thomas, P. (1989). Pocket money: A study of economic education. *British Journal of Developmental Psychology*, **2**, 205–212.

Furth, H. (1980). *The World of Grown-Ups*. New York: Elsevier.

Furth, H. Baur, M. and Smith, J. (1976). Children's conception of social institutions: a Piagetian framework. *Human Development*, **19**, 341–347.

Furth, H. and McConville, K. (1981). Adolescent understanding of compromise in political and social areas. *Merrill-Palmer Quarterly*, **27**, 412–427.

Gaines, L. and Esserman, J.F. (1981). A quantitative study of young children's comprehension of television programmes and commercials. In J.F. Esserman (Ed.), *Television Advertising and Children*. New York: Child Research Service.

Galst, J.P. (1980). Television food commercials and pro-nutritional public service announcements as determinants of young people's snack choices. *Child Development*, **51**, 3, 935–938.

Galst, J.P. and White, M.A. (1976). The unhealthy persuader: the reinforcing value of television and children's purchase-influencing attempts at the supermarket. *Child Development*, **47**, 1089–1096.

Gardner, C. and Sheppard, J (1989) *Consuming Passion: The Rise of Retail Culture*. London: Unwin Hyman.

Gardner, H. (1982). *Developmental Psychology: An Introduction*. Boston, MA: Little, Brown.

Gardner, H., Winner, E., Bechhofer, R. and Wolf, D. (1978). The development of figurative language. In K.E. Nelson (Ed.), *Children's Language*, 1–38. New York: Gardner.

Gilkison, P. (1973). Teenagers' perceptions of buying frame of reference: A decade of retrospect. *Journal of Applied Psychology*, **28**, 16–27.

Goldberg, M.E. (1990). A quasi-experiment assessing the effectiveness of TV advertising directed to children. *Journal of Marketing Research*, **27**, 445–454.

Goldberg, M.E., Gorn, G.J. and Gibson, W. (1987). TV messages for snacks and breakfast foods: Do they influence children's preferences? *Journal of Consumer Research*, **5**, 1, 73–81.

Goldstein, J.H. (1992). *Television Advertising and Children: A Review of Research*. Prepared for Toy Manufacturers of Europe, Brussels, April.

Gonzales, M. (1988). Aisles of teens. *American Demographics*, September, 19.

Gorn, G.J. and Goldberg, M.E. (1977). The impact of television advertising on children from low income families. *Journal of Consumer Research*, **4**, 86–88.

Gorn, G.J. and Goldberg, M.F. (1980). Children's responses to repetitive television commercials. *Journal of Consumer Research*, **6**, 421–424.

Gorn, G.J. and Goldberg, M.E. (1982). Some unintended consequences of TV advertising to children. *Journal of Consumer Research*, September, **4**, 86–88.

Goslin, D.A. (1969). *Handbook of Socialization Theory and Research*. Chicago: Rand McNally.

Greenberg, B.S., Fazal, S. and Wober, M. (1986). *Children's Views on Advertising*. London: Research Department, Independent Broadcasting Authority.

Greer, D., Potts, R., Wright, J.C. and Huston, A.C. (1982). The effects of television commercial form and commercial placement on children's social behaviour and attention. *Child Development*, **53**, 611–619.

Grossbart, S., Carlson, L. and Walsh, A. (1988). Consumer socialization and frequency of shopping with children. *Journal of the Academy of Marketing Science*, **19**, 155–163.

Grossbart, S. L. and Crosby, L.A. (1984). Understanding the basis of parental concern and reaction to children's food advertising. *Journal of Marketing*, **48**, 79–92.

GSI-CFRO (1989). L'argent des jeunes. *Sciences et Vie Economie*, **52**, 12–17.

Guest, L. (1964). Brand loyalty revisited: A twenty year report. *Journal of Applied Psychology*, **48**, 93–97.

Gunter, B. and McAleer, J.L. (1990). *Children and Television: The One-Eyed Monster?* London: Routledge.

Haedrich, G., Adam, M., Kreilkamp, E. and Kuss, A. (1984). Zur Verhaltenswirkung der Fernsehwerbung bei Kindern. *Marketing*, **6**, 129–133.

Hall, C. (1987). There's no place like home. *Marketing and Media Decisions*, July, pp. 26, 28.

Hamilton, J. and Warden, J. (1966). Student's role in a high school community and his clothing behaviour. *Journal of Home Economics*, **58**, 789–791.

Hansen, F. (1972). *Consumer Choice Behaviour*. New York: Free Press.

Hansen, H. (1985). The economics of early childhood education in Minnesota. *The Journal of Economic Education*, **16**, 219–224.

Haste, H. and Torney-Purta, J. (1992). *The Development of Political Understanding*. San Francisco: Jossey-Bass.

Hawkins, R. and Pingree, S. (1982) Television's influence on social reality. In D. Pearl, L. Bouthilet and J. Lazar (Eds), *Television and Behaviour: Ten Years of Scientific Progress and Implications for the Eighties*. Rockville, Maryland: Institute of Mental Health.

Hempel, D.J. (1974). Family buying decision: A cross-cultural perspective. *Journal of Marketing Research*, **11**, 295–302.

Hermann, R. (1991). Participation and leadership in consumer movement organizations. *Journal of Social Issues*, **47**, 119–33.

Hill, R. and Aldous, J. (1969). Socialization for marriage and parenthood. In D.A. Goslin (Ed.), *Handbook of Socialization Theory and Research*. Chicago: Rand McNally.

Himmelweit, H., Humphreys, P., Jaeger, M. and Katz, M. (1981). *How Voters Decide*. London: Academic Press.

Hite, R.E. and Eck, R. (1987). Advertising to children: Attitudes of business vs. consumers. *Journal of Advertising Research*, **27**, 5, 40–53.

Holicki, S. and Sonesson, I. (1991). TV in the socialization process: A study of preschool children in Sweden and Germany. *The Nordicom Review of Nordic Mass Communication*, **1**, 15–23.

Holman, J. and Braithwaite, V. (1982). Parental lifestyles and children's television viewing. *Australian Journal of Psychology*, **34**, 375–382.

Horton, R. and Weidenaar, D. (1975). Wherefore economic education? *The Journal of Economic Education*, **7**, 40–44.

Hower, J.T. and Edwards, K.J. (1978). Interparent factor analysis of children's perceptions of parental child rearing behaviours. *Journal of Genetic Psychology*, **132**, 261–266.

Huston, A.C., Wright, J.C., Wartella, E., Rice, M.L., Watkins, B.A., Campbell, T. and Potts, R. (1992). Communicating more than content: Formal features of children's television programmes. *Journal of Communication*, *31*, 32–48.

Irving, K. and Siegal, M. (1983). Mitigating circumstances in children's perceptions of criminal justice. *British Journal of Development Psychology*, **1**, 179–188.

Isler, L., Popper, E. and Ward, S. (1987). Children's purchase requests and parental responses. *Journal of Advertising Research*, **27**, 54–59.

Jackson, R. (1972). The development of political concepts in young children. *Educational Research*, **14**, 51–55.

Jaglom, L.M. and Gardner, H. (1981). The preschool television viewer as anthropologist. In H. Kelly and H. Gardner (Eds), *Viewing Children Through Television*. San Francisco: Jossey-Bass, pp. 9–30.

Jahoda, G. (1979). The construction of economic reality by some Glaswegian children. *European Journal of Social Psychology*, **9**, 115–127.

Jahoda, G. (1981). The development of thinking about economic institutions: The bank. *Cahiers de Psychologie Cognitive*, **1**, 55–73.

James, W. (1891). *The Principles of Psychology*. London: Macmillan.

Jaros, D. and Grant, L. (1979). *Political Behaviour: Choice and Perspective*. Oxford: Blackwell.

Jenkins, R.L. (1978). The influence of children in family decision-making: Parents' perceptions. In W.L. Wilkie (Ed.), *Advances in Consumer Research*, **6**, 413–419.

John, D.R. (1984). The development of knowledge structures in children. In E.C. Hirschman and M.B. Holbrook (Eds) *Advances in Consumer Research* 12, Chicago: Association for Consumer Research, pp.329–333.

John, D.R. and Whitney, J.C. (1986). The development of consumer knowledge in children: A cognitive structure approach. *Journal of Consumer Research*, **11**, 964–971.

Joossens, L. (1984). Het effect van cumulatieve blootstelling aan reclamescpots op kinderen. Een experimenteel onderzoek. *Communicatie*, **3**, 8–12.

Kagan,J., Moss, H. and Siegel, I. (1962). Psychological significance of styles of conceptualisation. In R. Brown (Ed.), *Cognitive Development in Children*. Chicago: Chicago University Press, pp. 73–112.

Kamptner, N. (1991). Personal possessions and their meaning: A life-span perspective. *Journal of Social Behaviour and Personality*, **6**, 209–228.

Kapferer, J.N. (1985). *L'Enfant et las Publicité. Les Chemins de la Seduction*. Pris: Dunod.

Kinsey, J. (1987). The use of children in advertising and the impact of advertising aimed at children. *International Journal of Advertising*, **6**, 169–177.

Kline, S. (1991). Let's make a deal: merchandising in US-kinderfernsehen. *Media Perspective*, **4**, 220–234.

Kohlberg, L. (1969). Sequence: The cognitive development approach to socialization. In D. Goslin (Ed.), *Handbook of Socialisation Theory and Research*. Chicago: Rand McNally, pp. 347–480.

Kojima, K. (1968). Youth and television in contemporary Japan: analytical framework, background and characteristics. *Gazette*, **37**, 87–102.

Kourilsky, M. (1977). The kinder-economy: a case study of kindergarten pupils' acquisition of economic concepts. *The Elementary School Journal*, **77**, 182–191.

Kourilsky, M. and Campbell, M. (1984). Sex differences in a simulated classroom economy: Children's beliefs about entrepreneurship. *Sex Roles*, **10**, 53–66.

Kourilsky, M. and Murray, T. (1981). The use of economic reasoning to increase satisfaction with family decision making. *Journal of Consumer Research*, **8**, 183–188.

Kunkel, D. (1988). From a raised eyebrow to a turned back: The FCC and children's product-related programming. *Journal of Communication*, **38**, 90–108.

Kunkel, D. (1991). Crafting media policy: The genesis and implications of the Children's Television Act of 1990. *American Behavioural Scientist*, **35**, 181–202.

Kunkel, D. and Roberts, D. (1991). Young minds and marketplace values: Issues in children's television advertising. *Journal of Social Issues*, **57**, 57–72.

Langman, L. (1992). Neon cages: Shopping for subjectivity. In R. Shields (Ed.), *Lifestyle Shopping: The Subject of Consumption*. London: Routledge.

Laurent, G. and Kapferer, J.N. (1985). Measuring consumer involvement profiles. *Journal of Marketing Research*, **22**, 41–53.

Leahy, R. (1981). The development of the conception of economic inequality: I. Descriptions and comparisons of rich and poor people. *Child Development*, **52**, 523–532.

Leiser, D. (1983). Children's conceptions of economics: The constitution of the cognitive domain. *Journal of Economic Psychology*, **4**, 297–317.

Leiser, D., Sevon, G. and Levy, D. (1990). Chidren's economic socialization of ten countries. *Journal of Economic Psychology*, **11**, 591–614.

Levin, S.R. and Anderson, D.R. (1976). The development of attention. *Journal of Communication*, **26**, 126–135.

Levin, S.R., Petros, T.V. and Petrella, F.W. (1982). Preschoolers' awareness of television advertising. *Child Development*, **53**, 933–937.

Liebert, D.E., Sprafkin, J.N., Liebert, R.M. and Rubinstein, E.A. (1977). Effects of television commercial disclaimers on the product expectations of children. *Journal of Communication*, **27**, 118–124.

Liebert, R,M. (1986). Effects of television on children and adolescents. *Journal of Developmental and Behavioural Paediatrics*, **7**, 43–48.

Linn, M.C., de Benedectis, T. and Delucchi, K. (1982). Adolescent reasoning about advertisements: Preliminary investigations. *Child Development*, **53**, 1599–1613.

Lull, J. (1980). The social uses of television. *Human Communication Research*, **6**, 97–209.

Lyle, J. and Hoffman, H.R. (1971). Children's use of television and other media. In E.A. Rubinstein, G.A. Comstock and J.P. Murray (Eds), *Television and Social Behaviour*. Washington DC: US Government Printing Office, pp. 129–256.

Macklin, C. (1985). Do young children understand the selling intent of commercials? *Journal of Consumer Affairs*, **19**, 293–304.

Macklin, C. (1987). Preschoolers' understanding of the informational function of advertising. *Journal of Consumer Research*, **14**, 229–239.

McDonald, W.J. (1982). Approaches to group research with children. *Journal of the Academy of Marketing Science*, **10**, 490–499.

McKenzie, R. (1971). An exploratory study of the economic understanding of elementary school teachers. *The Journal of Economic Education*, **3**, 26–31.

McLeod, J.M. and Becker, L.B. (1974). Testing the validity of television gratifications and avoidances through political effects analysis. In J. Blumler and E. Katz (Eds), *The Uses of Mass Communications: Current Perspectives on Gratifications Research*. Beverly Hills, CA: Sage.

McLeod, J.M. and Chaffee, S.H. (1972). The construction of social reality. In J.T. Tedeschi (Ed.), *The Social Influence Process*. Chicago: Aldine-Atherton, pp. 50–99.

McLeod, J.M., Fitzpatrick, M.A., Glynn, C.J. and Fallis, S.F. (1982). Television and social relations: Family influences and consequences for interpersonal behaviour. In D. Pearl, L. Bouthilet and J. Lazar (Eds), *Television and Behaviour: Ten Years of Scientific Progress and Implications for the Eighties*. Washington, DC: US Government Printing Office.

McLeod, J.M. and O'Keefe, G.J. (1972). The socialisation perspective and communication behaviour. In F.G. Kline and P.J. Tichenor (Eds), *Current Perspectives in Mass Communications Research*, Beverly Hill, CA: Sage, pp. 121–168.

McNeal, J.U. (1969). The child as consumer: A new market. *Journal of Retailing*. Summer, 15–22, 84.

McNeal, J.U. (1987). *Children as Consumers*. Lexington, MA: Lexington Books.

McNeal, J.U. (1992). *Kids as Customers: A Handbook of Marketing to Children*. New York: Lexington Books.

McNeal, J.U. and Yeh, C.H. (1990). Taiwanese children as consumers. *Asia Pacific Journal of Marketing*, **2**, 32–43.

Madison Avenue (1980). Seventeen makes a sales call. 22nd November, pp.85, 88–91, 94–96.

Marshall, H. and Magruder, L. (1960). Relations between parent money education practices and children's knowledge and use of money. *Child Development*, **31**, 253–284.

Mayer, R. (1991). Gone yesterday here today: Consumer issues in the agenda setting process. *Journal of Social Issues*, **47**, 21–39.

Mehotra, S. and Torges, S. (1976). Determinants of children's influence on mother's buying behaviour. In W.D. Perreault Jr. (Ed.), *Advances in Consumer Research*, **4**, 56–69.

Messaris, P. and Sarett, C. (1982). On the consequences of television-related parent–child interaction. *Mass Communication Review Yearbook*, Vol.3., pp. 365–383.

Meyer, M. (1983). *Children and the Formal Features of television: Approaches and Findings of Experimental and Formative Research*. Munich: K.G. Saur Verlag.

Meyer, T.P., Donohue, T.R. and Hencke, L.L. (1978). How black children see TV commercials. *Journal of Advertising Research*, **18**, 5, 51–62.

Milavsky, R., Pekowsky, B. and Stipp, H. (1975). TV drug advertising and proprietary and illicit drug use among teenage boys. *Public Opinion Quarterly*, **39**, 457–481.

Miller, L. and Horn, T. (1955). Children's concepts regarding debt. *The Elementary School Journal*, **56**, 406–412.

Millson, C.A. (1966). *Conformity to Peers versus Adults in Early Adolescence.* New York: Doctoral Thesis, Cornell University.

Mintel (1990). *Youth Lifestyles 1990.* London: Mintel Publications Ltd.

Moore, R.L. (1990). Effects of television on family consumer behaviour. In J. Bryant (Ed.), *Television and the American Family.* Hillsdale, NJ: Lawrence Erlbaum Associates.

Moore, R.L. and Moschis, G.P. (1978). Teenager's reactions to advertising. *Journal of Advertising*, **7**, 24–30.

Moore, R.L. and Moschis, G.P. (1979). Role perceptions in adolescent consumer learning. *Home Economic Research Journal*, **8**, 66–74.

Moore, R.L. and Moschis, G.P. (1981). The role of family communication in consumer learning. *Journal of Communication*, **31**, 42–51.

Moore, R.L. and Stephens, L.F. (1975). Some communication and demographic determinants of adolescent consumer learning. *Journal of Consumer Research*, **2**, 80–92.

Moschis, G.P. and Churchill, G.A. (1978). Consumer socialization: A theoretical and empirical analysis. *Journal of Marketing Research*, **15**, 599–609.

Moschis, G.P., Lawton, J.T. and Stampfl, R.W. (1980). Preschool children's consumer learning. *Home Economics Journal*, **9**, 64–71.

Moschis, G.P. and Moore, R.L. (1979a). Decision making among the young: A socialization perspective. *Journal of Consumer Research*, **6**, 101–112.

Moschis, G.P. and Moore, R.L. (1979b). Family communication and consumer socialization. In W. L. Wilkie (Ed.), *Advances in Consumer Research*, Vol.6. Ann Arbor, MI: Association for Consumer Research, pp. 359–363.

Moschis, G.P. and Moore, R.L. (1979c). Mass media and personal influences on adolescent consumer learning. *Developments in Marketing Science*, Vol.2.

Moschis, G.P. and Moore, R.L. (1980a). Purchasing behaviour of adolescent consumers. In R.P. Bagiozzi, K.L. Berhardt, P.S. Busch, D.W. Cravens, J.F. Hair and C.A. Scott (Eds), *AMA Educators' Conference Proceedings.* Chicago: American Marketing Association.

Moschis, G.P. and Moore, R.L. (1980b). Racial and socio-economic influences on the development of consumer behaviour. Georgia State University, Working Paper.

Moschis, G. P. and Moore, R.L. (1981a). A study of consumer skill acquisition. Georgia State University, Working Paper.

Moschis, G.P. and Moore, R.L. (1981b). The effects of family communication and mass media use on adolescent consumer learning. *Journal of Communication*, **31**.

Moschis, G.P. and Moore, R.L. (1981c). Anticipating consumer socialisation. Georgia State University, Working paper.

Moschis, G.P. and Moore, R.L. (1981d). A study of acquisition of desires for products and brands. *1981 AMA Educator's Conference Proceedings*. Chicago: American Marketing Association.

Moschis, G.P. and Moore, R.L. (1981e). A model of brand preference formation. Georgia State University, Working Paper.

Moschis, G.P. and Moore, R.L. (1982). A longitudinal study of television advertising effects. *Journal of Consumer Research*, **9**, 3, 279–286.

Moschis, G.P., Moore, R.L. and Smith, R.B. (1984). The impact of family communication on adolescent consumer socialization. In T.C. Kinnear (Ed.), *Advances in Consumer Research*, Vol.11. Provo, UT: Association for Consumer Research.

Moschis, G.P., Moore, R.L. and Stephens, L.F. (1977). Purchasing patterns of adolescent consumers. *Journal of Retailing*, **53**, 17–26, 92.

Murray, J.P. and Kippax, S. (1981). Television's impact on children and adults: International perspectives on theory and research. *Mass Communication Review Yearbook*, Vol. 2, pp. 582–639.

Neelankavil, J.P., O'Brien, J.V. and Tashjian, R. (1985). Techniques to obtain market-related information from very young children. *Journal of Advertising Research*. June/July, 41–47.

Nelson, J.E. (1979). Children as information sources in the family decision to eat out. *Advances in Consumer Research*, **6**, 419–423.

Newson, J. and Newson, E. (1976). *Seven Year Olds in the Home Environment.* London: Allen & Unwin.

Ng, S. (1983). Children's ideas about the bank and shop profit: Development, stages and the influence of cognitive contrasts and conflicts. *Journal of Economic Psychology*, **4**, 209–221.

Ng, S. (1985). Children's ideas about the bank: A New Zealand replication. *European Journal of Social Psychology*, **15**, 121–123.

Nikken, P. (1991). Ook Kinderen verdienen Kwaltiteit op Televisie. *Jeugd en Samenleving*. October, **10**, 630–640.

Nippold, M. A., Cuyler, J.S. and Braunbeck-Price, R. (1988). Explanation of ambiguous advertisements: A developmental study with children and adolescents. *Journal of Speech and Hearing Research*, **31**, 466–474.

O'Brien, M. and Ingels, S. (1985). The effects of economics instruction in early adolescence. *Theory and Research in Social Education*, **4**, 279–294.

O'Brien, M. and Ingels, S. (1987). The economic values inventory. *Research in Economic Education*, **18**, 7–18.

Paget, K.F., Kritt, D. and Bergemann, L. (1984). Understanding strategic interactions in television commercials: A developmental study. *Journal of Applied Developmental Psychology*, **5**, 145–161.

Palmer, E.L. (1988). *Television and America's Children: A Crisis of Neglect*. New York: Oxford University Press.

Palmer, E.L. and McDowell, C.N. (1979). Program/commercial separators in children's television programming. *Journal of Communication*, **29**, 197–201.

Palmer, E.L. and MacNeil, M. (1991). Children's comprehension processes: From Piaget to public policy. In J. Bryant and D. Zillmann (Eds), *Responding to the Screen: Reception and Reaction Processes*. Hillsdale, NJ: Lawrence Erlbaum Associates.

Parsons, T., Bales, R. and Shils, E.A. (1953). *Working Papers in the Theory of Action*. Glencoe, IL: The Free Press.

Peracchio, L.A. (1992). How do young children learn to be consumers? A cript-processing approach. *Journal of Consumer Research*, **18**, 425–439.

Pereira, J. (1990). Kids' advertisers play hide-and-seek, concealing commercials in every cranny. *Wall Street Journal*, April 30, pp. 131–136.

Pollio, H. and Gray, R. (1973). Change-making strategies in children and adults. *The Journal of Psychology*, **84**, 173–179.

Pope, D. (1991). Advertising as a consumer issue. *Journal of Social Issues*, **47**, 41–56.

Prasad, V.K., Rao, T.R. and Sheikh, A.A. (1978). Mother vis commercial. *Journal of Communication*, **28**, 91–96.

Prevey, E. (1945). A quantitative study of family practices in training children in the use of money. *The Journal of Educational Psychology*, **36**, 411–428.

Psathas, G. (1957). Ethnicity, social class and adolescent independence from parental control. *American Sociological Review*, **22**, 415–423.

Ramsett, D. (1972). Toward improving economic education in the elementary grades. *The Journal of Economic Education*, **4**, 30–35.

Remmers, H.H. and Radler, D.H. (1957). The basis of teenage behaviour. *The American Teenager*, New York: Boules-Mezri, 229–237.

Reynolds, F.D. and Wells, W.D. (1977). *Consumer Behaviour*. New York: McGraw-Hill Book Company.

Rice, M., Huston, A.C. and Wright, J.C. (1983). The forms of television: Effects on children's attention, comprehension and social behaviour. In M. Mayer (Ed.), *Children and the Formal Features of Television*. Munich: K.G. Saur, pp. 21–55.

Riecken, G. and Yavas, U. (1990). Children's general, product and brand-specific attitudes towards television commercials: Implications for public policy and advertising strategy. *International Journal of Advertising*, **9**, 136–148.

Riem, H. (1987). *Reclame en het Kind: de Invloed van TV-Reclame op Kinderen*. Antwerp: University of Antwerp.

Riesman, D., Glazer, N. and Denney, R. (1953). *The Lonely Crowd*. New York: Doubleday.

Riesman, D. and Roseborough, H. (1955). Careers and consumer behaviour. In L.C. Clark (Ed.), *Consumer Behaviour, Vol.II: The Life Cycle and Consumer Behaviour.* New York: New York University Press, pp. 1–18.

Robertson, T.S. (1976). Low-commitment consumer behaviour. *Journal of Advertising Research,* **16**, 19–24.

Robertson, T.S. (1979). Parental mediation of television advertising effects. *Journal of Communication,* **29**, 12–25.

Robertson, T.S. and Rossiter, J. (1974). Children and commercial persuasion: An attributional theory analysis. *Journal of Consumer Research,* **1**, 13–20.

Robertson, T.S. and Rossiter, J.R. (1977). Children's responsiveness to commercials. *Journal of Communication,* **27**, 101–106.

Robertson, T.S., Ward, S., Gatignon, H. and Klees, D.M. (1989). Advertising and children: A cross-cultural study. *Communication Research,* **16**, 459–485.

Roe, A. and Siegelman, M. (1963). Parent–child relations questionnaire. *Child Development,* **34**, 355–369.

Roedder, D.L., Sternthal, B. and Calder, B.J. (1983). Attitude-behaviour consistency in children's responses to television advertising. *Journal of Marketing Research,* **20**, 337–349.

Roger, R. and Nolf, S. (1980), *Education of the Consumer: A Review of Historical Developments.* Washington, DC: Consumer Education Resource Network.

Rolandelli, D.R. (1989). Children and television: The visual superiority effect reconsidered. *Journal of Broadcasting and Electronic Media,* **33**, 69–81.

Ross, A. (Ed.) (1990). *Economic and Industrial Awareness in the Primary School.* London: PNL Press.

Ross, R.P., Campbell, T., Wright, J.C., Huston, A. C., Rice, M.L. and Turk, P. (1984). When celebrities talk, children listen: An experimental analysis of children's response to TV ads with celebrity endorsement. *Journal of Applied Developmental Psychology,* **5**, 185–202.

Rossano, M.J. and Butter, E.J. (1987). Television advertising and children's attitudes towards proprietary medicine. *Psychology and Marketing,* **4**, 213–224.

Rossiter, J.R. (1980). Children and television advertising: Policy issues, perspectives and the status of research. In E.L. Palmer and A. Dorr (Eds), *Children and the Faces of Television.* New York: Academic Press, pp. 251–272.

Rust, L. (1986). Children's advertising: How it works, how to do it, how to know if it works. *Journal of Advertising Research,* **26**, RC-13–15.

Rust, L. (1993). Parents and children shopping together. *Journal of Advertising Research,* **4**, 65–70.

Ryan, M.S. (1965). Factors related to satisfaction with girls' blouses and slips: A comparison of mothers' and adolescent daughters' opinions. New York: Cornell University, Agricultural Experiment Station Bulletin 1003, May.

Salomon, G. (1983). Beyond the formats of television: The effects of student preconceptions on the experience of televiewing. In M. Mayer (Ed.), *Children and the Formal Features of Television.* Munich: K.G. Saur, pp. 209–232.

Samli, A.C. and Windeshausen, H.N. (1964). *Sacramento Teenage Market Study*. Sacramento, Calf: Advertising Club of Sacramento, pp.37–39.

Saunders, P. (1994). A global framework for teaching economics. In W. Walstad (Ed.), *An International Perspective on Economic Education*. Boston: Kluwer, pp. 37–45.

Saunders, P., Bach, G., Calderwood, G. and Hansen, W. (1993). *A Framework for Teaching the Basic Concepts* (3rd edition). New York: National Council on Economic Education.

Saunders, J.R., Samli, A.C. and Tozier, E.F. (1973). Congruence and conflict in buying decisions of mothers and daughters. *Journal of Retailing*, **49**, 3–18.

Schiffman, L.G. and Kanuk, L.L. (1991). *Consumer Behaviour*. Englewood Cliffs, NJ: Prentice Hall.

Schneider, C. (1987). *Children's Television: The Art, the Business and How It Works*. Lincolnwood, Chicago: NTC Business Books.

Schug, M. and Birkey, C. (1985). The development of children's economic reasoning. Paper presented at the annual meeting of the American Educational Research Association, Chicago.

Scott, L.M. (1990). Understanding jingles and needledrop: A rhetorical approach to music in advertising. *Journal of Consumer Research*, **17**, 223–236.

Sebald, H. (1968). *Adolescence: A Socio–Psychological Analysis*, New York: Appleton-Century-Crofts.

Sellers, P. (1989). The ABC's of marketing to kids. *Fortune*. May 8, p. 115.

Sepstrup, P. (1986). The electronic dilemma of television advertising. *European Journal of Communication*, **1**, 383–405.

Sevon, G. and Weckstrom, S. (1989). The development of reasoning about economic events: A study of Finnish children. *Journal of Economic Psychology*, **10**, 495–514.

Shaak, B., Annes, L. and Rossiter, J.R. (1975). Effects of the social success theme on children's product preference. Paper presented at the 1975 Conference on Culture and Communications, Philadelphia, PA: Temple University.

Sheikh, A.A. and Moleski, L.M. (1977). Conflict in the family over commercials. *Journal of Communication*, **27**, 152–157.

Sheikh, A.A., Prasad, V.K. and Rao, T.R. (1974). Children's TV commercials: A review of research. *Journal of Communication*, **24**, 126–136.

Shimp, T.A., Dyer, R.F. and Divita, S.F. (1976). An experimental test of the harmful effects of premium-oriented commercials on children. *Journal of Consumer Research*, **3**, 1–11.

Smith, G. and Sweeney, E. (1984). *Children and Television Advertising: An overview*. London: Children's Research Unit.

Sonuga-Barke, E. and Webley, P. (1993). *Children's Saving: Study in the Development of Economic Behaviour*. Hove, UK: Lawrence Erlbaum Associates.

Stacey, B. (1982). Economic socialization in the pre-adult years. *British Journal of Social Psychology*, **21**, 159–73.

Stacey, B. and Singer, M. (1985). The perception of poverty and wealth among teenagers. *Journal of Adolescence*, **8**, 231–241.

Stephens, N. and Stutts, M.A. (1982). Preschoolers' ability to distinguish between television programming and commercials. *Journal of Advertising*, **11**, 16–26.

Stevens, W. (1988). *Humor in de Reclame Een Literatuurstudie*. Leiven: Licentiaastverhandeling K.U.L.

Stewart, F. (1992) The adolescent as consumer. In J.C. Coleman and C. Warren-Adamson (Eds), *Youth Policy in the 1990s: The Way Forward* London: Routledge.

Stone, E.C. (1985). *Advertising and Children*. Presentation given to the Global Products/Services Marketing Commission of the International Advertising Association, December.

Stone, J. (1954). *The Measurement of Consumers' Expenditure and Behaviour in the United Kingdom*. Cambridge: Cambridge University Press.

Stoneman, Z. and Brody, G.H. (1982). The indirect impact of child-oriented advertisements on mother-child interactions. *Journal of Applied Developmental Psychology*, **2**, 369–376.

Stradling, R. (1977). *The Political Awareness of the School Leaver*. London: Hansarch Society.

Strauss, A. (1952). The development and transformation of monetary meaning in the child. *American Sociological Review*, **53**, 275–286.

Stutts, M.A. and Hunnicutt, G.G. (1987) Can young children understand disclaimers in television commercials? *Journal of Advertising*, **16**, 41–46.

Stutts, M.A., Vance, D. and Hudleson, S. (1981). Programme-commercial separators in children's television: Do they help a child tell the difference between Bugs Bunny and the Quick Rabbit? *Journal of Advertising*, **10**, 16–25.

Sutton, R. (1962). Behaviour in the attainment of economic concepts. *The Journal of Psychology*, **53**, 37–46.

Swinyard, W.R. and Sim, C.P. (1987). Perceptions of children's influence on family decision processes. *The Journal of Consumer Marketing*, **4**, 25–38.

Szybillo, G.J. and Sosanie, A. (1977). Family decision making: Husband, wife and children. In W.D. Perreault (Ed.) *Advances in Consumer Research*, **4**, 46–49.

Szybillo, G.J., Sosanie, A. and Tenebein, A. (1977). Should children be seen, but not heard? *Journal of Advertising Research*, **6**, 7–13.

Tootelian, D.H. and Gaedeke, R.M. (1992). The teen market: An exploratory analysis of income, spending and shopping patterns. *Journal of Consumer Marketing*, **9**, 35–45.

Tootelian, D.H. and Windeschausen, H.N. (1975). The teen-age market: A comparative analysis: 1964–1974. *Journal of Retailing*. Summer, 51–60, 92.

Vener, A.M. (1957). *Adolescent orientation to clothing: A social psychological interpretation.* Unpublished doctoral dissertation, Michigan State University, East Lansing, Michigan 48823.

Verhaeren, J. (1991). *Kinderen en Televisiereklame; Een Onderzoek naar de (wan)orde in Rehuleringen met betrekking tot Kinderen, Aanzet tot een bruikbaar Model voor Vlaaderen?* Brussel: Licentiaatsverhandeling, V.U.B.

Von Feilitzen, C. (1991). Children's and adolescents' media use: Some methodological reflections. *Communication Yearbook 14*, pp. 91–101. Beverly Hills, CA: Sage.

Waite, P. (1988). Economic Awareness: Context, issues and concepts. *Theory and Practice.*

Walls, Ltd (1983). *Pocket Money Monitor.* London: Walls.

Waldrop, J. (1990). Teens take control. *American Demographics*, March, p. 12.

Walstad, W. (1979). Effectiveness of a USMES in service economic education program for elementary school teachers. *The Journal of Economic Education*, **11**, 1–12.

Walstad, W. and Watts, M. (1985). Teaching economics in schools: A review of survey findings. *The Journal of Economic Education*, **16**, 135–146.

Ward, S. (1974). Consumer socialization. *Journal of Consumer Research*, **1**, 1–16.

Ward, S., Popper, E. and Wackman, D. (1977). *Parent Under Pressure. Influences on Mothers' Responses to Children's Purchase Requests.* Report No. 77–107. Cambridge, Mass: Marketing Science Institute.

Ward, S., Reale, G. and Levinson, D. (1972). Children's perceptions, explanations and judgements of television advertising: A further exploration. In E.A. Rubinstein, G.A. Comstock and J.P. Murray (Eds), *Television and Social Behaviour, Vol.4, Television in Day-to-Day Life: Patterns of Use.* Washington, DC: US Government Printing Office, pp. 468–490.

Ward, S. and Wackman, D. (1972). Television advertising and intra-family influence: Children's purchase influence attempts and parental yielding. *Journal of Marketing Research*, **9**, 316–319.

Ward, S. and Wackman, D. (1973). Children's information processing of television advertising. In P. Clark (Ed.), *New Models for Mass Communications Research.* Beverly Hills, CA: Sage.

Ward, S., Wackman, D. and Wartella, E. (1977). *How Children Learn To Buy: The Development of Consumer Information-Processing Skills.* Beverly Hills, CA: Sage.

Wartella, E. (1980). Individual differences in children's responses to television advertising. In E.L. Palmer and A. Dorr (Eds), *Children and the Faces of Television.* New York: Academic Press.

Wartella, E. and Ettema, J.S. (1974). A cognitive developmental study of children's attention to television commercials. *Communication Research*, **1**, 46–69.

References **209**

Wartella, E. and Hunter, L.S. (1983). Children and the formats of television advertising. In M. Meyer (Ed.), *Children and the Formal Features of Television*. Munich: K.G. Saur Verlag, pp. 144–165.

Wartella, E., Wackman, D., Ward, S., Shamir, J. and Alexander, A. (1979). The young child as consumer. In E. Wartella (Ed.), *Children Communicating: Media and Development of Thought, Speech, Understanding*. Beverly Hills, CA: Sage.

Webley, P. (1983). *Growing Up in the Modern Economy*. Paper at the Sixth International Conference on Political Psychology, Oxford, UK.

Webley, P., Levine, M. and Lewis, A. (1991). A study in economic psychology: Children's saving in a play economy. *Human Relations*, **44**, 127–146.

Weinberger, M.G. and Spotts, H.E. (1989). Humour in US versus UK television commercials: A comparison. *Journal of Advertising*, **18**, 39–44.

Wells, W. and LoSciuto, L. (1966). Direct observation of purchasing behaviour. *Journal of Marketing Research*, **3**, 227–233.

Werner, A. (1989). Television and age-related differences: A contribution to the debate on the 'Disappearance of Childhood'. *European Journal of Communication*, **4**, 33–50.

Whitehead, D. (1986). Student's attitudes to economic issues. *Economics*. Spring, 24–32.

Winick, C., Williamson, L.G., Chuzimir, S.F. and Winick, M.P. (1973). *Children's Television Commercials: A Content Analysis*. New York: Praeger.

Winick, M.P. and Winick, C. (1979). *The Television Experience: What Children See*. Beverly Hills, CA: Sage.

Winocur, S. and Siegal, M. (1982). Adolescents' judgements of economic arrangements. *International Journal of Behavioural Development*, **5**, 357–365.

Wittebroodt, I. (1990). *De Invloed van Televisiereclame op Kinderen. Literatuurstudie en Oonderzoek bij Schoolgaande Kinderen*. Leuven: Licentiaatsverhandeling K.U.L.

Wolf, M.A., Abelman, R. and Hexamer, A. (1981). Children's understanding of television: Some methodological considerations and a question-asking model for receivership skills. *Communication Yearbook 5*, pp. 405–431.

Wolfe, A. (1990). *Children and Advertising: An Advertising Association Monograph*. Henley-on-Thames, Oxon: NTC Publications.

Wosinski, M. and Pietras, M. (1990). Economic socialization of Polish children in different macro-economic conditions. *Journal of Economic Psychology*, **11**, 515–528.

Wright, P. and Barbour, F. (1975). The relevance of decision process models in structuring persuasive messages. *Communication Research*, **2**, 246–259.

Young, B.M. (1990). *Television Advertising and Children*. Oxford: Clarendon Press.

Zabucovec, V. and Polic, M. (1990). Yugoslavian children in a situation of rapid economic changes. *Journal of Economic Psychology*, **11**, 529–543.

Zajonc, R.B. (1968). Attitudinal effects of mere exposure. *Journal of Personality and Social Psychology*, **9**, 1–27.

Zinser, O., Perry, S. and Edgar, R. (1975). Affluence of the recipient, value of donations and sharing behaviour in preschool children. *The Journal of Psychology*, **89**, 301–305.

Zuckerman, P. and Gianioni, L. (1981). Measuring children's response to television advertising. In J. Esserman (Ed.), *Television Advertising and Children: Issues, Research and Findings*. New York: Child Research Service, pp. 83–93.

Zuckerman, P., Ziegler, M.E. and Stevenson, H.W. (1978). Children's viewing of television and recognition memory of commercials. *Child Development*, **49**, 96–104.

Author index

Abramovitch, R., 73
Adler, R. P., 10, 29, 56, 104, 107, 114, 121, 124, 138
Ajzen, I., 138
Aldous, J., 30
Anderson, D. R., 110, 112, 131
Angrist, S. S., 30
Annes, B., 29
Arens, W. F., 107, 128, 146
Argyle, M., 73
Armentrout, J., 22
Arnal, M.-J., 133
Assael, H., 51
Atkin, C. K., 18, 22, 28, 53, 55, 57, 108, 118, 127, 133, 139
Avery, R. K., 12

Bach, G., 96
Bahn, K. D., 9
Bales, R., 30
Banks, S., 101
Barbour, F., 130
Baumrind, D., 22, 23
Bayer, A., 30
Bechtel, R. B., 108
Becker, W. C., 22, 104
Bednall, D., 118, 119
Belch, G. E., 18, 41, 56
Belch, M. A., 18
Belk, R., 116
Bennett, W., 57
Berey, L. A., 55, 162
Berti, A., 65, 71, 72, 73, 74, 76
Birds Eye Walls, 6
Birkey, C., 68
Blatt, J., 111, 121
Blosser, B. J., 113, 114, 116, 126
Bocker, F., 18
Bombi, A., 65, 71, 72, 73, 74, 76
Bonnett, C., 82
Bovee, C. L., 107, 128, 146
Braithwaite, J., 32
Brittain, C. V., 29
Brobeck, S., 183
Brody, D. H., 57, 143
Bronson, W. C., 22
Brown, D., 116
Bruck, M., 120, 125
Bryant, J., 116, 131
Burgard, P., 89
Burger, E., 22
Burgess, E. W., 30
Burr, P. L., 22
Burr, R. M., 22
Burris, V., 68
Butter, E. J., 114, 115, 139, 140

Calvert, S. L., 109, 110
Campbell, E. Q., 28
Campbell, M., 81, 89
Cantor, J., 142
Carlens, D., 146
Carlson, L., 9, 22, 24, 63
Caron, A., 18, 60, 103, 130
Cateora, P. R., 31
Ceresino, G., 18
Chaffee, S., 27
Chaffee, S. H., 17, 28
Cheyne, W., 89
Childers, T., 22
Chizmar, J., 94
Christenson, P. G., 107, 181
Churchill, G. A., 12, 13, 16, 17, 25, 26, 28, 30, 31, 103, 104
Clancy-Hepburn, K., 22
Cleare, A., 74
Coleman, J. S., 12, 29
Collins, J., 133
Condry, J., 57, 112, 127, 133
Cram, F., 76
Crosby, L. A., 19, 23
Cummings, S., 71

Dailey, 160
Danziger, K., 66, 69
Davidson, D., 93
Davis, H. L., 30
Davis, J., 1
Davis, K., 87
Dawson, B. L., 143
de Beni, R., 73, 74
de Bens, E., 150
Denney, R., 24
Department for Education and Employment 2
Desmond, R. J., 146
Dibbs, S., 141
Dickinson, J., 89
Dittmar, H., 43
Donahue, T. R., 122, 123, 125, 128, 145
Donahue, W. A., 125
Dorr, A., 56, 107, 109, 114, 117, 118, 120, 128, 132, 138, 145, 146, 181
Doubleday, C., 146
Duffy, J., 118, 119
Dunlop, R., 36

Eck, R., 133
Eckstein, J., 36
Edgar, R., 78
Edwards, K. J., 22
Emler, N., 89
Emmerich, W., 30
Enis, B. M., 22

Ermisch, J., 2
Esserman, J. F., 121, 122, 133
Ettema, J. S., 112, 158

Faber, R. J., 129
Feshbach, S., 195
Fierman, J., 41
Fishbein, M., 138
Fox, K., 83, 84, 93
Foxman, E. R., 21
Friedman, M., 182, 186, 187
Fry, J. N., 16
Furby, L., 43, 45, 77, 88
Furnham, A., 13, 35, 66, 70, 73, 74, 77, 78, 79, 82,
    84, 86, 87, 90, 175, 181
Furth, H., 74

Gaedeke, R. M., 2, 5, 47, 49
Gaines, L., 121, 122, 133
Galst, J. P., 57, 58, 60, 63, 107, 127, 142
Gardner, C., 8
Gardner, H., 22, 23, 115
Gianioni, L., 115
Gilkison P., 12
Glazer, N., 24
Goldberg, M. E., 139, 141, 142, 144, 145, 148, 149,
    151, 152
Goldstein, J. H., 102
Gonzales, M., 3
Gorn, G. J., 139, 141, 142, 144
Goslin, D. A., 13
Graves, S. B., 181
Gray, R., 72
Greenberg, B. S., 29, 57, 59, 105, 110,
    127
Greer, D., 109, 110
Grossbart, S., 9, 10, 63
Grossbart, S. L., 19, 22, 23, 24
GSI-CFRO 41
Guest, L., 25
Gunter, B., 106, 133

Haedrich, G., 139
Halinski, R., 94
Hall, C., 2
Hamilton, J., 30
Hannaford, M., 118, 119
Hansen, F., 51
Hansen, H., 94
Haste, H., 65
Hawkins, R., 28
Heald, G., 133
Hencke, L. L., 125
Hermann, R., 185
Hill, R., 30
Hite, R. E., 133
Hoffman, H. R., 12
Holicki, S., 106
Holman, J., 32
Horn, T., 79
Horton, R., 95
Hower, J. T., 22
Hunnicutt, G. G., 128
Hunter, L. S., 108
Huston, A. C., 126

Ingels, S., 65, 90, 91
Irving, K., 77, 80
Isler, L., 19, 56, 57

Jaglom, L. M., 115
Jahoda, G., 68, 73, 74, 89

James, W., 6
John, D. R., 10, 177
Jones, S., 77
Joossens, L., 126, 144

Kagan, J., 22
Kamptner, N., 37
Kapferer, J. N., 138, 144
Kilgore, J., 93
Kinsey, J., 131, 144
Kippax, S., 106
Kline, S., 106
Kohlberg, L., 13
Kojima, K., 106
Kourilsky, M., 12, 65, 81, 89, 91, 92
Kovaric, P., 146
Kunkel, D., 107, 115, 117, 119, 120, 124, 126, 167,
    184

Langman, L., 51
Leahy, R., 78, 79
Leiser, D., 68, 88
Levin, S. R., 112, 114, 115, 118
Levine, M., 81
Lewis, A., 81
Liebert, D. E., 129
Liebert, R. M., 106, 110
Linn, M. C., 126
Lis, A., 76
Locke, H. J., 30
Lorch, E. P., 110
LoSciuto, L., 53
Lull, J., 26
Lyle, J., 12

McAleer, J. L., 106, 133
McDonald, W. J., 160
McDowell, C. N., 114, 115, 118
McKenzie, R., 94
Macklin, C., 123, 125
McLeod, J. M., 13, 17, 26, 27, 28, 104
McNeal, J. U., 1, 2, 3, 4, 6, 7, 9, 10, 16, 29, 31, 32–3,
    35, 36, 41, 46, 47, 49, 52, 54, 55, 60, 62, 66,
    156, 161, 164, 165, 166, 167, 168, 169, 177,
    178, 179, 180
MacNeil, M., 124
Madison Avenue 10
Magruder, L., 83
Marshall, H., 83
Mayer, R., 183
Mehotra, S., 16, 55
Messaris, P., 146
Meyer, M., 109
Meyer, T. P., 124, 128, 145
Milavsky, R., 139
Miller, L., 79
Mintel 5, 36
Moleski, L. M., 57
Moore, R. L., 10, 12, 13, 15, 16, 17, 25, 26, 27, 28,
    41, 50, 56, 104, 149
Moschis, G. P., 10, 12, 13, 15, 16, 17, 25, 26, 27, 28,
    30, 31, 41, 50, 56, 103, 104
Murray, J. P., 12, 106

Neelankavil, J. P., 162
Newson, E., 84, 87
Newson, J., 84, 87
Ng, S., 75, 76, 79, 91
Nikken, P., 106
Nippold, M. A., 116
Nolf, S., 179

O'Brien, M., 65, 90, 91
O'Keefe, G. J., 13

Paget, K. F., 121
Palmer, E. L., 114, 115, 118, 124
Parsons, T., 15, 18, 29, 30, 103
Pekowsky, B., 139
Peracchio, L. A., 9
Pereira, J., 61
Perry, S., 78
Phelps, E., 181
Pietras, M., 79, 90, 91
Pingree, S., 28
Polic, M., 71
Pollay, R. W., 55, 162
Pollio, H., 72
Pope, D., 183
Popper, E., 19, 57
Prasad, V. K., 148
President's Committee on Consumer Interests, 179
Psathas, G., 15, 25

Radler, D. H., 29
Ramsett, D., 94
Rao, A., 22
Remmers, H. H., 29
Reynolds, F. D., 9, 10, 103
Rheingold, C., 53
Rice, M., 109
Riecken, G., 107, 133, 140, 141
Riem, H., 59, 60
Riesman, D., 15, 18, 24, 27, 29, 103
Roberts, D. F., 113, 114, 115, 116, 119, 126, 184
Robertson, T. S., 17, 25, 27, 29, 56, 57, 58, 59, 60, 101, 103, 121, 122, 126, 144, 145
Roe, A., 22
Roedder, D. L., 148, 149
Roger, R., 179
Rolandelli, D. R., 109, 110, 132
Roseborough, H., 15, 18, 27, 29, 103
Ross, A., 98, 100
Ross, R. P., 120, 128, 129, 148, 149
Rossano, M. J., 140
Rossiter, J. R., 25, 29, 103, 104, 118, 119, 121, 122, 126, 130, 140, 144
Rust, L., 18, 163
Ryan, M. S., 29

Samli, A. C., 50
Sarett, C., 146
Saunders, J. R., 16, 18, 29, 50
Saunders, P., 95, 97
Schneider, C., 15, 150
Schug, M., 68
Scott, L. M., 109, 132
Scott, M. C., 109, 110
Sebald, H., 30
Sepstrup, P., 107, 117
Sevon, G., 68, 78
Shaak, B., 29
Sheikh, A. A., 57, 124
Sheppard, J., 8
Shils, E. A., 30
Siegal, M., 77, 78, 80
Siegelman, M., 22
Sim, C. P., 18
Singer, M., 78
Smith, G., 52, 64, 120, 150
Sonesson, I., 106
Sonuga-Barke, E., 80
Spotts, H. E., 116

Stacey, B., 13, 66, 70, 78, 82, 175
Stephens, L. F., 15
Stephens, N., 123
Stevens, W., 110
Stevenson, H. W., 112
Stewart, F., 2, 3, 6, 36
Stipp, H., 139
Stone, E. C., 29
Stoneman, Z., 57, 143
Strauss, A., 66, 72
Stutts, M. A., 123, 128
Sutton, R., 67
Sweeney, E., 52, 114, 120, 150
Swinyard, W. R., 18
Szybillo, G. J., 55, 56

Taebel, D., 71
Taylor, T., 87
Thomas, P., 84, 86, 87
Tootelian, D. H., 2, 3, 5, 47, 49
Torges, S., 16, 55
Torney-Purta, J., 65

Vandenbruane, P., 150
Vener, A. M., 29, 103
Verhaeren, J., 109, 117, 118
Von Feilitzen, C., 106

Wackman, D., 15, 17, 18, 27, 53, 55, 57, 63, 104, 111, 120, 121, 158
Waite, P., 94
Waldrop, J., 39
Walls Ltd 83
Walstad, W., 94, 180
Ward, S., 10, 13, 15, 16, 17, 18, 19, 22, 24, 25, 26, 27, 51, 53, 55, 57, 60, 63, 103, 104, 111, 112, 120, 121, 122, 123, 130, 132, 133, 158
Warden, J., 30
Wartella, E., 10, 108, 110, 112, 120, 125, 130, 131, 132, 158
Watts, M., 94, 180
Webley, P., 70, 79, 80, 81, 93
Weckstrom, S., 68, 78
Weidnaar, D., 95
Weinberger, M. G 116
Wells, W., 53
Wells, W. D., 9, 10, 103
Werner, A., 128
White, M. A., 57, 107, 127
Whitehead, D., 91
Windeshausen, H. N., 3, 50
Winick, C., 108, 139
Winick, M. P., 108
Winocur, S., 78
Wittebroodt, I., 106, 107, 126, 129
Wolf, M. A., 109
Wolfe, A., 150
Wosinski, M., 79, 90, 91
Wright, P., 130

Yavas, U., 107, 133, 140, 141
Yeh, C. H., 36, 54
Young, B. M., 57, 58, 59, 101, 106, 109, 111, 113, 117, 120, 123, 124, 125, 126, 127, 130, 131, 133, 144, 145, 147, 148, 149

Zabucovec, V., 71
Zajonc, R. B., 133
Ziegler, M. E., 112
Zinser, O., 78
Zuckerman, P., 112, 115

Subject index

Adolescents:
  brand loyalty, 10
  buying power, 65
  changes in consumer behaviour, 10
  family influence, 16
  peer group influence, 28–30
Adult-Oriented Approach, 160
Advertising, 10, 165
  celebrity endorsement, 129
  children's degree of attention, 105–11
  children's memory, 130–1
  comprehensibility, 128–9
  as consumer issue, 183–4
  effect on consumer behaviour, 36, 101–5, 137–8, 155–6
  as information source, 60
  McNeal's model, 165–7
  misleading presentation, 127–8
  regulation, 173–4, 175–9
  repetition effect, 144
  truthfulness and accuracy, 127–8
  see also television advertising
Age/life cycle position, 14
Allowances see pocket money
American Federal Trade Commission (FTC), advertising ban, 184
Attentional inertia, 110–11
Audience factors, 110
Authoritarian parents, 23, 63
Authoritative parents, 23, 63

Baby Boomers 5
Banking, children's understanding, 74–5
Basic Economic Test (BET), 94
Boycotts:
  marketplace-oriented, 186–7
  media-oriented, 186–7
Brand loyalties, 10, 41
Businesses:
  influence on consumer behaviour, 32, 176
  role as educators, 180

Celebrity endorsement, in advertising, 129
Child market, 1, 155
  allocation of expenditure, 4
  demands, 7–8
  market research, 157–8, 164–5
  satisfaction of needs, 7
  size, 4–7
  targeting, 169–70, 171–2
Children:
  as consumers, 178–9
  financial resources, 3
  independent purchases, 3
  influence on decision-making, 3
  memory of advertising, 130–2

research difficulties, 164–5
shopping behaviour pattern, 54
sources of purchasing power, 5–6
spending power, 6–7
Co-shopping experiences, 9–10
Cognitive development, Piagetian model, 13, 66, 69–70
Comprehensibility, in advertising, 128–9
Consumer education, 179–87
  by businesses and manufacturers, 180
  by parents and families, 33, 180
  by schools, 180
  developing knowledge, 10
  early training, 3–4
  and quality patterns, 17
  and socialization process, 17
Consumer movement organizations, 185–7
Consumer socialization, 13–14
  and behaviour modification, 12
  conceptual model, 13–14
  direct, 12
  family communications influence, 24–8
  indirect, 12
  individual rights, 182
  and parental styles, 22–4
  protectionism, 175
  starting age, 9
  training period, 176
Creative Drama Approach, 160
Cross-cultural differences, 88–9

Department store shopping, 47
Depth-interviewing technique, 161–2

Economic education, 91–2
  children's development of ideas, 66–71
  children's understanding of values, 90–1
  in primary grades, 92–5
  setting goals, 95–8
Economic relations, children's understanding, 79–80
Economic socialization:
  basic concepts, 95
  of children, 65–6
  knowledge and understanding objectives, 98
  pocket money, 82–8
  research studies on children's understanding, 71–82
Economic Values Inventory (EVI), 91
Education see consumer education
Entrepreneurship, children's understanding, 81–2
Event marketing, child-targeted, 168–9

Family communication:
  concept-oriented, 27
  indirect influences, 26–7

and mass media effects, 17
  mediating effects, 27–8
  and social class, 26
  and socialization, 17
  source of consumer information, 16
Family conflicts:
  due to children's requests, 56–7
  in family context, 57
  from advertising commercials, 102–5, 174
Family consumer decisions
  children's influence, 18–19
  parental influence, 18
Favourite possessions, 37–8
  importance, 43–5
Federal Communications Commission (FCC),
      advertising time control, 184
Focus groups, 158–60
Food advertising, 141–3
Food-choice behaviour, 143
Food shopping, 47

Gender differences, 89–90
  attention to advertising, 110
  effect on parental role, 15
Generation X, 5
Gratification delay, 143
Grocery shopping, teenagers, 41
Group discussions, 160

Household decision-making, 51–2
  children's influence, 41, 52–3, 53–7
  see also family consumer decisions

Information sources, for purchase requests, 60–1

Justice, children's understanding, 80

Kinder-Economy, 92

Laboratory research, 163–4
Learning processes, 14
  models, 13, 14
Learning properties, 14
Legal protection, 154
Leisure activities, 36

McNeal's advertising model, 165–7
Market research, children's market, 157–8, 164–5
Marketing, child-targeted, 169–70
Mass media:
  exposure to, 26–7
  and family influences, 17
  see also television advertising
Materialistic orientations, 27
Medicine, television advertising, 139–40
Memory of advertising:
  advertising-related factors, 132
  child-related factors, 131–2
Mere exposure effect, 104, 133, 139
Money-related concepts, children's development, 66,
      72–3
Mothers:
  influence on decision making, 18
  teaching methods, 23–4
Music, memory role, 132

Neglecting parents, 23, 63
Non-food shopping, 47

Observational techniques, 162–3
Ownership, children's understanding, 76–7

P-tests (advertising effectiveness), 167
Parent-child conflict see family conflicts
Parental decision-making see household decision-
      making
Parental role:
  authoritarian, 23, 63
  authoritative, 23, 63
  and child gender, 15
  as educators, 33–4, 145–6, 180
  importance, 15
  incidental nature, 16
  mediation effect, 28, 146
  overt communication, 17
  permissive, 63
  responses to product requests, 62
  and social class, 15, 145
  socialization styles, 22–4, 31
  studies, 18–22
  type of product, 16
  yielding to children's requests, 55
  see also mothers
Parental socialization, 22–4
Peer group influence, 22, 28–30, 32, 159
Permissive parents, 63
Persuasive intent, in television advertising, 119–24
Pestering action, 56, 58
Picture-drawing technique, 160–1
Pocket money, 6
  understanding, 82–8
Possessions:
  children's understanding, 76–7
  favourite see favourite possessions
Postponing response, 63
Poverty, children's understanding, 78–9
Prices, children's understanding, 73–4
Primary Test of Economic Understanding (PTEU), 93
Product, role in consumer socialization, 32
Product purchase patterns, 35–6
  effect of child's age, 58
  effect of cultural background, 59
  effect of socio-economic class, 58
  effect of television exposure, 59
  influence of advertising, 58
  international, 36–7
  preferences, 49, 172
Product requests:
  by type, 59–60
  location, 61
  parental responses, 62
  sources for, 60–1
Profit, children's understanding, 73–4
Programme-length commercials, 167–8, 174
Promotions, child-targeted, 168–70
Protectionism, 33, 175, 187–8
  policy forms, 182–3
Public relations, child-targeted, 168–70
Public Service Announcements (PSAs), 148
Publicity, child-targeted, 168
Purchase behaviour, 146–7
Purchase-request behaviour, 153

Recall tests, 131
Recognition tests, 131
Reformists, 182–3
Refusal response, 63
Regulation of advertising, 173–4, 175–9
Requests see product requests
Retailing practices, for young, 156–7, 171
Retroactive socialization, 29
Rigid controlling parents, 23
Role-playing technique, 164

Saving habits, 36, 42
    children's understanding, 80–1
Schools:
    public relations role, 169
    role as consumer educators, 32, 180
Secret balloting, 159
Self-identity, 43
Self-regulating codes, advertising, 154
Separation devices, television advertising, 118
Sex-role differences, 30–1
    and peer groups, 30
    see also gender differences
Shopping:
    behaviour/patterns, 32, 45–6, 50, 177
    meaning, 47–9
    selectivity, 50
    social function, 49
Shopping mall shopping, 47, 51
Slogans, memory role, 132
Social class:
    differences, 89
    parental role, 15, 145
    and television watching, 18
Social learning model, 13
Social structure variables, 14
Socialization process, 13
    agents in, 14, 175–6
    and family communication, 17, 176
    see also economic socialization; consumer
        socialization
Socio-economic background, and decision-making
        patterns, 24–6
Specialty store shopping, 47
Stores:
    as information sources, 61
    loyalty, 50
    preferences, 49, 62
Structural Approach, 160
Substitution response, 62
Supermarket shopping, 47
    parent-child interaction, 18

Teacher's influence *see* schools
Teenage market *see* child market
Teenagers:
    affluence, 2

as distinct phase, 1
grocery shopping, 41
market size, 2
purchase patterns, 39–43, 46
shopping likes/dislikes, 49
slackers, 5
Television advertising:
    ability to distinguish, 114–17
    attitudes, 133–4
    child's processing stages, 134–5
    clustering technique, 118–19, 133
    data on children's exposure, 106–7, 126
    degree of attention, 108–10
    distinction from programmes, 111–13, 118–19
    effect of child's age, 144–5
    effect on consumer behaviour, 18, 28, 36, 58, 59,
        102–5, 153
    effect on knowledge, attitudes and values,
        138–41
    effect of social class, 154
    experimental research, 147–9
    of food products, 141–3
    interpretation of content, 127–33
    mediating factors, 143–6
    of medicines, 139–40
    parental attitudes, 22, 32
    persuasive intent, 119–24, 126
    programme length commercials, 167–8
    quasi-experimental research, 151–3
    research methodology, 124–6
    scheduling, 132
    and social class, 18
    survey research, 149–51
    time control, 184
    truthfulness, 127–8
    understanding, 111
'Trade-offs' *see* Basic Economic Test (BET)
Treasured possessions, 37–8
Truthfulness, in advertising, 127–8

Wealth, children's understanding, 78–9
Work experience, for children, 87

Yankelovich Partners Youth Monitor Survey, 1993, 7
Youth market *see* teenagers